FROM
WATERGATE
TO
MONICAGATE

Contents

Introduction

The *Oxford Modern English Dictionary* defines the term "media" as "the main means of mass communication (esp. newspapers and broadcasting)." The term has variously been defined to include print journalism, broadcasting, cinema, and more recently, the Internet. This book will concentrate on the news media and therefore will exclude cinema.

There is no shortage of controversy in the American media. In the competition for profits, publishers have virtually destroyed the traditional wall between their news and advertising departments. Harried editors have adopted the journalistic values of the tabloid press as reporters concentrate on crime, scandal, and "puff pieces."

Media lawyer Bruce Sanford admits, "A canyon of disbelief and distrust has developed between the public and the news media. Deep, complex and so contradictory as to be airless at times, this gorge has widened at an accelerating rate during the last decade. Its darkness frightens the media. It threatens not just the communication industry's enviable financial power but its special role in ordering American democracy."[1]

The press establishment has always been nervous about its delicate relationship with the public. In 1938 James Stahlman, publisher of the *Nashville Banner* and former president of the American Newspaper Publishers Association, complained of the "growing tendency on the part of the public to look with disfavor and distrust upon the press." But during that same year a Roper poll for *Fortune* magazine found that 78 percent of respondents thought newspaper stories were either "almost always" or "usually" accurate.[2] Compare that with a 1994 Times Mirror survey in which 71 percent of respondents said, "The news media gets in the way of society solving its problems," whereas only 25 percent said, "The news media help society to solve its problems." Four percent didn't know.[3]

In 1995 an NBC/*Wall Street Journal* poll found that only 26 percent of Americans had a "very positive" or even "somewhat positive" view of the news media. That same year the cover of *The American Editor*, the publication of the ASNE, declared, "It's Official: Most People Don't Like Us Anymore." An article within entitled "Under Siege" presented the journalist's view of the media, and no punches were pulled. Marvin Kalb, a Harvard professor and former NBC reporter, posed a rhetorical question to his colleagues and answered it: "Why do Americans hate the press? Because you deserve it."[4]

There was more bad news to come. A 1997 Roper Center survey revealed public complaints about the press that are covered in various chapters of this book:

82% think reporters are insensitive to people's pain when covering disasters and accidents (see Chapter 6).

64% think the news is too sensationalized (see Chapters 5 and 6).

64% think reporters spend too much time offering their own opinions (see Chapters 4 and 7).

76% think reporters focus too much on the private lives of public officials (see Chapters 5 and 6).

63% think the news is too manipulated by powerful interests (see Chapters 1–3), including: elected officials (81%), big business (87%), corporate media owners (88%), advertisers (88%), and the media's desire to make profits (91%).

60% think reporters too often quote sources whose names are not given in news stories (see Chapter 8).

52% think the news is too biased (see Chapters 1–4 and 7).

46% think the news is too negative (see Chapters 5 and 6).

Only 2 percent of respondents said they believe all of what newspaper reporters write, but at the same time 80 percent said the press is crucial to the functioning of a free society.[5]

As one might expect, the public's growing hostility toward journalism has affected the morale of reporters. "I think we bear 95 percent of the responsibility for the low repute in which we are held," said Howard Kurtz, media reporter for the *Washington Post*. "In no other profession would top executives scratch their heads and wonder why it is that a substantial proportion of the customers think they're scum." When asked to characterize the current attitude of news professionals, Sandra Mims Rowe, editor of the Portland *Oregonian*, said, "Mistrustful. Cynical. Re-

sentful." David Shaw, media critic for the *Los Angeles Times*, characterized his colleagues as "Critical, skeptical, hostile, unhappy." Jim Gels,
publisher of the Duluth *News-Tribune*, said, "Angry. At times hostile.
Almost, in some cases, unwilling to listen."[6]

Richard Harwood, while serving as the *Washington Post*'s ombudsman,
noted that "[m]any of today's newspeople feel overworked, overstressed,
underpaid and assigned to too many trivial tasks. They complain in great
numbers about the lack of 'leadership' in newsrooms." The excitement
and glamour of journalism, which once led reporters to overlook long
hours and low pay, have been lost. More disturbing, says Harwood, are
"the insecurities and fears of the future communicated by corporate leaders whose dedication to journalism and its essential role in a democratic
society is suspect. . . . In the search for ever greater profitability they
have, in many cases, diversified their companies to a degree that con-
fuses everyone—themselves included—as to what business they are really in or really care about."[7]

Another former *Post* ombudsman, Joann Byrd, concludes that "people
don't see journalism as public service anymore." Instead, they believe
that "journalists are engaged in self-service—getting ratings, selling
newspapers or making their careers." The public, says Byrd, regards the
journalist's claim of detachment as "so much hogwash." The *Boston
Globe*'s Mark Jurkowitz worries that "the media seem to have given up
all pretense of being objective middlemen, simple purveyors of information. . . . If that's the case, they are much fairer game for people who
are unhappy with the news that they read and see."[8]

Americans feel they have been dislodged from meaningful participation in our democracy by three powerful groups: politicians, lobbyists,
and the press. As indicated in this book, those three groups have become
close allies, compounding the threat to democracy.

William Greider, a former *Washington Post* assistant managing editor,
says, "Like the other primary political institutions, the press has lost
viable connections to its own readers and grown more distant from
them. . . . As an institution, the media have gravitated toward elite interests and converged with those powerful few who already dominate politics. People sense this about the news, even if they are unable to describe
how it happened or why they feel so alienated from the newspapers that
purport to speak for them."[9]

A number of surveys have shown public concern over the close relationship between the press and political power. Barry Sussman, a public
opinion–polling consultant, says, "Instead of seeing the major media as
out to get the political establishment, most people, when asked, say that
reporting on public figures is too soft and that the media are in bed with
the leadership in Washington."[10]

After a decade of major journalistic scandals, the public hostility toward the media came as no surprise, but when newspaper executives gave themselves bad grades, it made news. In 1998 a poll sponsored by *Editor & Publisher* magazine found that nearly half of America's editors and publishers think press coverage is "shallow and inadequate." In addition, 55 percent of the executives believe the press is too cynical, two-thirds say that newspapers concentrate on personalities rather than policy, and more than 75 percent say that print and broadcast organizations go beyond reporting the news and actually create controversy. Almost one out of five of executives contacted believes that press coverage is "often inaccurate."[11]

Although this book examines journalism in a very critical way, the author takes no pleasure in the current plight of the media. A robust and independent press is essential to our democracy, and it is the author's hope that this exposition of media controversies will help reform and strengthen a free press. Unfortunately, the public's growing hostility toward the media suggests an inclination to repress, not reform, the American press.

Bruce Sanford warns, "The consequences of the growing canyon of distrust between the public and the media are already discernible and should worry us even more than the knowledge that we understand the situation poorly. For the result of the public's misplaced fury has been a palpable willingness to silence the media—and to curtail its ability to gather and report the news, and to make us more dependent than ever on the government for our understanding of human events. There is no more certain road to the loss of freedom."[12]

In this era of journalistic controversy, the courts seem to be as deeply contemptuous of the media as is the public. Lawsuits against the media have become a spectacularly profitable enterprise, leading to decisions that threaten many of the traditional press freedoms. A North Carolina jury recently awarded $5.5 million in punitive damages against ABC over a 1992 *Prime Time Live* show that accused the Food Lion supermarket chain of selling spoiled meat. The accuracy of the report was not at issue, but the jury rejected ABC's use of undercover reporters with hidden cameras. Such a legal judgment insulates powerful institutions from a form of investigative journalism that has historically exposed corporate wrongdoing, as well as swindlers and charlatans.

Given the hostile attitude of the courts, most media executives today are willing to settle lawsuits at a significant financial loss rather than suffer defeat in court. In 1995 ABC issued a public apology and agreed to pay $16 million in legal expenses to the Philip Morris and R. J. Reynolds tobacco companies rather than fight a lawsuit over a *Day One* documentary about the addictiveness of nicotine. The following year CBS censored a *60 Minutes* exposé on the tobacco industry in the face of a similar lawsuit (see Chapter 1).

In December 1996 NBC paid more than $500,000 to Richard Jewell, the Atlanta security guard wrongfully implicated in the bombing at the 1996 Summer Olympics, simply because Tom Brokaw had cited police sources on the air saying they had enough evidence to arrest Jewell. CNN paid Jewell an undisclosed amount in a separate settlement, and he subsequently used his new wealth to fund a lawsuit against the *Atlanta Journal and Constitution*, claiming he was unfairly portrayed as the bomber at the Summer Olympics.

The courts have also begun to show animosity toward "ride-alongs," the common practice whereby reporters accompany police to crime scenes and photograph their activities. Historically, this press oversight of police activity has been recognized as a way to hold law enforcement practices up to public scrutiny, but no more. In a 1995 case involving a CBS team's presence during a police raid on a private home, Judge Jack Weinstein said, "CBS had no greater right than that of a thief to be in the home."[13] In 1999 the Supreme Court ruled unanimously that media ride-alongs violate the Fourth Amendment, which prohibits "unreasonable searches and seizures." The Court was silent on First Amendment implications with respect to "freedom of speech, or of the press."

The result of such decisions serves no one's interests. The public now sees only what the police want it to see. The police are now unable to defend themselves against scurrilous accusations, and reporters on the law enforcement beat must patch together the truth from second-hand reports.

The new judicial hostility toward the press has no ideological origin. Indeed, many liberal judges are leading the charge against the media, whereas some of the strongest support for press freedom is coming from conservatives. For example, when special prosecutor Kenneth Starr was a Washington, D.C., appeals court judge, he wrote an important First Amendment decision in *Ollman v. Evans* that was characterized as being worthy of the liberal Supreme Court Justice William Brennan. Starr's colleague on the D.C. court was Robert Bork, President Ronald Reagan's nominee for the Supreme Court who was deemed too conservative to be confirmed. In *Ollman*, Bork warned that the growing stream of lawsuits against the press could threaten the people's right to know. He concluded that "an upsurge in libel actions, accompanied by a startling inflation of damage awards, . . . threaten[s] to impose a self-censorship on the press which can as effectively inhibit debate and criticism as could overt government regulation that the First Amendment most certainly would not permit."[14]

When esteemed appeals court judge Abner Mikva recently retired from the D.C. circuit, he spoke candidly about the impending legal storm building around the media. "A feeling is abroad among some judges that the Supreme Court has gone too far in protecting the media from defamation actions resulting from instances of irresponsible journalism," he told members of Georgia State University's law school. "I've been a judge for fifteen years, and now that I've taken off my robes, one of the first things I must say is—Watch Out! There's a backlash coming in First Amendment doctrine."[15]

Some in the media are attempting to regain the trust of the American people. At the 1999 national roundtable sponsored by the Scripps Howard Foundation, eleven journalists from around the country examined journalism's "growing credibility crisis with the American people." They referred to a new survey by Scripps Howard News Service showing that fewer than 15 percent of Americans think newspapers are very reliable and more than 75 percent think reporters are biased, inaccurate, and prying. Moderator Judy Woodruff, CNN senior correspondent, encouraged the other journalists to go beyond criticism and suggest what can be done to protect the public's faith in the media. Among the suggested solutions to the credibility crisis were:

- The media should pay attention to the basics, respecting what the reader wants and avoiding doing harm in any way.

- When reporters "fall in love" with their big stories, editors should take a step back before printing them.

- The media should be more independent and avoid the so-called herd mentality.

- Reporters, producers, and writers should be taught a "higher consciousness of ethics." When reporters cover a story, the first filter should be, "Is it right and is it ethical?"

- The media should ask advice from customers more frequently than it does now.[16]

The American Society of Newspaper Editors (ASNE) has begun what it calls the Journalism Credibility Project, a million-dollar initiative to improve the credibility of newspapers and journalism. The project began in April 1998 with an in-depth survey of 3,000 Americans and was followed by sixteen focus groups. In the spring of 1999, eight daily newspapers agreed to serve as "test sites" in a three-year program to develop innovative solutions to the four major areas of concern revealed in the ASNE survey: accuracy, sensationalism, bias, and alienation from readers.

The survey had shown that the public finds too many factual errors in newspapers, believes that newspapers fail to show respect for their readers, suspects that the biases of journalists influence what stories are covered and how they are covered, believes that sensational stories get heavy news coverage not because they are important but because they sell newspapers, and feels that newsroom values and practices conflict with their own priorities.

ASNE president Edward L. Seaton said, "We expect each test-site newspaper to develop concrete, actionable, effective solutions to the credibility problems that can be used in a variety of newspapers and markets—with effectiveness evaluated by market impact. . . . The real goal is to understand the problem and then alter the content of the paper." Seaton described the changes that the test sites hope to implement. "[T]here will be attempts to desensationalize the news report; connect with customers and communities; get the facts right and learn to spell; explain ourselves and our decisions; show more respect for the public and news sources; and be more open-minded, unbiased and absent of favoritism."[17]

The Radio and Television Directors Foundation has initiated the Journalism Ethics and Integrity Project with the intention of reinforcing core journalism values through training in ethical decision-making skills. Another organization, the Committee of Concerned Journalists, has enlisted over a thousand members dedicated to creating a national conversation among journalists about core principles. The purposes of this conversation would be to renew journalists' faith in the principles of their profession, to provide the public with a better understanding of those principles, and to inform media management of the financial and social value of those principles.

A recent survey about the modern media crisis, published in the March 2000 issue of the media watchdog journal *Brill's Content*, produced some disturbing conclusions. In describing the results of the survey, Frank Luntz, the chief pollster, said, "In essence, we gave 822 randomly selected Americans a paintbrush and an empty canvas, and asked them to portray their media masterpiece. And what did they paint? Handcuffs."[18] For example, a majority of respondents (48% Yes to 45% No) would compel journalists to disclose their political leanings, and over one-quarter (26% to 67%) would bar them from participating in any political activity.

Some of the other questions answered in the survey were:

In general, does the press make conditions in America seem better or worse than they are?

Better, 45%; Worse, 48%

Should media outlets be licensed like hospitals?

Yes, 42%; No, 36%

Should journalists be licensed like doctors?

Yes, 41%; No, 50%

One of the important revelations of the *Brill's* survey was that the public must share responsibility for the media's current sad state. Part of the problem concerns the changing public definition of "news." Significant percentages of survey respondents considered TV shows like *America's Most Wanted* or the *Today Show* to be "news." Five percent of respondents said they get most of their information about the law from *Ally McBeal*.

The *Brill's* survey revealed a strong streak of hypocrisy in respondents' indictment of the media. Even though most Americans complained that the media goes too far in the pursuit of truth, the survey showed that respondents would avidly consume the very sort of news that they decried. Pollster Luntz put together a "voyeur index" with respect to four hypothetical excesses in news reporting. Fully 39 percent of respondents said the media should not have covered any of the four scenarios, yet 79 percent would have viewed at least one of them. "These results confirm a longstanding assumption," said Luntz. "What Americans say they want in news and how they will actually behave are entirely different."[19]

Luntz concluded, "We complain there is not enough substance, and yet many of us consider shows like *America's Most Wanted* to be hard news. We would tell television news producers to limit what they broadcast, yet most of us admit we want to see more. We are a mass of contradictions, just like the news."[20]

The ten controversies that constitute the focus of the chapters of this book were chosen on the basis of their journalistic significance, timeliness, and historical depth. There were, of course, abundant examples to choose from. Some were too recent in origin to represent long-standing controversies (e.g., the recent revelation that the White House had been reviewing scripts for all six major TV networks and providing financial rewards for anti-drug messages[21]). Other issues, such as censorship of the school press, were worthy of inclusion but have been covered in depth in previous books.

Of the ten controversies presented, the one from which most other journalistic problems stem is the media monopoly, which forms the basis for Chapter 1. The following three chapters discuss the controversy over ceding control of the news to public relations agencies, the Central Intelligence Agency, and the forces of wartime censorship. Chapters 5 and 6 examine a pair of related issues, the role of the tabloid press and the paparazzi. Chapters 7 and 8 address breaches of traditional journalistic ethics, including plagiarism, fabrication, unsubstantiated charges, and the use of confidential sources. The final two chapters cover what many believe represent the media's hope for the future: the Internet and microradio. As you will see, even these vital and independent media formats face daunting obstacles.

NOTES

1. Bruce W. Sanford, *Don't Shoot the Messenger: How Our Growing Hatred of the Media Threatens Free Speech for All of Us* (New York: The Free Press, 1999), p. 11.

2. "The Press and the People—A Survey," *Fortune* (August 1939), pp. 64, 70.

3. Times Mirror Center for the People & the Press, "The People, the Press & Politics: The New Political Landscape," October 1994, p. 160.

4. Linda Fibich, "Under Siege," *American Journalism Review* (September 1995), p. 18.

5. "Do You Believe What Newspeople Tell You?" *Washington Post Parade Magazine* (March 2, 1997), p. 4.

6. Fibich, "Under Siege," pp. 16, 20.

7. Richard Harwood, "A Loss of Nerve in the News Business," *Washington Post* (May 31, 1997), A19.

8. Fibich, "Under Siege," pp. 18, 20.

9. William Greider, *Who Will Tell the People: The Betrayal of American Democracy* (New York: Simon & Schuster, 1992), p. 288.

10. Quoted in Ibid, p. 302.

11. Robert Neuwirth, "Press Flawed, News Chiefs Admit," *Editor & Publisher* (January 17, 1998), p. 10.

12. Sanford, *Don't Shoot the Messenger*, p. 10.

13. *Ayeni v. CBS, Inc.*, 848 F.Supp., 362, 368 (E.D.N.Y.), *aff'd* 35 F. 3d 680 (2d Cir. 1994).

14. *Ollman v. Evans*, 750 F. 2d 970, 997 (D.C. Cir. 1984).

15. A. J. Mikva, "In My Opinion, Those Are Not Facts," *Georgia State University Law Review*, 1995, pp. 291, 296.

16. Jan Jaben, "Credibility Crisis in the Newsroom," *Editor & Publisher* (February 27, 1999), p. 12.

17. "Why Newspaper Credibility Has Been Dropping: Remarks by Edward L. Seaton" (December 15, 1998), p. 4, www.asne.org/works/jcp/seaton/htm.

18. Frank Luntz, "Public to Press: Cool It," *Brill's Content* (March 2000), p. 76.

19. Ibid., p. 79.

20. Ibid., p. 114.

21. Howard Kurtz, "White House Cut Anti-Drug Deal with TV," *Washington Post*, January 14, 2000, A1.

C H A P T E R

Monopolistic Control of Journalism

THE MEDIA'S BRAVE NEW WORLD

"The defining fact of American life in the 1990s is its reorganization around the needs of the corporations," says Thomas Frank, editor in chief of *The Baffler*, a Chicago-based political journal. "[T]hose of us who are concerned about the concentration of the media see the big change as essentially a negative one: the sky really is falling, civilization is wandering into a cultural catastrophe."[1]

The business community regards such hyperbole as an attack on free market society. The press is, after all, a business, and every business must pursue growth and profit. To do otherwise would ill serve its stockholders. But do unlimited corporate growth and centralization serve the media, and American society, well?

Ben Bagdikian's trail-blazing book *The Media Monopoly* (1983) revealed that more than half of all media business in the United States was controlled by just fifty corporations. By 1987 the book's second edition reported that the number of these "controlling corporations" had shrunk to twenty-nine. By the time of the fourth edition in 1992 there were just twenty such controlling corporations, and in 1996 Bagdikian reported that the following ten corporations now controlled American media: Time Warner, Disney, Viacom, News Corp Ltd., Sony, Telecommunications Inc., Seagram, Westinghouse, Gannett, and General Electric. In 1999 Viacom bought CBS/Westinghouse, reducing the exclusive media club to nine members.

In the preface to the fifth edition of *The Media Monopoly* Bagdikian explains, "Nothing in earlier history matches this corporate group's power to penetrate the social landscape. Using both old and new technology, by owning each other's shares, engaging in joint ventures as partners, and other forms of cooperation, this handful of giants has created what is, in effect, a news communications cartel within the United States.... At issue is the possession of power to surround almost every man, woman, and child in the country with controlled images and words, to socialize each new generation of Americans, to alter the political agenda of the country."[2]

These new private information power centers have successfully persuaded the public that their corporate control of the media is an exercise in individual free expression. This effective use of the First Amendment as a shield for corporate power relies in large part on a century-old Supreme Court ruling that a corporation is an individual and on the subsequent corporate presumption that abridgement of expression can come only from the state.

Herbert Schiller, professor emeritus of communications at the University of California at San Diego, says, "Our whole constitutional heritage rebels at the thought of giving giant information corporations the power to control people's minds." He believes that corporate speech has become the dominant discourse both nationally and internationally, changing dramatically the context in which the concepts of freedom of speech and press must be interpreted. "Whereas the corporate voice booms across the land, individual expression, at best, trickles through tiny, constricted public circuits," says Schiller. "This has allowed the effective right to free speech to be transferred from individuals to billion-dollar companies that, in effect, monopolize public communication."[3]

George Gerbner, dean emeritus of the Annenberg School for Communication at the University of Pennsylvania, says the corporate media force out thoughtful programming through "a complex manufacturing and marketing machine" that is fueled by "[m]ergers, consolidation, conglomerization, and globalization."[4] Gerbner says, "Censorship is what we have now—the imposition of a marketing formula on journalists and creative people, which is then foisted on the children of the world. That is not an expression of freedom. What we want is greater freedom for the journalists and the creative people, a loosening of the noose on the market formula, and a greater diversity of perspectives. The First Amendment has been perverted to shield monopolies as censors, and that's unacceptable."[5]

Bagdikian believes that future prospects for the media are even worse than what was portrayed in Aldous Huxley's *Brave New World*. They represent the same nightmare of mass conformity, but created by a family of powerful private corporations four hundred years before Huxley's twenty-fifth century prediction. In today's brave new world, a few conglomerates make maximum profits through their closely held control of the world's cultural and informational systems. According to Bagdikian, the "news" is cleansed of information about any public alternatives beyond the corporate agendas. The media giants frame the public agenda on all issues, including communications policy. They use powerful law firms, influential lobbyists, and massive campaign contributions to manufacture popular consent on the major political and economic issues of the day.

CONGRESS FOR SALE

The power of mega-corporations is increasingly used to determine the fate of legislation affecting the media itself. The passage of the landmark Telecommunications Act of 1996 is a case in point. The corporate leaders in the telephone, cable, satellite, and broadcast industries gathered in Washington to craft and pass this revolutionary revision of America's communications law. President Clinton spoke of the great advantages the new law would bring to the American people, but the bill's real beneficiaries were the media giants.

The bill extended the duration of broadcast licenses from five to eight years, making it increasingly difficult to hold even the most irresponsible broadcasters accountable. The bill also removed all numerical limits on radio and TV station ownership, allowing one individual to own an *unlimited* number of stations. For the first time in history, one company can own radio, TV, and cable stations in the same market. The bill also increased what is called the national "audience cap" to 35 percent, allowing all the news media in the nation to be owned by just three individuals or companies.

Few Americans were aware of these provisions, because the media didn't report them. "Self-interested corporate-owned news outlets did not critically debate the most important communications legislation passed by Congress in the past 60 years," says Peter Phillips, editor of *Censored 1997: The News that Didn't Make the News.*[6]

For example, the media chose to ignore a provision deep within the Act that stood to make them billions of dollars: free access to the "digital spectrum." Jeff Chester of the Center for Media Education says having a piece of the digital spectrum is "like having the keys to Fort Knox." This is because digital technology will enable broadcasters to take a single channel that they may own and turn it into twenty or more channels, making significant amounts of money in the process. Because the federal government owns the digital spectrum, media experts expected the government to auction it off to the broadcasters in a public auction, earning the public up to $70 billion. Instead, the lobbying power of the broadcast industry convinced Congress to give it to them free of charge. "The broadcasters had hundreds of lobbyists spread all over the Hill for a couple of years leading up to that period," says Charles Lewis of the Center for Public Integrity. "They have one advantage that no one else has. They control the fate of all politicians."

"Let me tell you how they do that," explained Senator John McCain (R-Idaho). "There's an issue before the Congress that affects their industry. They call in the station managers from the congressman's district or the senator's state. They sit down in a room with a senator or representative. Now there are never any threats made. . . . But they are the messengers. They portray you in the work you do here in Washington to the people in your state or district. It's incredibly power."[7]

Dean Alger, who has authored a study of corporations and mass media, examined nightly network coverage of the Telecommunications Act from the beginning of the Senate debate until the night before it was passed. During that nine months, the three network news shows aired only nineteen minutes on the Act, none of which included a single mention of the debate over whether broadcasters should pay for the use of the digital spectrum.

Senator Bob Dole (R-Kans.) wondered why the supposedly aggressive media couldn't cover its own scandal. "When it comes to a billion dollar giveaway to them," he said, "mum's the word."

Senator McCain told his colleagues in the Senate, "You will not see this story on any television or hear it on any radio broadcast, because it directly affects them."

Charles Lewis explains that because the networks will make billions of dollars as the result of the Telecommunications Act, the last thing they wanted was a public airing of the issue. "The media did not want to discuss what it was doing," he said. "It would be like a bank robber stopping the robbery and saying, 'Look what we're doing here. Let's have a press conference in front of the bank.' "[8]

Even as the media maintained silence on the digital spectrum controversy, it was the recipient of substantial revenues from an advertising blitz by the broadcast lobby that railed against any congressional intrusion. Congress quickly capitulated, and the broadcasters got $70 billion worth of free airwaves in a political process that the then head of the Federal Communications Commission called the biggest corporate giveaway of this century.[9]

Gene Kimmelman, co-chairman of Consumer's Union, explained, "When there are very few companies that control the most popular media outlets and there's a policy issue that comes up that could hurt them financially, it is very unlikely we're going to get a full airing of that kind of an issue."[10]

Another example of the power of the media monopoly over Congress was evident in 1998, when the tobacco industry used its advertising dollars and the influence of its corporate media holdings to control broadcast coverage of an anti-smoking bill introduced by Senator McCain. During the months of debate over McCain's bill, the tobacco industry spent millions in media ads to defeat it, but only one nightly news broadcast ran a story addressing the industry's claims. Coverage on cable TV was also minimal. Bill Moyers, who hosted a public television exposé on the subject, noted, "Tobacco won the war. Corporate spending had turned the tide against a popular bill."[11]

The most recent example of congressional subservience to the corporate media is the Radio Broadcasting Preservation Act, a bill introduced by congressional allies of the National Association of Broadcasters in an effort to countermand the FCC's February 2000 decision to allow low power noncommercial broadcasting. The bill, passed in December 2000, rendered null and void the FCC's new regulations authorizing Low Power FM (LPFM) community radio, feared by the major broadcasters as a threat to their control of the airwaves (see Chapter 10).

MERGER MANIA

Predictably, the passage of the Telecommunications Act of 1996 set off a massive wave of corporate mergers and acquisitions. On June 21, 1996, Westinghouse (number one nationally in radio revenues) acquired Infinity Broadcasting (number two in radio revenues), making it three times larger than its closest competitor. In July 1996 Rupert Murdoch acquired New World Communications Group, making his News Corporation the biggest owner and operator of TV stations in the United States. Also in July, Time Warner and Turner Broadcasting merged to form Time Warner-Turner, the world's largest media conglomerate with more than $20 billion in annual revenue. In October, British Telecommunications acquired U.S. phone giant MCI in a deal worth $20.3 billion.

As the twentieth century drew to a close, the merger momentum grew. In the biggest media merger ever, Westinghouse, after acquiring CBS and assuming the corporate name CBS Corp., was itself acquired by Viacom in September 1999. Viacom's press release expressed pride and optimism: "Reaching the greatest number of viewers and listeners of any media enterprise, spanning all ages and demographics, the new Viacom will be the premier outlet for advertisers in the world."[12]

With Viacom's 19 television stations and CBS's 15, the new company would own stations in 18 of the top 20 markets and reach 41 percent of the population. Viacom would now own more local TV stations than any other entity as well as the nation's biggest group of radio stations. The rest of Viacom's portfolio includes such profitable cable networks as MTV, VH1, and Nickelodeon; the Paramount film studio; and the Block-

Author and former *Washington Post* editor Ben Bagdikian has documented the potentially dangerous power of media corporations in his seminal work, *The Media Monopoly*, now in its sixth edition. Photo by Ted Streshinsky, courtesy of Ben Bagdikian.

Media tycoon Rupert Murdoch heads the News Corporation, one of the nine conglomerates that control the world's media. Photo reproduced from the collections of the Library of Congress.

buster video rental chain. "The deal is obscene," said Jean Pool, director for North American Media at J. Walter Thompson in New York.[13]

Even ethnic and racial identities within the media are being threatened by new megacorporations like Viacom. On November 1, 2000, Black Entertainment Television (BET), one of the nation's premier black-owned media companies, announced its pending sale to Viacom. "This kind of consolidation is undermining diversity throughout the communications industry," warned James L. Winston, executive director of the National Association of Black Owned Broadcasters. "We see it in radio station and TV ownership, where a small number of companies are consolidating ownership across the country of media voices. And we have always had only one independent African American voice in the cable industry, and it sounds like we may be about to lose that as well."[14]

There seems no end to the corporate appetite. On the eve of the new millennium, the front page of the *Washington Post*'s Business Section declared, "The industrial world has approached the turn of the century in a frenzy of merger madness, capping a dramatic wave of global corporate consolidation that has been gaining momentum through much of this century."[15]

Barely had the new millennium begun when the largest corporate merger in history was announced, and of course it was another media merger. America Online (AOL), the world's largest Internet provider, acquired Time Warner, creating a media super giant that straddled cyberspace and the traditional mass media. AOL's Steve Case, now chairman of AOL Time Warner, and Time Warner's Gerald Levin, AOL Time Warner's new chief executive officer, became instant media celebrities. On the *NewsHour With Jim Lehrer*, Case denied reports that he wanted AOL to be "the king of the world," but he was dogged with questions about the compromised independence of Time Inc., the publishing arm of Time Warner.

When asked if he was prepared to pick up a copy of *Time* and see a negative story about AOL, he answered, "I think the coverage of AOL and me is going to get tougher in the Time Warner publications . . . , because you want to make sure nobody thinks there is any favoritism. . . . This not about trying to have some influence over all these media properties for some kind of self-serving reason. This is about trying to help consumers." Levin agreed. "In the first conversations that Steve [Case] and I had," said Levin, "I established as a benchmark the independence of our journalism, regardless of how we were restructuring the company."[16]

If the sprawling new media empire of AOL Time Warner can demonstrate journalistic independence, it will contradict all precedent. Tom Rosenstiel, director of the Project for Excellence in Journalism, anticipates that the AOL Time Warner merger will produce even more journalistic conflicts of interest than those that emerged after Disney's acquisition of ABC. "You just multiply that beyond comprehension and that's how many conflicts there are," he said of the AOL purchase. "It's a serious problem: Will people believe them?"

Fortune magazine reporter Marc Gunther is unsure of his own independence now that his magazine is owned by AOL. "When I wrote about AOL before, it was clean," he said. "Now I'm covering our parent company.... Readers and viewers have to approach these big companies with a high degree of skepticism."

James Ledbetter, New York bureau chief of *Industry Standard* magazine, points out the monumental dimensions of the credibility problem faced by AOL Time Warner. "Virtually every company they could possibly report on is now either a partner or a competitor."[17]

On February 29, 2000, Steve Case and Gerald Levin defended the AOL Time Warner merger before the Senate Judiciary Committee. Committee chairman Orrin Hatch (R-Utah) warned the two moguls of the danger of having a single company or a handful of companies control who can access the Internet or develop content.

Senator Mike DeWine (R-Ohio), chairman of the antitrust subcommittee, added, "The more I examine this deal the more I am convinced that it does raise very significant competition and public policy issues that must be thoroughly explored."[18]

Such congressional hand-wringing would do little to slow the pace of the media mergers. On March 13, 2000, the Chicago-based Tribune Co. announced its purchase of the Los Angeles-based Times Mirror Co., creating the nation's third-largest newspaper chain and combining massive multimedia holdings. The Tribune Co. already owned newspapers such as the *Chicago Tribune* and the *Orlando Sentinel* as well as TV and cable stations, radio stations, Internet sites, media companies, and the Chicago Cubs baseball team. With the acquisition of the Times Mirror Co., it would now own seven additional newspapers, including the *Los Angeles Times*, the *Baltimore Sun*, and *Newsday*, as well as magazines such as *Field and Stream* and *Popular Science*, Internet sites, and a variety of professional and publishing operations.

In addition to its traditional media acquisitions, the new company's combined Web sites would give them 3.4 million online visitors per month, putting them in the forefront of such activities. In explaining that "size and scale are essential" in the media industry, John W. Madigan, Tribune Co.'s chief executive, said, "We think we're creating the premier multimedia company in America."[19]

"This is negative for everyone except the shareholders," said Robert McChesney, a professor of communications at the University of Illinois. "This deal in particular takes control over delivering information in major markets and puts it in fewer and fewer hands." Newspaper analyst

John Morton said the Tribune Co. acquisition would cause smaller media companies to ask, "Are we going to be on a dance floor full of elephants?"[20]

In the past, media mergers usually involved smaller local newspapers, but the Tribune–Times Mirror merger showed that even prominent national newspapers with strong family ownership were targets for the big media conglomerates. "It's impossible to resist the pressures of the market for very long, no matter how prestigious your owner's name," said Mark Crispin Miller, director of the Project on Media Ownership at New York University. "We're talking about a media landscape that's dominated by a few brands and increasingly is all about sales. . . . There's nothing sacred in this climate. Everything and everyone's up for grabs."[21] Even European media companies are joining the American game of merger mania. On June 20, 2000, the French media conglomerate Vivendi announced a $34 billion takeover of the Canadian-American company Seagram, which owns Universal Studios and Polygram records. Jean-Marie Messier, chief executive of Vivendi, said the new company would rival AOL Time Warner in its ability to both produce and distribute entertainment worldwide. Anticipating what he said were inevitable questions about the propriety of a media baron owning the services that report on his empire, Messier said he would avoid the situation in the United States where the major news media are owned by conglomerates. "News is a very sensitive issue," said Messier. "I would feel uncomfortable controlling news media. In Europe, the very day you do that, people will raise objections."[22]

In the United States, on the other hand, neither public opinion nor the media industry itself seems able to halt the decline of independent news. David Halberstam, Pulitzer Prize–winning journalist and author, concludes, "The object of these mergers is never to improve the service. . . . [T]here is less and less real commitment to the reader of news. . . . I don't think there's anybody at the head of one of these large corporations that cares very much about journalism."[23]

CORPORATE TENTACLES

There have always been "bottom line" pressures on the media to accommodate stockholders, advertisers, or political interests. What is different today is that the media is controlled by so few owners. For example, if you're watching ABC News, the History Channel, sports on ESPN, a movie on Lifetime, or commentary on E!, you're watching Disney. That's only a fraction of Disney's media holdings, which include newspapers, magazines, radio stations, local TV stations, and, of course, motion picture production.

Similarly, if you're watching FOX News, the FX Channel, or the Family

Channel, you're watching a small part of Rupert Murdoch's News Corporation, a global media giant that controls newspapers, book publishers, regional sports networks, and satellites delivering programming to 75 percent of the world.

If you're watching CBS-TV, MTV, Nickelodeon, a film from Paramount Pictures, or a video rented at Blockbuster, you're watching a small part of Viacom, whose massive holdings span television, cable, motion pictures, video, radio, publishing, online media, theme parks, and billboards.

If you're watching NBC-TV, Bravo, or A&E; listening to NBC Radio; or using GE appliances or power generation, you're using General Electric, ranked number one with General Motors in Forbes 500. GE's ownership of NBC includes CNBC and MSNBC, through which NBC is tied to Dow Jones and Co. and Microsoft Corp. In another era, these media outlets would be competitors. Today they are partners.

And, of course, AOL Time Warner is now the big boy on the corporate block. These megacorporations have extensive media holdings, but they have an unprecedented amount of broader interests that they must promote and protect through their media outlets. Indeed, because these vast holdings are generally more profitable than their media interests, the modern media corporations subordinate public information to those profits. General Electric is a good example. In addition to its media holdings, such as NBC, GE is involved in everything from jet engines to abrasives to nuclear and electrical generating systems, as well as hotels, insurance, and finance.

Dean Alger, author of *Megamedia*, asks, "When NBC reporters come upon some issue involved in those industrial areas, are they going to think twice about what they cover? There's a built-in conflict of interest." Charles Lewis of the Center for Public Integrity agrees. "It means you're not going to be investigating certain subjects. It means that you're not going to see NBC investigating General Electric. You're not going to have ABC doing a big investigation covering Disney."[24]

Disney's Michael Eisner, chairman of ABC, admitted as much when he stated, "I would prefer ABC not to cover Disney. . . . [T]he way you avoid conflict of interest is to, as best you can, not cover yourself." Just a few days after Eisner's statement, ABC News killed a story about convicted pedophiles employed at Disney's theme parks.[25]

The giant media conglomerates have such broad and interlocking business interests that companies that would normally be competitors function as partners. For example, the Discovery Channel, the Learning Channel, and Animal Planet are all joint ventures between cable giant Telecommunications Inc. (TCI) and Cox Communications, another media giant. In addition, TCI jointly owns the QVC shopping channel with the cable giant Comcast. TCI also shares ownership of BRAVO with GE and

Cablevision, and TCI owns one-third of Cablevision. TCI even owns two-thirds of the company that produces public television's *NewsHour With Jim Lehrer*.

AOL Time Warner's cable operation ought to be a fierce competitor to TCI, but TCI's 10 percent stake in AOL Time Warner gives them common interests that reduce competition. The growth of interlocking media conglomerates is typified by the 1999 acquisition of TCI by AT&T, the monopolistic corporation that regulators had earlier broken up to spur competition.

Competition and diversity in the news have been reduced dramatically in a single generation. Of the 1,500 daily newspapers in the United States, 99 percent are the only daily in their cities. Of the 11,800 cable systems, all but a handful are monopolies in their cities. The 11,000 radio stations and the four TV networks carry monotonously similar programming. Editors and journalists are reluctant participants in this process. In a 1992 Marquette University poll of editors, 93 percent of them said advertisers tried to influence the news. A majority of the editors said their own management condoned the pressure, and 37 percent admitted that they succumbed to the pressure. Peter Phillips, editor of *Project Censored*, says, "Gone are the days when journalists were semi-free to write the stories they chose to expose the corruption of the powerful and the abuses of the business corporate elite."[26]

Project Censored's research during 1998 showed that the eleven largest media corporations are connected through shared boards of directors to 144 of the Corporate 1000 companies in the United States. For example, the *Washington Post* has a shared board director with Gillette, as does CBS, which shares board directors with Wal-Mart and Pharmacia & Upjohn. The *Los Angeles Times* shares board directors with Procter & Gamble and Nordstrom. The *New York Times* shares a board member with Bristol-Meyers Squibb, as does NBC. Gannett shares a board member with DuPont, and AOL Time Warner shares board members with Colgate-Palmolive, K-Mart, and Sears.

One example of the dangers of these shared boards occurred in 1999 when NBC's parent company, General Electric, caved in to pressure from the Nuclear Energy Institute (NEI). Steven Specker, president of GE's nuclear energy division, is on the executive board of the NEI. When NBC attempted to promote its "Atomic Train" miniseries about a train loaded with nuclear waste that goes out of control near Denver, NEI complained about making a public issue of the dangers of nuclear waste. The NEI issued a report detailing a "containment strategy" for the series, describing it as "an aggressive effort prior to the broadcast" to "validate our point of view." The report concluded, "We certainly do not want to provide news outlets a reason to air a 'could this happen in our town?' story."

NBC promptly removed all references to nuclear waste in the mini-series and announced that it would run a disclaimer at the start of the series saying the events depicted were "pure fiction." The cave-in was disturbing, not only to media critics but to the U.S. Senate as well. Senator Richard Bryan (D-Nev.) charged that the NEI would stop at nothing to keep information about nuclear danger from the public, including manipulating the content of a fictional movie. "My sense is the network did an 'el foldo,' " said Bryan. "I cannot in all honesty prove that, but the circumstantial evidence is pretty strong—just days before the program was to air!"[27]

The news alliance announced in November 1999 by NBC and the *Washington Post* raised more concerns about conflict of interest. The *Post* is now in business with a network that is owned by General Electric and is partners with Microsoft, both companies frequently covered by the *Post*. "This will not change or color our coverage," said Executive Editor Leonard Downie, but he admitted, "I know it will be more difficult for readers to see it that way."[28]

In 1998 Mark Crispin Miller, a professor of media studies at New York University, prepared a set of "media maps" designed to display the tentacles connecting some of the vast holdings of the major media conglomerates. Figures 1 through 4—updated maps of four of those conglomerates—were derived in part from Miller's original data.

When the media maps were first published in 1995, they were an eye-opener for many prominent individuals within the media whose reactions were published in *The Nation*. TV producer Norman Lear said the maps were "like the picture that speaks a thousand (in this case a million) words. It should be clear to any reasonable person that there are too few funnels through which will flow most of the world's entertainment and information. Too few funnels suggests too few individuals making too many decisions about what the world's population needs to know." Motion picture director Oliver Stone wrote, "We pride ourselves on having a 'free press.' But how free is it when we are given the same stories by every major media conglomerate in the country, when alternative viewpoints are not accessible to most Americans? The power to control the flow of information is the power to control the way people think. That power should not be concentrated in the hands of a few conglomerates."[29]

Media author Herbert Schiller said, "Packaged consciousness . . . is made by the ever-expanding goliaths of the message and image business. Gigantic entertainment-information complexes exercise a near-seamless and unified private corporate control over what we think and think about. The national symbolic environment has been appropriated by a few corporate juggernauts in the consciousness business." Leslie Savan of *The Village Voice* complained that "the entertainment and news products of these few companies determine more and more of the nation's emotional gram-

Figure 1
The Media Map: General Electric

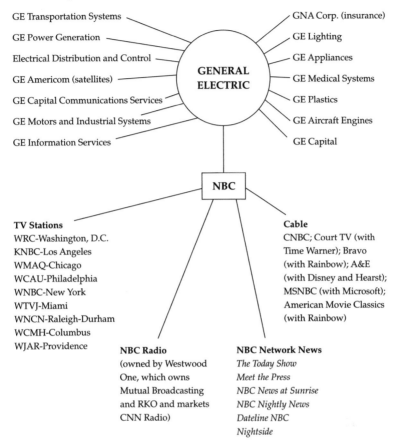

GE Transportation Systems

GE Power Generation

Electrical Distribution and Control

GE Americom (satellites)

GE Capital Communications Services

GE Motors and Industrial Systems

GE Information Services

GENERAL ELECTRIC

GNA Corp. (insurance)

GE Lighting

GE Appliances

GE Medical Systems

GE Plastics

GE Aircraft Engines

GE Capital

NBC

TV Stations
WRC-Washington, D.C.
KNBC-Los Angeles
WMAQ-Chicago
WCAU-Philadelphia
WNBC-New York
WTVJ-Miami
WNCN-Raleigh-Durham
WCMH-Columbus
WJAR-Providence

NBC Radio
(owned by Westwood
One, which owns
Mutual Broadcasting
and RKO and markets
CNN Radio)

Cable
CNBC; Court TV (with
Time Warner); Bravo
(with Rainbow); A&E
(with Disney and Hearst);
MSNBC (with Microsoft);
American Movie Classics
(with Rainbow)

NBC Network News
The Today Show
Meet the Press
NBC News at Sunrise
NBC Nightly News
Dateline NBC
Nightside

Note: NBC owns 25 to 50 percent of the following: History Channel; Independent Film Channel; News Sports; Prime; Prism; and Women's Entertainment; plus seven Sports Channels in Cincinnati, Chicago, Florida, New England, the Pacific region, Ohio, and Philadelphia.

Source: Revised and updated from data in *The Nation* (June 3, 1996; June 8, 1998) and *Censored 1997*.

Figure 2
The Media Map: AOL Time Warner

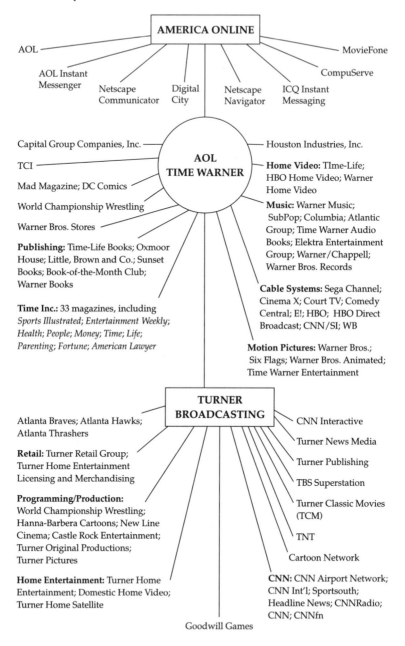

Source: Revised and updated from data in *The Nation* (June 3, 1996; June 8,1998) and *Censored 1997*.

On November 12, 1995, Mike Wallace told 21 million shocked television viewers that he could not present an interview with tobacco industry whistleblower Jeffrey Wigand because "the management of CBS had seen fit to give in to perceived threats of legal action" by the tobacco companies. Photo reproduced from the collections of the Library of Congress.

Walter Cronkite, regarded as America's most trusted man during his years as CBS News' anchorman, believes that there are few people in the corporate media environment today who have a background of journalistic ethics or responsibility. Photo reproduced from the collections of the Library of Congress.

Frequently, the corporate media censor their outlets for merely criticizing the corporate structure itself. Jim Hightower, who had a syndicated radio show on ABC, criticized Disney's acquisition of Capital Cities/ABC, saying it did not serve the people. "We're not talking about monopoly here over toasters," said Hightower. "We're talking about monopoly over your access to news and information, and it's information that you and I need if we're going to have a democracy in this country."

Within a short time, Hightower was off the air. ABC said his ratings weren't good enough. Hightower said, "I see the ABC action as the result of what I call the three M's: my message, the merger with Disney, and marketing. . . . I think somebody higher up began to listen to the show and decided this is not a message for the new Disney/ABC."[36]

A few years ago, *Saturday Night Live* did a satire of media monopoly in which it mocked the power of conglomerates like GE and Disney to control the media. The TV parody, titled "Media-opoly," ran only once, on a live broadcast, after which it mysteriously disappeared from reruns.

MAINTAINING THE WALL BETWEEN THE BOARDROOM AND THE NEWSROOM

In 1997 Richard M. Cohen, former senior producer for CBS Evening News, expressed fear for the future of the media. Complaining that the press had sacrificed traditional journalistic standards for profit, Cohen said, "The landscape is bleak. The sword has been blunted. The mission abandoned. The marketplace has triumphed, and we are all the losers. . . . Available political solutions to this problem would involve crossing swords with some of the wealthiest, most powerful corporate forces in America. . . . We live in the shadow of that corporate monolith extending ever upward into the sky. Corporations have been called private governments, and they are becoming the state. . . . The small issue of news quality is probably not even on the corporate radar screen. Conglomerates only grow greedier and fatter for their own purposes."[37]

Cohen fondly recalled the days when there was an impenetrable wall between the newsroom and the boardroom, but he declared that the wall had crumbled. "Corporate ownership of the networks and local stations is destroying the integrity of news," he said. "The dumbing down, the demise of news is all about the hunger for advertising revenues and how that plays out in the newsroom. . . . The corporate culture has met the news culture. They are, and are supposed to be, diametrically opposed to each other. Neither can function with integrity or effectiveness when they merge."[38]

There have been numerous highly publicized incidents proving Cohen's point. In 1997 the *National Review*'s advertising director sent an advance copy of an article prominently citing the Enron electric company to Enron's chairman. The cover note concluded, "Will Enron consider an ad in *National Review*'s June 16 issue?"[39] John O'Sullivan, the magazine's editor, said he had "no objection" to the tactic. "I'm an editor who believes you've got to help advertising if possible. Every now and then I talk to advertisers. That pays the bills."

Increasingly, companies are demanding to see a publication's content in advance in order to decide whether to include an ad. The American Society of Magazine Editors has cautioned its members "that some advertisers may mistake an early warning as an open invitation to pressure the publisher or editor to alter, or even kill, the article in question." William Kristol, editor of the *Weekly Standard*, warned against giving advertisers the impression that editorial content can be affected by advertising decisions. "That is a bright line you don't want to cross," he said.[40]

In 1999 a scandal at the *Los Angeles Times* highlighted the dimming of that bright line. The *Times* had been taken over in 1995 by Mark Willes, a former General Mills executive with no journalistic experience, who appointed himself publisher. Willes declared that he would use a "bazooka" to destroy the traditional wall separating the advertising department from the newsroom. In 1999 he selected Kathryn Downing, an attorney with no journalistic experience, to succeed him as publisher, and Downing intensified the merging of the paper's news and business interests.

The *Times* soon signed a partnership agreement with the Staples Center, a new $400 million sports and entertainment complex in Los Angeles. As part of its financial commitment to the Staples Center, the *Times* published a 168-page Sunday magazine supplement extolling the Center. This apparent merging of reporting and advertising brought quick criticism from the news industry, including reporters and editors at the *Times*. Adding to the controversy, the *Times* split the $2 million in advertising revenues with the Center. The reporters and editors working on the magazine supplement were not told about the revenue-sharing agreement.

Alice Short, editor of the *Times Magazine*, said, "If people in editorial had known about it ahead of time, they would have refused to work on it. That's why no one told us." Within hours of the revelation of the deal with the Staples Center, over 300 members of the *Times* editorial staff signed a statement expressing what Short called "their anger and disgust and sense of betrayal."

Henry Weinstein, the *Times*'s legal reporter, explained, "A fundamental premise of journalism is that a journalist should not be sharing revenue or have a business relationship with somebody that he's writing a story about. In fact, our own code of ethics for reporters specifically forbids this. What we saw in this deal was that the people who run the newspaper had done something that just flagrantly violated our own rules."[41]

Weinstein said that the *Times*'s inappropriate alliance with the Staples

Center justified the traditional separation of the newsroom from advertising pressures. "It confirmed your worst suspicions of what would happen if this wall was broken down, and it showed the need for maintaining the wall."[42]

The top executives at the *Times* were dismayed at the public response to the deal. *Times* editor Michael Parks said, "We entered into a business relationship, including revenue sharing, with an institution we were covering. That's a major problem. It suggests to a reader that we can be bought. We cannot be bought. But there's an appearance of an ethical breach." Publisher Downing admitted she had a "fundamental misunderstanding" of the principles of editorial independence.[43] Chief executive officer Willes said, "I didn't realize it was wrong. Shame on me for that. It didn't register the way it should have."[44]

In response to Downing's comments, *Washington Post* columnist Richard Cohen said, "I, too, have a 'fundamental misunderstanding' of how such an ignoramus could become the publisher of a major—and very important—newspaper." Cohen notes that the price of Times Mirror stock has risen under Willes, and "the board is pleased as punch" with his approach. Yet Cohen concludes, "Willes and Downing have cheapened their own product. After all, some of what their ad salesmen are selling is the reputation of a fine newspaper."[45]

A look at fellow CEOs and publishers reveals that Willes and Downing are not regarded as pariahs by their peers. A recent survey by *Editor and Publisher* magazine showed that 72 percent of top newspaper executives want closer cooperation between news and business departments, and 67 percent of them concede that guidelines separating their advertising and editorial operations are occasionally breached.[46]

The news media seem unconcerned about this phenomenon. In 1992 the nonprofit Center for the Study of Commercialism invited some 200 journalists to a Washington news conference at which it released a report entitled *Dictating Content: How Advertising Pressure Can Corrupt a Free Press*. Almost none of the invited journalists came to the news conference, and the report was ignored by the press, prompting the media watchdog group Project Censored to name *Dictating Content* as one of the ten "best censored" stories of 1992.

CONCLUSION: THE HOPE FOR JOURNALISTIC INDEPENDENCE

Even as the pace of mergers accelerates and the corporate mentality becomes the norm in newsrooms, there are some journalists and scholars who see hope in the Internet and grass roots movements. Steve Coll, managing editor of the *Washington Post*, says, "At the same time that this consolidation is occurring, a countervailing trend—technology—is opening an infinite number of channels, literally infinite on the web. It is making possible inexpensive self-publishing and community publishing to a scale and to an effect that America hasn't witnessed since the penny press."[47]

Michael Kinsley, editor of the Microsoft-owned online magazine *Slate*, believes that easy access to Internet publishing will counter the effects of the media monopoly. "A. J. Liebling said that freedom of the press is for those who own one," said Kinsley. "And now anyone for a few hundred dollars can be his own press lord . . . and have the kind of scope that only a few people had as recently as ten years ago."[48]

James Cramer, cofounder of a financial news Web site, says his experience contradicts Kinsley's optimism. "[O]ne of the great things about this medium that everyone says is 'Anybody can have a website.' . . . That is perhaps the most incorrect statement," says Cramer. "It's getting read that matters, and you can't be read unless you're connected with one of these big media outfits. . . . As a creator of content, if you're not affiliated with Time Warner or Disney or CBS . . . or News Corp./Fox or GE, NBC, or CNBC, I think you're finished."[49]

Some journalists believe individual reporters and editors can protect their profession from the dangers of corporate influence and "bottom line" journalism. "I reject a construct that suggests that *only* commercial goals are important, that the obligations of a journalist in a democracy do not have an *equal* importance," says Maxwell King, editor of the *Philadelphia Inquirer* from 1990 to 1998. "I will not permit myself, my journalism or my company to be defined only in terms of these commercial goals."[50]

Mark Crispin Miller says that shedding light on corporate power is the first step in escaping its grasp, and he calls for more maps of the contracting media universe. "Such maps will point us toward the only possible escape from the impending blackout," says Miller. "They would suggest the true causes of the enormous ills that now dismay so many Americans: the universal sleaze and 'dumbing down,' the flood tide of corporate propaganda, the terminal inanity of U.S. politics. These have arisen not from any grand decline in national character, . . . but from the inevitable toxic influence of those few corporations that have monopolized our culture. The only way to solve the problem is to break their hold; and to that end the facts of media ownership must be made known to all." Miller concludes that the time has come to free the media by creating a new, broadly based movement dedicated to an all-important mission: antitrust. "This movement must start by getting out the word— and there's the rub," says Miller. "Our problem has no precedent, for what's monopolized today is no mere staple such as beef or oil but the very media whereby the problem could be solved. . . . Today's antitrust campaign will therefore have to be a thorough grass-roots effort—one that will work around the mainstream media so as to free them by and by."[51]

Media scholar Robert McChesney warns that the nine massive conglomerates that now dominate the media cannot be tamed by current antitrust law. "It is not merely their economic power, or even their cultural power, that causes concern," says McChesney. "It is their political power. They have grown so large that they are close to being untamable by government. . . . Applying antitrust to media will not be enough. Even with an enlightened policy of media ownership in the digital age, there would still be too much power in the hands of owners and advertisers. That is why antitrust must be complemented by an aggressive and wide-ranging program to establish a viable nonprofit and noncommercial media sector."[52]

Robert Lande, professor of law at the University of Baltimore, urges Congress to create what he calls a Temporary Committee to Study Media Mergers and Media Convergence. "If the committee concludes that existing antitrust laws are inadequate, it should recommend that new antimerger legislation be enacted. This may be the only way to prevent the nightmare scenario of a media oligopoly."[53]

NOTES

1. Thomas Frank, "Liberation Marketing and the Culture Trust," in *Conglomerates and the Media*, eds. Erik Barnouw et al. (New York: The New Press, 1997), pp. 173–74.

2. Ben H. Bagdikian, Preface to the Fifth Edition, *The Media Monopoly*, 5th ed. (Boston: Beacon Press, 1997), p. ix.

3. Herbert I. Schiller, "Information Deprivation in an Information-Rich Society," in *Invisible Crises*, eds. George Gerbner, Hamid Mowlana, and Herbert Schiller (Boulder, Colo.: Westview Press, 1996), p. 17.

4. George Gerbner, "The Hidden Side of Television Violence," in *Invisible Crises*, pp. 31–32.

5. Quoted in Sara Kelly, "To Free the World," *The Utne Reader* (January–February 1997), p. 80.

6. Peter Phillips and Ivan Harslof, "Censorship within Modern Democratic Societies," in *Censored 1997: The News That Didn't Make the News*, ed. Peter Phillips (New York: Seven Stories Press, 1997), p. 148.

7. "Free Speech for Sale," PBS documentary hosted by Bill Moyers, June 6, 1999.

8. Ibid.

9. Ibid.

10. Ibid.

11. Ibid.

12. Verlyn Klinkenborg, "The Vision behind the CBS-Viacom Merger," *New York Times* (September 9, 1999), A24.

13. Stuart Elliott, "Advertising," *New York Times* (September 8, 1999), C8.

14. Greg Schneider, "Disbelief in the Air at BET," *Washington Post* (November 2, 2000), E15.

15. Sandra Sugawara, "Merger Wave Accelerated in '99," *Washington Post* (December 31, 1999), E1.

16. "Megamerger Masters," Online NewsHour, January 12, 2000, pp. 13–14, www.pbs.org/newshour.

17. Howard Kurtz, "It's All in the Family: Mega-Media's Tricky Ethics," *Washington Post* (January 11, 2000), C1.

18. "AOL, Time Warner Try to Allay Fears," *Washington Post* (March 1, 2000), E1, E4.

19. Howard Kurtz, "Tribune to Buy Times Mirror Co.," *Washington Post* (March 14, 2000), A1.

20. Sharon Walsh, "Tomorrow's Merger Today," *Washington Post* (March 14, 2000), E1, E13.

21. Ibid.

22. "Vivendi Deal Shifts Balance of Power in Global Media," *Washington Post* (June 23, 2000), E4.

23. David Halberstam, "On Serving Only One God," *Brill's Content* (December 1999/January 2000), p. 96.

24. "Free Speech for Sale," PBS documentary hosted by Bill Moyers, June 6, 1999.

25. Rifka Rosenwein, "Why Media Mergers Matter," *Brill's Content* (December 1999/January 2000), p. 94.

26. Peter Phillips, "Building Media Democracy," in *Censored 1999: The News That Didn't Make the News*, ed. Peter Phillips (New York: Seven Stories Press, 1999), p. 130.

27. Lisa de Morales, "Did the Nuclear Energy Lobby Derail 'Atomic Train?' " *Washington Post* (May 13, 1999), C7.

28. Howard Kurtz, "Post Co., NBC Announce Alliance," *Washington Post* (November 18, 1999), A24.

29. "On That Chart," *The Nation* (June 3, 1996), pp. 16–19.

30. Ibid.

31. Advertisement by the Philip Morris Corp., *Washington Post* (August 24, 1995), A16.

32. Smoke in the Eye," *Frontline* television series, PBS, April 2, 1996.

33. "Self-censorship at CBS," *New York Times* (November 12, 1995), E14.

34. Frank Rich, "Fear and Favor," *New York Times* (November 15, 1995), A23.

35. "Smoke in the Eye," *Frontline* television series, PBS, April 2, 1996.

36. Evan Smith, "Jim Hightower," *Mother Jones* (November/December 1995), p. 58.

37. Richard M. Cohen, "The Corporate Takeover of News: Blunting the Sword," in *Conglomerates and the Media*, pp. 31–33, 36.

38. Ibid.

39. Howard Kurtz. "At the National Review, Does 'Ad' Stand for 'Advance?' " *Washington Post* (July 7, 1997), C1.

40. Ibid., C4.

41. "Trouble at the L.A. Times," Online NewsHour, December 16, 1999, pp. 1–3, www.pbs.org/newshour.

42. Sharon Waxman, "Los Angeles' Troubled Times," *Washington Post* (November 9, 1999), C8.

43. Howard Kurtz, "Ex-Publisher Slams L.A. Times," *Washington Post* (November 5, 1999), C2.

44. Howard Kurtz, " 'Ethical Iceberg' Seen in L.A. Times Scandal Probe," *Washington Post* (December 21, 1999), C9.

45. Richard Cohen, "No Way to Do News Business," *Washington Post* (November 11, 1999), A43.

46. "Trouble at the L.A. Times," Online NewsHour, December 16, 1999, pp. 1–3, www.pbs.org/newshour.

47. "Joining Forces," Online NewsHour, January 19, 2000, p. 8, www.pbs.org/newshour.

48. "The New Age of Journalism," Online NewsHour, January 19, 2000, pp. 1, 3, www.pbs.org/newshour.

49. James Cramer, "On How the Little Guy Doesn't Have a Chance," *Brill's Content* (January 2000), p. 104.

50. Maxwell E. P. King, "Journalism in an Egalitarian Society" (lecture given at Washington and Lee University, Lexington, Virginia, 1998).

51. Mark Crispin Miller, "Free the Media," *The Nation* (June 3, 1996), pp. 10, 12.

52. Robert W. McChesney, "Antitrust & the Media—I," *The Nation* (May 22, 2000), p. 5.

53. Robert H. Lande, "Antitrust & the Media—II," *The Nation* (May 22, 2000), p. 6.

CHAPTER 2

Public Relations and the News

SELLING THE NEWS

Public relations may be the phenomenon that best defines the twentieth-century media. The power of the public relations (PR) industry to determine the commercial tastes of the American public is widely acknowledged and, in some circles, admired. But few Americans understand the process by which their opinions are molded, and fewer still know how much of the news and information originates from the desks of PR agents, popularly known as "flacks." That vernacular term for press agents or PR people now pervades press coverage.

What began as the work of small-time show men hawking cheap products is today a $10 billion industry conducted by former journalists, retired politicians, and ambitious young college graduates. Press agents who once relied on news releases and publicity stunts now produce entire stories for every major newspaper in the country. In addition, PR firms write, film, and produce "news" shows that are transmitted by satellite feed to hundreds of TV stations around the world. These "video news releases" (VNRs) are designed to be indistinguishable from real news and are frequently used on TV news shows without any attribution or disclaimer.

"Most of what you see on TV is, in fact, a canned PR product," says a senior vice president with Gray & Company public relations. "Most of what you read in the paper and see on television is not news."[1]

In addition to direct manipulation of the media, the PR industry funds and orchestrates many of the apparently grass roots campaigns that lobby federal and state governments. Such lobbying receives major media coverage, but the corporate hand behind the campaigns remains invisible.

"The best PR ends up looking like news," says one PR executive. "You never know when a PR agency is being effective; you'll just find your views slowly shifting."[2]

PR executives today mediate public communications in ways few people could have imagined a generation ago. "PR has become a communications medium in its own right, an industry designed to alter perception, reshape reality and manufacture consent," says Mark Dowie, editor and publisher of *Mother Jones* magazine.[3] Dowie says PR professionals can look at the front page of any newspaper or listen to any news broadcast and identify which of their peers placed, handled, or "massaged" a particular story, managed the spin, or wrote the CEO's quotes.[4]

"The news media have progressively abandoned their news-gathering function to public relations practitioners," says public relations scholar Scott Cutlip. "Studies show that some 40% of media content comes from public relations sources."[5] This prepackaged "news" flows virtually unedited from public relations offices.

The ease with which PR professionals have taken over the news is reflected in the fact that about one-third of them began their careers as journalists. Indeed, the 150,000 PR professionals in the United States outnumber the nation's 130,000 reporters, and the gap is widening. Some of the nation's top journalism schools now send more than half of their graduates directly into public relations. As the media becomes dependent on PR for more and more of its content, the PR executives have become powerful media figures. Today's reporters are deferential to publicists such as Frank Mankiewicz or Harold Burson, knowing that their firms (Hill & Knowlton, and Burson-Marsteller) represent many of the most quotable sources in the country.

PR firms provide both "paid media" (advertising) and "free media" (public relations). The public recognizes that an ad in the local newspaper is a form of commercial propaganda, but the public doesn't realize that the story on page one may have been placed by the same firm that placed the ad. Corporations use the phrase "integrated communications" to describe this combination of advertising and public relations. In the past, such an approach was used to sell products. Today it is used to "sell" ideas, policies, political candidates, ideologies, and even foreign dictators. This new propaganda, aimed at the subconscious, has dangerous consequences for a free press and a democratic society. Mark Dowie warns, "This is an awesome power we give to an industry that gravitates to wealth, offers surplus power and influence to those who need it least, and operates largely beyond public view."[6]

The descent of the American press into tabloid journalism during the 1990s has expanded the opportunities for PR practitioners to increase their influence in the news room. In their 1985 book, *PR: How the Public Relations Industry Writes the News*, authors Jeff Blyskal and Marie Blyskal say, "PR people know how the press thinks. They are able to tailor their publicity so that journalists will listen and cover it. As a result much of the news that you read in newspapers and magazines or watch on television and hear on radio is heavily influenced and slanted by public relations people. Whole sections of the news are virtually owned by PR. . . . Unfortunately, news hatched by a PR person and journalist working together looks like real news dug up by enterprising journalists working independently. The public thus does not know which news stories and journalists are playing servant to PR."[7]

Working reporters receive dozens, often hundreds, of PR contacts each day. PR Newswire, a leader in the distribution of corporate and institutional information to the media and the financial community, sends some 100,000 news releases a year to some 2,000 newsrooms. Other PR distribution services specialize in placing stories in newspapers through the mass distribution of PR-written feature articles and opinion pieces that are picked up as real news. The North American Precis Syndicate, for example, sends camera-ready stories on behalf of most of the top PR firms and Fortune 500 companies to 10,000 newspapers, almost all of which reprint some of the material. The stories are designed to promote products or serve clients' political agendas.

A similar business, Radio USA, writes, typesets, prints, and distributes broadcast-quality news scripts to 5,000 radio stations throughout the country. Busy radio journalists have little hesitation about using these scripts. "When your job is to come up with hundreds of story ideas every month, Radio USA helps," says Susan Vaughan, news director at KVEC in San Luis Obispo, California.[8]

The use of radio and video news releases (VNRs) is a little-known practice that mushroomed during the 1980s when PR firms found that they could film, edit, and produce their own news segments, even entire programs, and that broadcasters would run the segments as "news," often without editing. When the PR firm Gray & Co. began producing a radio program for its clients called "Washington Spotlight," they didn't have to force it on the media. Outlets such as the Mutual Radio Network actually requested the packaged "news."

In 1985 Gray & Co. distributed a VNR featuring an interview with one of its clients, King Hassan II of Morocco. After CNN's airing of the PR segment, some journalists claimed that they had been tricked into running propaganda, but an executive at Gray pointed out the media's hypocrisy: "I used to read in *Broadcasting* the cache of letters from directors after the story broke about electronic news releases saying, 'How despicable. Never in a thousand years.' And they were people I had talked to who had called me back so that they had the right coordinates on the satellite so that they could take the feed. They knew exactly who we were. They called us all the time." The Gray executive said these were the same people who would call them to request an overnight FedEx of a PR story because they forgot to turn their downlink on. "I was personally aggrieved at all this sort of self-righteousness of the media when that story broke," said another Gray executive. "Most of them take it straight off the air[satellite] and broadcast it. Rip and read."[9]

Packaged "news" supplied by PR firms is attractive to news organizations because it is cost effective. When a TV news show airs a VNR, the PR firm that produced it pays all the costs of scripting, filming, and editing. PR-supplied experts enable reporters to quickly and easily produce authentic-sounding stories, and the public thinks it is seeing objectively reported news.

PR firms usually produce VNRs with two versions of the story being touted. The first is fully edited, with voiceovers or with a script indicating where the station's local news anchor should read his or her lines. The second version, known as "B-roll," consists of the raw footage used to produce the fully edited version. The local station can edit the B-roll itself or combine it with footage from other sources. "The big stations don't want pre-packaged, pre-taped," explains a Gray & Co. executive. "They have the money, the budget, and the manpower to put their own together. But the smaller stations across the country lap up stuff like this."[10]

MediaLink, a PR firm that distributed about half of the VNRs made available to newscasters in the early 1990s, surveyed ninety-two newsrooms and found that all of them used VNRs supplied free by PR firms, despite the fact that they were slanted to sell a client's products or views while appearing to be news. For example, on June 13, 1991, *CBS Evening News* ran a segment on the dangers of automatic safety belts although it was part of a VNR created by a lawyers' lobby group.

George Glazer, a senior vice president of Hill & Knowlton, says VNRs are as much a public relations fixture as the print news release is. Given this reality, one would expect the journalistic profession to impose some restrictions on the use of VNRs, but no formal guidelines have ever been promulgated. "With few exceptions, broadcasters as a group have refused to participate in any kinds of standards establishment for VNRs, in part because they rarely will admit to using them on the air," explains Glazer. "There are truly hundreds of examples of self-denial on the part of broadcasters when it comes to admitting that VNRs are used."[11]

In an effort to promote a more open relationship between the media and PR firms, Glazer has called for "the admission by broadcasters that VNRs are useful, that they are used on the air regularly by virtually every station and network in the country and that usage will increase rather than disappear." Glazer admits that the public relations people who produce VNRs are slanting the content to present their client favorably, but he says there is no conspiracy to mislead. "In many cases, the producers are former broadcasters, and it's hard to believe that there has been a mass sellout as they left stations or networks and moved to 'the other side.' They are still working pretty much the same as when they were journalists—and that's what makes them valuable in their new roles."[12]

The PR industry knows that it must do more than make stories available to journalists. In order to market its packaged news, it must know the personalities, needs, and weaknesses of the reporters themselves. Former *Wall Street Journal* reporter Dean Rothbart makes his living by providing PR firms with dossiers on journalists so that the firms will be better able to manipulate the media. Rothbart's firm, TJFR Products and Services, communicates this information in high-priced newsletters and customized workshops. Rothbart places the bios of over 6,000 journalists in his computer system and offers to fax a requested bio to a PR firm within an hour.

One Rothbart publication, *TJFR Environment News Reporter*, tells PR executives, "Let us be your eyes and ears when the environmental media convene. . . . Gather vital information on key journalists. . . . Not only will you find news on journalists, we'll tell you what they want from you and what strategies you can employ with them to generate more positive stories and better manage potentially negative situations."[13]

PR agents for the DuPont company have actually recruited selected members of the media as paid participants in laboratory research to develop a PR strategy for dealing with media controversies. The participating journalists were assured, "Your ethics as a journalist (and that of your news organization) will not be violated or jeopardized in any way." Afterwards one of the participating reporters said, "They would give us small pieces of paper which would say something like, 'Dupont makes very wonderful chemicals, and no one needs to worry.' " The journalists were then asked to develop stories based on that theme, while DuPont researchers observed from behind a mirrored window.[14]

Robert J. Myers and Associates, a Houston firm, hired journalists to help ARCO Petroleum practice its PR strategies for handling the news media following environmental disasters. In a staged oil spill controversy, reporters were assigned the role of the "predatory press." Professional actors played the part of environmentalists, and ARCO employees and government officials played themselves. "The drills gave company flacks the opportunity to practice varnishing the truth just in case the mop-up doesn't go as planned," said one participating journalist, Dashka Slater. "Mostly the company and government spokespeople did what they had learned to do in numerous media-training workshops: convey as little information as possible in as many words as possible."[15]

An increasingly effective way for the PR industry to influence reporters is through the Internet. For example, an on-line service called Profnet invites journalists in search of information to e-mail their requests to the service, which distributes them to more than 800 PR representatives of research institutions. The service then finds professors or researchers to answer the questions in a way that shapes the spin of the story in the direction determined by the PR representative.

THE ORIGINS OF PUBLIC RELATIONS

The media's dependence on advertising began in the 1830s, when "penny presses" combined low sales price with mass circulation to attract expensive advertising. This gave advertisers the power to influence news and editorial sections. By the turn of the century, most companies employed press agents to feed advertising and publicity to newspapers. Often these agents were former reporters who saw this as a way to make more money. According to the authoritative *History of Journalism*, by the end of the nineteenth century advertisers could "insert at a higher cost almost any advertisement disguised as a bit of news. Sometimes these paid reading notices of advertisers were distinguished by star or dagger, but more frequently there was no sign to indicate to the readers that the account had been bought and paid for and was not a regular news item."[16]

Ivy Lee was one of the earliest PR consultants to emphasize corporate image-building. Lee's first major job was to paper over the Rockefeller family's brutal union-busting tactics, including the machine-gunning of striking mine workers and their families. During World War I, Lee and other PR pioneers joined the government's campaign to mobilize support for the war effort and turned it into the most effective large-scale war propaganda ever seen. After World War I, Lee's firm once more defended the Rockefellers in a private war between coal mine owners and striking mine workers in West Virginia that left at least seventy miners dead. Lee's success in cleaning up the reputation of the coal companies soon made him the most sought-after advisor of his day. Indeed, many historians consider him to have been the "father of public relations," though his own reputation was tainted late in his career by his association with Nazi Germany.[17]

After Lee's death in 1934, Edward L. Bernays assumed leadership of the PR industry. Bernays was a nephew of Sigmund Freud, and he pioneered the use of psychology in public persuasion. "If we understand the mechanism and motives of the group mind," wrote Bernays, "it is now possible to control and regiment the masses according to our will without their knowing it."[18] Bernays expanded on this technique of opinion-molding in his book *The Engineering of Consent* (1955).

In his most important book, *Propaganda* (1928), Bernays justified his techniques of mind control: "The conscious and intelligent manipulation of the organized habits and opinions of the masses is an important element in democratic society. Those who manipulate this unseen mechanism of society constitute an invisible government which is the true ruling power of our country.... In almost every act of our daily lives, whether in the sphere of politics or business, in our social conduct or our ethical thinking, we are dominated by the relatively small number of persons ... who understand the mental processes and social patterns of the masses. It is they who pull the wires which control the public mind."[19]

Among the earliest clients for PR pioneers like Bernays, Ivy Lee, and John Hill were the tobacco companies, for whom they used psychological marketing techniques, subliminal message reinforcement, phony front groups, and the purchase of favorable news reporting to motivate women and children to use cigarettes.[20] In the early 1950s, when the first scientific studies showing tobacco's role in cancer and other fatal illnesses began to surface, John Hill, founder of the giant PR firm Hill & Knowlton (H&K), designed the costliest and most successful PR crisis management campaign in history. In 1958 H&K formed the Tobacco Institute, a PR and lobbying organization that by 1990 had grown into one of the most formidable public relations/lobbying machines in history.

Atomic energy was another early client for the burgeoning PR industry, which produced propaganda labeled as "educational" materials and targeted all levels of American society, including the grade schools. Films, comic books, and cartoon graphics were particularly effective. By the 1990s the storage of nuclear waste had become the nuclear power industry's major public relations problem. Whenever a major waste storage program was announced, it was accompanied by a massive PR campaign, including the hiring of local reporters to present the atomic industry's side of the story and to convince the public that atomic energy was safe.

PUBLIC RELATIONS FOR FOREIGN POWERS

On February 4, 1963, Senator J. William Fulbright, chair of the Senate Foreign Relations Committee, convened hearings to scrutinize PR firms that represented foreign nations. In its testimony, the Hamilton Wright Organization described PR services to its client, nationalist China, that included the creation of feature stories for newspapers and magazines and movie short subjects. Wright said it was his practice to make such material available to editors and producers free of charge. When Wright

Edward L. Bernays, a nephew of Sigmund Freud, pioneered the use of psychology in public relations. In 1928 he wrote, "If we understand the mechanism and motives of the group mind, it is now possible to control and regiment the masses according to our will without their knowing it." Photo reproduced from the collections of the Library of Congress.

During the 1950s, Don Knowlton (left) and John W. Hill (right) used the public relations firm Hill & Knowlton to mold public opinion. Among their major accomplishments was convincing the public that smoking was not harmful to one's health. Photo reproduced from the collections of the Library of Congress.

was asked whether these editors knew that the material had been paid for by a foreign government, he said that some did and some did not. Committee members expressed concern that the American public was unaware that Wright's organization was functioning as a foreign agent.

Scott Cutlip, a prominent public relations scholar, says, "The 1963 hearings made it abundantly clear that these practitioners had assumed a substantial portion of the news-gathering functions in foreign news, and yet these agencies cannot be expected to report objectively in the public interest. . . . The Fulbright record is replete with examples of foreign news produced by public relations agencies and used in dead-pan fashion by the nations' media."[21]

Anastasio Somoza was one of several Latin American dictators who exploited American PR. During the 1970s the Nicaraguan tyrant employed the Mackenzie and McCheyne firm in New York, which was paid $300,000 in fees during Somoza's last full year in power. Mackenzie said of his client, "By the sheer law of averages, Somoza has to have done some good. Even Mussolini did some good for Italy."[22]

After Somoza's business partners gunned down the editor of the independent Nicaraguan newspaper *La Prensa*, Somoza turned to a new agent, Norman L. Wolfson of the New York PR firm Norman, Lawrence, Patterson, & Farrell. Somoza paid $7,000 a month to Wolfson, who spent most of his time convincing reporters that they had not been fair in their coverage of Somoza. Wolfson's memoir of the experience, "Selling Somoza: the Lost Cause of a PR Man," appeared in the July 20, 1979, issue of William Buckley's conservative *National Review*, just in time to accompany Somoza's hasty flight from Nicaragua into exile, to be replaced by the Sandinista revolutionaries.

When the triumphant Sandinistas took power in Nicaragua, the U.S. government and the PR firms that had promoted Somoza had to create a credible insurgent force from the defeated "Somocistas." Toward this end, Somoza's National Guard, notorious for its brutality, was reorganized into a counter-revolutionary force known as the Contras.

Despite a 1913 law that prohibits federal government agencies from engaging in public relations activities, including the use of the media, to influence members of Congress, President Ronald Reagan had CIA director William Casey set up a "public diplomacy" machine that was described as "America's first peace-time propaganda ministry . . . a set of domestic political operations comparable to what the CIA conducts against hostile forces abroad." The scientific methods of modern public relations were used to build an unprecedented bureaucracy designed to keep the news media in line and to restrict conflicting information from reaching the American public.[23]

In August 1983, as Reagan's PR operation was taking shape, CIA director Casey summoned a group of top public relations executives to a

Senator J. William Fulbright (D-Ark.) is shown speaking with Senate colleague Theodore F. Green (D-R.I.). Fulbright's Foreign Relations Committee held hearings in 1963 to scrutinize public relations firms that represented foreign nations. Testimony indicated that these firms had assumed a substantial portion of America's news gathering functions. Photo reproduced from the collections of the Library of Congress.

Despite a 1913 law prohibiting federal agencies from engaging in public relations activities, President Ronald Reagan had CIA director William Casey create the Office of Public Diplomacy (OPD), described by *Washington Post* editor Ben Bradlee as "the wholesale integration of intelligence and PR." Photo reproduced from the collections of the Library of Congress.

full-day secret strategy meeting. Four of the five executives were prominent members of the Public Relations Society of America, the industry's leading professional association. They advised the Reagan administration to set up a classic corporate communications function within the White House and dramatize the Contra cause by creating a privately funded public education program. The White House responded by bringing together a coalition of retired military men and right-wing millionaires to support the Nicaragua Freedom Fund, the main purpose of which was to divert attention from the administration's covert funding of the Contras. One channel for such funding was a specialized PR firm, International Business Communications, which pleaded guilty in 1987 to income tax fraud in raising funds for the Contras.

Following the advice of the PR executives, the White House appointed Walter Raymond Jr., a twenty-year veteran of the CIA's clandestine overseas media operations, as head of the administration's new Office of Public Diplomacy (OPD) for Latin America and the Caribbean, an action described by *Washington Post* editor Ben Bradlee as "the wholesale integration of intelligence and PR."[24] In its first year, the OPD's activities included booking more than 1,500 speaking engagements, including radio, television, and editorial board interviews; publishing three books on Nicaragua; and distributing materials to 1,600 college libraries, 520 political science faculties, 122 editorial writers, and 107 religious organizations. Prominent journalists were the focus of special attention.[25]

In 1985 the OPD used a "cut-out" (i.e., a person whose ties to the OPD were concealed) to arrange visits by Contra leader Alfonso Robelo to news organizations such as the Hearst newspapers, *Newsweek*, Scripps Howard newspapers, the *Washington Post, USA Today*, CNN, the McNeil-Lehrer Report, the Today Show, and CBS Morning News.[26]

In private memos to the National Security Council, the OPD boasted of having "killed" news stories opposing the Reagan administration's Nicaragua policies, using tactics that included intimidation and character assassination of journalists. The OPD also funded conservative organizations such as Accuracy in Media, which aggressively attacked journalists who criticized Reagan's foreign policy. In July 1985 the OPD helped spread a fabricated story that some American reporters had slanted their stories after receiving sexual favors from Sandinista prostitutes.[27]

The OPD staged publicity stunts and news stories such as the fictional 1984 "MIGs crisis," which claimed that Nicaragua was about to receive a delivery of Soviet fighter planes. The story was prominently played on TV news, with "special bulletins" interrupting regular programming. Though the story was eventually proven to be false, it helped create the public perception that Nicaragua posed a military threat to the United

States and it diverted attention from Nicaragua's first free elections, in which the Sandinistas received 67 percent of the vote.

The White House dismissed the elections as "a sham" and accused the Sandinistas of drug running and terrorism. To press the terrorism charge, the White House employed Neil Livingstone, senior vice-president with the PR firm Gray & Co. By the late 1980s the PR campaign to demonize the Sandinistas had become so successful that American newspaper editors felt the need to fall in line. "In the first couple of years I was here," said Judy Butler, a journalist living in Nicaragua, "there was an interest, at least on the part of some reporters, to try to write about what they saw in Nicaragua. . . . Increasingly, their stories were changed in the States and the reporters started carrying telexes to show that what got published was not what they had written. Now, they don't even bother."[28]

The Office of Public Diplomacy was disbanded in 1988, after the U.S. comptroller general concluded that it had "engaged in prohibited, covert propaganda activities designed to influence the media and public to support Administration Latin American policies."[29]

Having been crucial in directing the Reagan administration's successful PR campaign in Nicaragua, private PR firms were much in demand to provide independent representation of controversial Latin American nations. When the nation of Colombia grew concerned about its international image as a compliant host for the world's largest drug cartel, it turned to the Sawyer/Miller Group, a top media consulting firm. Sawyer/Miller devised a program to change the public image of Colombia from that of villain to hero, a leader in the war on drugs. In 1991 alone, Colombia spent $3.1 million on the PR campaign, including newspaper and TV ads aimed at Washington policymakers. The campaign blamed the drug problem on drug users, whose demand was said to fuel the entire drug trade. "Look at the press clips from then on," said Sawyer/Miller's Jack Leslie proudly. "News stories, columns, editorials, all start talking more and more about demand."[30]

Sawyer/Miller produced pamphlets, video news releases, and letters to editors signed by Colombian government officials. All requests for press interviews were channeled through Sawyer/Miller, which provided ready access to sympathetic journalists while turning away those who were critical. The firm also organized meetings between Colombian government officials and newspaper editorial boards, at which favorable stories were proposed. Following a meeting with *New York Times Magazine* editor Warren Hoge, the *Times* ran a lengthy profile glorifying Colombian president Cesar Gaviria Trujillo, whose election campaign had been heavily funded by the drug cartels. The Colombian embassy sent thousands of copies of the article to journalists around the United States.

The propaganda campaign was effective, but in 1992 the Center for

Public Integrity published a damning report, *The Torturers' Lobby*, show-ing that PR firms were earning more than $30 million a year helping repressive governments improve their images. The giant firm Hill & Knowlton topped the list with $14 million in payments from countries with records of abuse, torture, and political imprisonment. During the period 1991–1992, while hundreds of Guatemalans were executed for political reasons, $220,000 in fees were paid by the Guatemalan govern-ment to the Washington firm of Patton, Boggs, & Blow. During the same period Nigeria's military government spent $2.6 million to cover its crimes, much of which went to a Burson-Marsteller subsidiary.

In his pre-Clinton days, Ron Brown, secretary of commerce under President Clinton, personally represented the Haitian dictatorship of "Papa Doc" Duvalier. Duvalier fled Haiti in 1986, and Jean Bertrand Aristide won Haiti's first democratic election in 1990 with 67 percent of the vote. Eight months later, soldiers led by Lieutenant General Raoul Cédras and Colonel Michel François sent Aristide into exile. Cédras then began a smear campaign against Aristide in America, using PR firms to spread the charges in the U.S. media.

The Haitian regime's most prominent lobbyist was Robert Mc-Candless, who circulated position papers and editorials in Washington. In his PR work, McCandless exploited his friendship with conservative columnist Robert Novak, who wrote a series of columns in support of the junta. Even after the return of civilian rule to Haiti, PR firms suc-cessfully continued to demonize Aristide in the American press.

PUBLIC RELATIONS FOR WAR

Wartime propaganda has a long and sordid history, but only in the twentieth century has it become closely integrated with public relations. President Reagan's military invasion of tiny Grenada was a PR triumph orchestrated by advisers Mike Deaver and Craig Fuller, who had pre-viously worked for the Hannaford Company, a PR firm that represented the Guatemalan military dictatorship. On his advisers' recommendation Reagan imposed a total media blackout on the Grenada invasion.

A more subtle and effective strategy was used by Reagan's successor, President George Bush, who, in concert with private PR firms, organized public support for the Persian Gulf War through one of the most inten-sive and successful PR campaigns in American history. Almost over-night, Bush was faced with the need to transform the public image of Iraqi leader Saddam Hussein from that of trusted ally to demon. Iraq's invasion of oil-rich Kuwait, an autocratic feudal state that had been an independent nation for only a quarter-century, did not initially arouse public support for sending American troops to the Gulf. "If and when a shooting war starts, reporters will begin to wonder why American soldiers are dying for oil-rich Sheiks," warned Hal Steward, a retired army PR official. "The U.S. military had better get cracking to come up with a public relations plan."[31]

Such a plan was soon under way, paid for by the oil-rich sheiks themselves. The government of Kuwait funded as many as twenty PR, law, and lobby firms in a campaign to mobilize U.S. public opinion against Saddam Hussein. Among the firms were the Rendon Group, which received a $100,000 per month retainer for media work, and Neill & Co., which received $50,000 per month. Sam Zackhein, a former U.S. ambassador to Bahrain, another feudal oil producer, channeled $7.7 million in advertising and lobbying money through two front groups—the Coalition for Americans at Risk, and the Freedom Task Force. The Coalition, which had been formed in the 1980s as a front for the Nicaraguan Contras, prepared and placed TV and newspaper ads and maintained a large source of speakers for pro-war events.[32]

Of all the PR firms working on the campaign, Hill & Knowlton, then the world's largest PR firm, was the most effective. As the mastermind behind the Persian Gulf War, H&K's activities alone would have constituted the largest foreign-funded PR campaign ever directed at molding American public opinion. Nine days after Iraqi troops entered Kuwait, H&K signed a contract to represent "Citizens for a Free Kuwait," a PR front group whose connections to the Kuwaiti government and the Bush administration were hidden. Over the next six months the Kuwaiti government provided $11.9 million to Citizens for a Free Kuwait, virtually all of which went to H&K.[33]

Craig Fuller, a close friend and political adviser to President Bush, was the man running H&K's Washington office. The news media didn't bother to examine Fuller's role in the Kuwaiti publicity campaign until after the war was over, but even before the fighting began they could have read in O'Dwyer's PR Services Report that Fuller had been on the Kuwaiti account at Hill & Knowlton since the first day. They would also have learned that the Wirthlin Group, a research arm of H&K, was the pollster for the Reagan administration, and that Robert K. Gray, chair of H&K/USA based in Washington, D.C., had a leading role in both Reagan campaigns.

In addition to such Republican partisans as Gray and Fuller, H&K employed a well-connected group of Democrats who helped develop bipartisan support for the Persian Gulf War. Lauri Fitz-Pegado, who headed the Kuwait campaign, had formerly worked with Democratic lobbyist and later Clinton appointee Ron Brown, representing Haiti's Duvalier dictatorship. H&K senior vice president Thomas Ross had been Pentagon spokesperson during the Carter administration. H&K vice-chair Frank Mankiewicz, former press secretary and adviser to Robert F. Kennedy and George McGovern, managed the news media, arranging hundreds of meetings, briefings, calls, and mailings directed toward the editors of daily newspapers and other media outlets.

"Hill & Knowlton has assumed a role in world affairs unprecedented for a PR firm," said Jack O'Dwyer, head of *O'Dwyer's PR Services*. "H&K has employed a stunning variety of opinion-forming devices and techniques to help keep U.S. opinion on the side of the Kuwaitis."[34]

H&K's activities included arranging media interviews for visiting Kuwaitis, organizing public rallies, releasing letters to the media, distributing news releases and information kits, contacting politicians, producing a nightly radio show in Arabic from Saudi Arabia, and producing dozens of video news releases that were given "free" air time around the country.

Public relations authors John Stauber and Sheldon Rampton noted, "The video news releases (VNRs) were shown by eager TV news directors around the world who rarely (if ever) identified Kuwait's PR firm as the source of the footage and stories. TV stations and networks simply fed the carefully crafted propaganda to unwitting viewers, who assumed they were watching 'real' journalism."[35]

Citizens for a Free Kuwait published a 154-page book entitled *The Rape of Kuwait*, copies of which were included in media kits and featured on TV talk shows and in newspapers. It soon became clear that stories of Iraqi brutality were the most effective PR tool. On October 10, 1990, the Congressional Human Rights Caucus held a hearing on Capitol Hill concerning Iraqi human rights violations. The hearing, chaired by Representative Tom Lantos (D-Calif.) and Representative John Porter (R-Ill.), had the outward appearance of an official congressional proceeding. In reality, it was a meeting of a separate and unofficial entity called the Congressional Human Rights Foundation, an H&K front group cochaired by Lantos and Porter. The foundation was housed in free office space at H&K and had its telephones answered by the H&K switchboard. In addition, Citizens for a Free Kuwait made a $50,000 donation to the foundation.

The emotionally moving testimony before the caucus came from a 15-year-old Kuwaiti girl known only by her first name, Nayirah. Her written testimony was passed out in a media kit prepared by Citizens for a Free Kuwait. The caucus claimed that her full name was being kept confidential to prevent Iraqi reprisals against her family. A much more compelling reason for anonymity would later be discovered.

In testimony frequently interrupted by sobbing, Nayirah gave an eyewitness account of shocking Iraqi brutality. "I volunteered at the al-Addan hospital," she testified. "While I was there, I saw the Iraqi soldiers come into the hospital with guns, and go into the room where . . . babies were in incubators. They took the babies out of the incubators, took the incubators, and left the babies on the cold floor to die."[36]

Three months passed between Nayirah's testimony and American military action, and during those months Nayirah's story was the most effective tool in mobilizing American public opinion in support of war. The story was repeated over and over in the media. President Bush told it. It was recited as fact on TV and radio, on the floor of Congress, even in the UN Security Council. Of all of the news reports about Iraq, none had more impact on public opinion.

"H&K sent its own camera crew to film this hearing that it had helped cast and direct. It then produced a film that was quickly sent out as a video release used widely by a gullible media," recalls Scott Cutlip. "Once more the public served as patsies for the public relations staged event."[37]

Only after the war was over did the press discover and reveal to the public that the testimony before the Human Rights Caucus was a PR hoax. Hill & Knowlton and Congressman Tom Lantos had failed to reveal that Nayirah was the daughter of Kuwait's ambassador to the United States and that she had been coached in her testimony by H&K vice-president Lauri Fitz-Pegado. Even Kuwait's own investigators admitted that Nayirah's testimony was false. John McArthur, in his book *Second Front*, noted, "The Human Rights Caucus is not a committee of Congress, and therefore it is not encumbered by the legal accoutrements that would make a witness hesitate before he or she lied. . . . Lying under oath before a congressional committee is a crime; lying from under the cover of anonymity to a caucus is merely public relations."[38]

If Nayirah's testimony had been exposed by the press at the time, Congress and the media might have looked behind the PR campaign that was leading the nation toward war. As late as December 1990, polls indicated that about half of the American public wanted President Bush to wait beyond his January 15 deadline for military intervention. On January 15 the U.S. Senate voted by a narrow five-vote margin to support a declaration of war. The fabricated incubator story probably determined that margin.

Following the war, human rights investigators could find no witnesses or other evidence to support H&K's story. Amnesty International was forced to issue an embarrassing retraction. Nayirah herself had no comment. Her father angrily rejected all requests to interview her. As for the architect of the fraud, H&K's Lauri Fitz-Pegado was nominated to be assistant secretary of commerce, but the Senate Banking Committee, which considered her nomination, was uncomfortable with her background. "Lauri Fitz-Pegado has coached perjured testimony before congress," said the committee report. "She has been a hired gun for disreputable foreign interests. She has deliberately attempted to mislead Senators about her past. In short, Lauri Fitz-Pegado has disqualified herself from service in the position to which she has been nominated."[39]

Meanwhile, the American press was disturbingly silent about its role in hoodwinking the public. After the war, the Canadian Broadcasting Corporation produced an Emmy award–winning documentary on the Persian Gulf War PR campaign titled "To Sell a War," but the few American reporters who pursued the documentary found it hard to come by. Hill & Knowlton refused to discuss the controversy or even show its VNRs to the press, choosing instead to recirculate the phony TV "news" reports.

Arthur Rouse, author of *Slanted News*, wrote, "The press, which had shown little interest in questioning the credibility of the atrocity reports when those reports were having such a tremendous impact on U.S. policy, seemed reluctant to reconsider the evidence—or its own reporting."[40]

A PR PROJECT FOR THE 1990s: DISMEMBERING THE BALKANS

With the end of the Persian Gulf War, Hill & Knowlton's clients were significantly fewer and its rival, Burson-Marsteller, took over as the world's largest PR firm, followed by firms such as Ruder Finn that specialize in representing foreign powers. The American public and media soon became subject to a new PR campaign in the Balkans that many believe has been the most successful in American history.

The focus of the new campaign was to exploit business opportunities in the multiethic nation of Yugoslavia by first breaking away its constituent republics (e.g., Slovenia, Croatia, and Bosnia) and then separating ethnic regions (e.g., the Serbian province of Kosovo) from what remained. Initially, Germany provided the main financial and political support for the dismemberment of Yugoslavia in an attempt to reestablish its influence over Croatia and Bosnia, which had been Nazi puppets during World War II. The United States soon entered the international competition for influence in the Balkans and the adjoining oil-rich Caspian Sea region, at which time American PR firms became dominant. The encouragement of Bosnian secession was particularly risky, because that Yugoslav republic had no modern history of sovereignty and there was a clear danger that the long-dormant hostility between Bosnian Croats, Muslims, and Serbs would be reignited. When the inevitable civil war began, the American press became a pawn in the public relations game.

In her book *Belgrade*, Florence Levinsohn describes how the political leadership of Bosnia, Croatia, and Kosovo each paid $30,000 a month to Ruder Finn to advance their interests. "They hired foreign propagandists to help them with their wars," writes Levinsohn. "The propagandists of their own governments had neither the credibility nor the skills to carry out this mission. The American media and government are well used to dealing with public relations firms, and they would be much more likely to accept information as reliable coming from fellow Americans than from the government of the obscure and unknown Bosnia, for example."[41]

James Harff, co-manager of Ruder Finn's Washington office, directed a fierce PR defense of the Muslims and Croatians while characterizing the Serbs as war criminals. Ruder Finn's campaign was constantly at odds with the UN, whose investigations lent some credence to the Serbs' claims that attacks on Muslims were staged by Bosnian government troops in order to precipitate Western intervention.

From the beginning of the Yugoslav wars, Ruder Finn sent a steady stream of press releases to American and European media and to the United Nations, with the primary purpose of painting the Serbs as barbarians. The American media was compliant in the PR campaign, but the UN was a frequent obstacle. For example, the claim (reminiscent of Nayirah's baby-killing charges against the Iraqis) that Serbian men had raped 50,000 Muslim women went unchallenged in the American media, but the United Nations was skeptical.

As of July 1994 the UN reported that it could document only 800 rapes and that they had been committed by Serbs, Croatians, and Bosnian Muslims alike. Levinsohn asks, "Where did the 50,000 figure come from? From the heads of the Bosnian Muslim leaders. How did it miraculously reach us in the United States and Europe? Through the good offices of Ruder Finn, which made no effort to check out such improbable numbers."[42]

When the Bosnian Muslims blamed the Serbs for the February 5, 1994, attack on the Markale Market in Sarajevo, a few enterprising journalists began to investigate for themselves. They discovered a classified UN report that unequivocally blamed the Muslims for the Markale massacre. Reporters in the United States, Israel, England, Italy, Greece, and France actually examined the evidence and concluded that the attack could not have been carried out by the Serbs. A French reporter, Bernard Volker, who claimed to have seen the UN report, broadcast that the UN privately held the Muslims responsible for the explosion.

Nonetheless, Ruder Finn's carefully orchestrated media campaign against the Serbs overwhelmed UN reports, and the resulting outrage resulted in an economic embargo of Yugoslavia. Because of the American-led embargo applied against Yugoslavia, its remaining republics, Serbia and Montenegro, did not have the funds to avail themselves of Western PR services. As a result, their story was seldom seen in the American press.

When Mirjana Kameretzy, Belgrade correspondent for the *New York Times* since 1952, noticed the increasingly rigid anti-Serb editorial policy at the *Times*, she ceased filing stories. "The other sides have been much more able in their efforts to tell their story the way they want to," she said. "Every single day I get releases from this Ruder Finn in Washington. First it was for Slovenia, then for Croatia, then it was Bosnia. And then it was Kosovo."[43]

In Kosovo, a tiny province of Serbia, a little-known secessionist group, the Kosovo Liberation Army (KLA), emerged in the early 1990s. Initially the world largely ignored the unilateral demands of the mysterious KLA, but after Ruder Finn wrote the documents codifying the declaration of the new "Republic of Kosovo," the world's media ran with the story. James Harff, president of Ruder Finn's global network, explained, "We helped them [the Kosovans] formulate the message in a way that Americans could understand."[44]

To convince the American public that Serbia, a republic within the nation of Yugoslavia, should itself be dismembered, Ruder Finn staged an intensive PR campaign, including a six-city American tour in March 1993. In an extraordinarily revealing interview in October 1993, Harff told French journalist Jacques Merlino, "We have been working for the republics of Croatia, Bosnia-Herzegovina and for the opposition in Kosovo for 18 months. During this period we have had a number of successes that gave us a formidable reputation on the international stage. We planned to take advantage of this conflict to develop commercial ties in business and tourism with these countries."

Harff described his simple public relations tools, including files containing the names of hundreds of journalists, politicians, representatives of humanitarian organizations, and university officials. He described how his computer system organizes and cross-indexes the files, feeding them to a fax in order to quickly distribute his information to anyone who might help his cause. Speed was essential, he said, because the spin favoring his cause had to be the first to hit the public. "We know quite well that only the first message is important," said Harff. "Subsequent denials have no effect whatsoever."[45]

Harff emphasized that the most important PR tactic was to intervene at the right moment with the right people. He noted that in just a few months he had organized 30 meetings with the major press organizations, distributed 13 exclusive stories, 37 faxes, 17 letters, and 8 official reports. He had also set up meetings between Bosnian representatives and vice presidential candidate Al Gore, former secretary of state Lawrence Eagleberger, and influential senators such as George Mitchell and Robert Dole. He boasted of conducting 48 phone conversations with White House officials, 20 with senators, and almost 100 with journalists, editors, TV reporters, and other influential members of the media. In every case, the message was that Serbs were responsible for all the carnage in the Balkans.

When asked how he could accept the enormous responsibility of demonizing an entire people, Harff answered, "We had a job to do and we did it. We are not paid to do a moral job, and if there is to be a debate on this issue, our conscience will be clear. If you want to prove that the Serbs are poor victims in this matter, go ahead."

When asked to identify the one accomplishment of which he was most proud, Harff answered without hesitation: "To have succeeded in putting Jewish public opinion on our side. It was very delicate work, and the dossiers of our clients posed a great danger for our side."

Harff explained that President Tudjman of Croatia had been "very imprudent" in making anti-Semitic statements in his book *Wastelands of Historical Reality* (1989). Similarly, said Harff, President Izetbegovich of Bosnia-Herzegovina "came off no better" in his Islamic Declaration of 1970 in which he strongly favored an Islamic fundamentalist state.

"Moreover," said Harff, "the historical past of Croatia and Bosnia was characterized by very real and cruel antisemitism. Many thousands of Jews were massacred in Croatian concentration camps. For these and other reasons, Jewish intellectuals and Jewish organizations were hostile to the Croatians and Bosnians. Our challenge was to reverse this state of affairs, and we succeeded splendidly."

To accomplish this feat, Ruder Finn capitalized on a story in *New York Newsday* in early August 1992 that included reports of alleged "death camps" in Bosnia. Harff said he immediately contacted the three major Jewish organizations—B'nai B'rith Anti-Defamation League, the American Jewish Committee, and the American Jewish Congress—to convince them that a new holocaust was being conducted. He suggested that the organizations publish a letter of concern in the *New York Times* and stage protests in front of the United Nations.

"All of this succeeded formidably," said Harff. "With the entrance of Jewish organizations on the side of the Bosnians, we hit the jackpot. Immediately we had the Serbs equated to Nazis in public opinion."[46]

Some Jewish organizations were uncomfortable as the object of such blatant manipulation. *Midstream: A Monthly Jewish Review* wrote, "This organized anti-Serb and pro-Muslim propaganda should cause anyone believing in democracy and free speech serious concern. It recalls Hitler's propaganda against the allies in World War II. . . . The Western governments do not control their media sufficiently to be responsible for it. So who is?"[47]

Midstream then answered its question by quoting James Harff. "We were quickly able to present the conflict as a simple matter, a short story with good people and evil people," said Harff. "And we were successful because we focused on a good target, that is, the Jewish target. One saw an immediate change in the language of the press, with the introduction of very emotional terms such as 'ethnic cleansing,' 'concentration camps,' etc., everything evoking Nazi Germany, gas chambers and Auschwitz.

The emotional charge was so strong that no one could oppose it without being accused of revisionism. We totally hit our target."

Midstream concluded, "The American Jewish organizations and leaders outwitted by Ruder & Finn can now pat themselves on the back. They have played a major role in gaining the world's sympathy for antisemitic regimes."[48]

William Markiewicz, in his newsletter *Vagabond*, asked, "How can we understand that the Jewish establishment was sucked into the anti-Serbian machine so easily? They have nothing to be proud of. Like sheep they accepted Harff's claims, without making the slightest effort to verify the claims. They knew that Harff was paid to do a job. And the rest of the world, like sheep, followed the Jews, as who can be more expert on Nazism than the Jews?"[49]

American Jews are not the only ones expressing belated concern at the media control exercised by PR firms such as Ruder Finn. The journal *Intelligence Digest* reported on Ruder Finn's control of the media with the following comment: "Most people are aware of the biases . . . of the everyday media. What is less well known is the way the media themselves can be the subject of manipulation. The following example, taken from the Yugoslav civil war, is an object lesson in media-manipulation."

Intelligence Digest quotes James Harff's response to the charge that Ruder Finn has publicly indicted Serbia without providing proof of its allegations. "Our job is not to verify information," responded Harff. "Our job . . . is to accelerate the distribution of all information which is favorable to us and to make sure it is seen by the proper people. This is what we did. We did not affirm the statement that there were death camps in Bosnia, only that *Newsday* had published it."

Intelligence Digest concludes, "This is a remarkable confession. . . . It goes a long way to explaining why the Serbs have had such bad press. . . . There are wider implications, too. For all their image of professionalism and hard-bitten cynicism, the Western media are clearly easier to manipulate than their operatives would like to admit. This is an important consideration in understanding the reactions of Western democracies to world events."[50]

As the Balkan spotlight shifted from Bosnia to Kosovo, James Harff left Ruder Finn to form his own PR company, Harff Communications Inc., and its marketing division, Global Communicators (GC). With Ruder Finn, Harff had worked with Kosovo Albanians and particularly with the terrorist KLA, but his new company represents Albanian business interests and Albanian Americans, for whom he has used his public relations skills to raise funds, organize demonstrations, and generate media coverage in support of the KLA's Kosovo agenda. GC also represents Albanian tycoon Velija, who dreams of a greater Albania that would include Kosovo and Macedonia.

Florence Levinsohn was prescient when she wrote, "Bosnia, Croatia, and Kosovo hired the American firm of Ruder Finn to take their story to the American and European publics and to the United Nations because they believed their struggles would be won in the hearts and minds of the Western public. . . . Only with an intervention, especially an American intervention, against the Serbs, could Bosnia and Croatia (and Kosovo) hope to win. To gain that intervention, it was crucially required that the Serbs be demonized, that the West sympathize with the plight of the former republics in their heroic struggle against the barbarians."[51]

Other American PR firms joined the rush to judgment against Serbia. For example, the Washington International Group (WIG) was hired by Bosnia to convince American and European reporters that charges of genocide against Serbians should be pushed before the International Court of Justice. WIG is headed by Marshall Harris, a former State Department official who resigned in protest over what he considered America's failure to take action against Serbia.

But despite the massive PR blitz that accompanied NATO's war on Serbia, the American public never bought the sales pitch. This public relations failure was revealed in Michael Powell's trenchant article, "How to Bomb in Selling a War." Powell quoted advertising executive Jeffrey Goodby who doubted that "any self-respecting image welder would touch the NATO account." Goodby put the "selling of this righteous war up there with the Ford Pinto, the smokeless cigar and the new Coke. . . . It's bombs going awry, and us denying it, and then saying we're sorry. . . . We're beyond imagemaking now."[52]

Powell noted that the war was "packaged, animated and broadcast by techno-enraptured reporters," feeding upon an "imbecilic optimism" about the nature of the war. Even Hank Sheinkopf, a Democratic political consultant, had difficulty justifying his party's war. "From a PR standpoint, America loves to go to war for a moral cause," he said. "But we don't look good bombing embassies. This show doesn't exactly excite the moral conscience right now."[53]

CONCLUSION

At the start of the twenty-first century, the growing power of a handful of giant corporations has removed the barriers among news reporting, advertising, and public relations. The fact that a small number of corporations controls most of today's media has been described in Chapter 1 of this book. In addition, two of the largest global PR firms, Burson-Marsteller and Hill & Knowlton, are owned by two of the largest advertising conglomerates, Young & Rubican and the WPP Group. These two PR/advertising giants alone exert a powerful influence on media editorial policies through the billions of dollars in print space and radio and TV time they purchase. Just as the media has failed to investigate the influence of PR on news coverage, it shows little interest in the danger posed by the mergers of PR and advertising interests. To do so would reveal their own dependency on those interests.

Authors Jeff Blyskal and Marie Blyskal say "the press had grown frighteningly dependent on public relations people. Outsiders—the reading and viewing public—would have a hard time discovering this on their own because the dependence on PR is part of behind-the-scenes press functioning.... Meanwhile, like an alcoholic who can't believe he has a drinking problem, members of the press are too close to their own addiction to PR to realize there is anything wrong. In fact, the press ... seems sadly self-deceptive about the press/PR relationship."[54]

Indeed, as the news becomes the captive of PR and advertising, cynical and underpaid reporters, like former politicians, are using the revolving door to go where the action, and the money, is. "The revolving door ... contributes to the blurred reality projected by the powerhouse PR firms," writes Vermont reporter John Dillon. "This door not only spins between the government and lobbies but between the press corps and PR firms. Like Capitol Hill aides who trade in their access and expertise for a lobbyist's salary, burned-out or broke reporters can be tempted by the greener and more lucrative pastures offered by PR companies."[55]

Author Susan Trento believes the revolving door among Washington's three elite groups accounts for much of the nation's social and political ills, yet all three are mostly silent on the process. "The triangle—the media, the government, and the lobbying and PR firms—protect each other," says Trento.[56]

In this unhealthy environment, even some in the PR industry are expressing concern about the crumbling credibility of the media. "Every time that a newspaper produces an advertorial section that offers free puff pieces to advertisers, and every time that a television station presents an infomercial in the guise of programming," writes Kirk Hallahan in *Public Relations Journal*, "media organizations cheapen the value of their product.... When a news medium covered a story in the past, the information sponsor gained more than mere exposure. The client, product or cause gained salience, stature and legitimacy." This legitimacy will be lost, warns Hallahan, if the public no longer sees a difference between news and paid propaganda. "While PR people might circumvent the press occasionally, we aren't going to want to do so all the time," Hallahan advises his PR colleagues. "We can't kill the goose that laid the golden egg. A loss of public reliance upon and confidence in the mass media could be devastating."[57]

NOTES

1. Susan B. Trento, *The Power House: Robert Keith Gray and the Selling of Access and Influence in Washington* (New York: St. Martin's Press, 1992), p. 23.

2. Ibid., p. 62.

3. John Stauber and Sheldon Rampton, *Toxic Sludge Is Good for You: Lies, Damn Lies and the Public Relations Industry* (Monroe, Maine: Common Courage Press, 1995), p. 2.

4. Ibid., p. 3.

5. Scott H. Cutlip, *The Unseen Power: Public Relations. A History* (Hillsdale, N.J.: Lawrence Erlbaum, 1994), p. 87.

6. Cited in Stauber and Rampton, *Toxic Sludge Is Good for You*, p. 4.

7. Jeff Blyskal and Marie Blyskal, *PR: How the Public Relations Industry Writes the News* (New York: William Morrow, 1985), p. 28.

8. Radio USA promotional material, 1984.

9. Trento, *Power House*, pp. 231, 233.

10. Ibid., p. 245.

11. George Glazer, "Let's Settle the Question of VNRs," *Public Relations Quarterly* (spring 1993), p. 44.

12. Ibid., pp. 44, 46.

13. TJFR promotional material, 1985. Quoted in Stauber and Rampton, *Toxic Sludge Is Good for You*, p. 186.

14. "12 Reporters Help Shape Pesticides PR Policy," *Environment Writer*, vol. 6, no. 11 (February 1995), pp. 1, 4–5.

15. Dashka Slater, "Dress Rehearsal for Disaster," *Sierra* (May/June 1994), p. 53.

16. *History of Journalism* cited in Edward L. Bernays, *Public Relations* (Norman: University of Oklahoma Press, 1957), p. 60.

17. Stauber and Rampton, *Toxic Sludge Is Good for You*, p. 22.

18. Edward L. Bernays, *Propaganda* (New York: H. Liveright, 1928), pp. 47–48.

19. Ibid., p. 7.

20. Stauber and Rampton, *Toxic Sludge Is Good for You*, p. 26.

21. Cutlip, *Unseen Power*, p. 87.

22. Cited in Rudy Mara, "Managua, Nicaragua, Is a Hell of a Spot," *Washington Post Magazine* (November 13, 1977), p. 5.

23. Robert Parry and Peter Kornbluh, "Iran/Contra's Untold Story," *Foreign Policy*, no. 72 (fall 1988), p. 4.

24. *O'Dwyer's PR Services Report* (October 1989), p. 1.

25. Parry and Kornbluh, "Iran/Contra's Untold Story," p. 24.

26. "Alleged 'White Propaganda' of S/LPD Criticized by Comptroller General," *O'Dwyer's PR Services Report* (January 1989), p. 42.

27. Parry and Kornbluh, "Iran/Contra's Untold Story," p. 25.

28. Judy Butler, interview with George Vukelich, January 1987, in *Toxic Sludge Is Good for You*, p. 166.

29. "Gelb Fights to Restore USIA Satellite TV Network, *O'Dwyer's PR Services Report* (October 1989), p. 1.

30. Cited in Barry Siegel, "Spin Doctors to the World," *Los Angeles Times Magazine* (November 24, 1991), p. 18.

31. Hal D. Steward, "A Public Relations Plan for the U.S. Military in the Middle East," *Public Relations Quarterly* (Winter 1990–1991), p. 10.

32. Stauber and Rampton, *Toxic Sludge Is Good for You*, p. 169.

33. Ibid.

34. *O'Dwyer's PR Services Report*, vol. 5, no. 1 (January 1991), pp. 8, 10.

35. Stauber and Rampton, *Toxic Sludge Is Good for You*, p. 171.

36. Cited in John R. MacArthur, *Second Front: Censorship and Propaganda in the Gulf War* (Berkeley: University of California Press, 1992), p. 58.

37. Cutlip, *Unseen Power*, p. 771.

38. MacArthur, *Second Front*, p. 58.

39. "Lantos Caught in Shady Deal," Senate Record Vote Analysis, 103rd Congress, 2d Session, June 16, 1994, p. S-6983 Temp. Record, *www.FreeRepublic.com*. http://209.67.114.212/forum/a153619.htm.

40. Cited in Cutlip, *Unseen Power*, p. 771.

41. Florence Levinsohn, *Belgrade: Among the Serbs* (Chicago: Ivan R. Dec, 1994), p. 313.

42. Ibid., p. 314.

43. Ibid., p. 32.

44. Cited in Cutlip, *Unseen Power*, p. 771.

45. Jacques Merlino, *Les Verités Yougoslaves Ne Sont Pas Toutes Bonne à Dire* (Paris: Editions Albin Michel, 1993), pp. 126–28.

46. Ibid.

47. Yohanan Ramati, "Stopping the War in Yugoslavia," *Midstream: A Monthly Jewish Review* (April 1994), p. 2.

48. Ibid.

49. William Markiewicz, " 'Golem' (Serbs and Jews)," *Vagabond*, no. 34 (May 1998), p. 2.

50. "Manipulating the Media," *Intelligence Digest: A Review of World Affairs* (February 4, 1994), pp. 1–2.

51. Levinsohn, *Belgrade*, p. 312.

52. Michael Powell, "How to Bomb in Selling a War," *Washington Post* (May 27, 1999), C1, C8.

53. Ibid.

54. Blyskal and Blyskal, *PR: How the Public Relations Industry Writes the News*, p. 34.

55. John Dillon, "Poisoning the Grassroots," *Covert Action*, no. 44 (spring 1993), p. 36.

56. Trento, *Power House*, p. xi.

57. Kirk Hallahan, "Public Relations and Circumvention of the Press," *Public Relations Quarterly* (summer 1994), pp. 17–19.

CHAPTER 3

Spies in the Media

A MEDIA CONTROVERSY UNEARTHED

It goes without saying that a free press risks being compromised, even corrupted, by any association with an agency dedicated to secrecy, propaganda, and disinformation. Yet claims of national security have often forced the American media into an uneasy relationship with the Central Intelligence Agency (CIA). This controversy was most prominent during the Cold War, but it surfaced again in February 1996 when a Council on Foreign Relations (CFR) task force recommended that restrictions on the CIA's relationship with journalists be removed.

The CFR's initial report, officially released on February 2, 1996, recommended that the CIA "resume sending out spies posing as American journalists." Richard Haass, the council's project director, said he was calling for the Senate Intelligence Committee "to take a fresh look" at the existing policy prohibiting the agency's use of American journalists or the use of CIA agents posing as journalists.

Almost immediately the Senate Intelligence Committee called on CIA director John M. Deutch to testify on the subject, and Deutsch dropped a bombshell: the CIA restraints dating to 1977 had already been modified by "waivers" that would allow CIA agents to pose as journalists or to enlist American journalists in clandestine operations under "extraordinary circumstances." Former CIA director Stansfield Turner had signed an addendum during his 1977 term that allowed such exceptions to the prohibition. Turner's directive also allowed the CIA to use non-journalist staff members of the American media (e.g., camera operators) as long as the arrangement was approved by the employee's news organization.

Even the CFR's Richard Haass said he was unaware of the waiver provision. "Our assumption was the use [of journalists] was totally banned," said Haass.[1] Professional news organizations were dismayed. "We thought this was a dead issue," said G. Kelly Hawes, president of the Society of Professional Journalists. "We thought the ban prohibited any use of any kind. It's 19 years later and no one knew about a loophole or exception to the rule."[2] David Bartlett of the Radio-Television News Directors Association expressed his surprise at Deutch's testimony. "We always assumed the CIA was following the rules," he said.[3]

On April 24, 1996, Jane Kirtley, executive director of the Reporters Committee for Freedom of the Press, wrote the following letter to CIA Director Deutch:

I am writing to express our deep concern over CIA policies regarding the use of journalists and news organizations in intelligence activities. During your testimony before the Senate in February, you acknowledged that the use of journalists as "cover" or as intelligence agents is not precluded by current agency policy.... [W]e are dismayed that you have failed to unequivocally repudiate the practices or to rule out their implementation in the future.

As you can surely understand, anything less than an unqualified rejection of these practices poses a palpable threat to the safety of countless American journalists working abroad. It also undermines the independence of the press by compromising the First Amendment–mandated separation of the government and the news media.

We join our colleagues in urging you to rescind the policy that would permit the CIA to recruit journalists for intelligence work or to allow agents to impersonate journalists.[4]

CHRONOLOGY OF CIA GUIDELINES ON USE OF THE MEDIA

The journalistic community had been caught off guard, misled by the ambiguous language in a succession of secretive CIA guidelines on its media activity, dating back to 1967. During the 1960s, stories of CIA-sponsored publishing houses here and abroad became public, and the agency sought to preempt further disclosures by issuing guidelines on the use of such institutions. In 1967 Desmond Fitzgerald, the CIA's deputy director for plans, declared, "We will, under no circumstances, publish books, magazines or newspapers in the United States."[5]

The 1967 order maintained the CIA's substantial publications program abroad, and many of those books and periodicals were routinely circulated in the United States. The agency's broader association with the mainstream media had not yet been revealed to the general public, but an entire postwar generation of American journalists had come to believe that complicity with the CIA was simply "the thing to do." The details of this cozy relationship had been kept discreetly in-house, but by the early 1970s it was common knowledge among the press corps.

Even CIA director William Colby was said to have been disturbed by the extensive and indiscriminate use of journalists by the agency during the 1960s. In anticipation of an impending public controversy, Colby released public guidelines minimizing the extent and significance of the CIA's use of journalists and announced that he was scaling down the program. In reality, Colby had decided to protect his most valuable media assets while severing formal relationships with those who were inactive or unproductive. Colby told important CIA operatives on the staffs of major newspaper and broadcast outlets to resign and become "stringers," that is, freelance reporters whose work was used piecemeal. This would allow Colby to assure editors that members of their staffs were not CIA employees.[6]

This was the period of Vietnam War protests, the Pentagon Papers, and Watergate. Investigative reporting was popular, and the CIA was coming under scrutiny. To ensure that reporters would not blow the cover of some of the more important stringers on the CIA's payroll, Colby had some of them reassigned to jobs on so-called proprietary publications—foreign periodicals or broadcast outlets secretly funded and staffed by the agency. Some journalists who had signed formal contracts with the CIA were released from their contracts and asked to continue their work under less formal arrangements.

As part of his public relations program, CIA director Colby instituted a regular series of lunches with the editorial boards of some of the major newspapers and weekly magazines. In his book *Honorable Men* (1978), Colby recalled one such lunch in November 1973:

"I was asked whether CIA used American newsmen in its work abroad. I knew we had done so in the past, but I also knew that the employment of those whom I had handled had been terminated. . . . So I answered, 'No.' But when on my return to Langley I checked . . . , I learned that while most had indeed been phased out, there were about five staff members of general-circulation media and about twenty-five in the stringer or free-lance category still working. . . . I thought the period long passed when I could follow [former CIA director] Allen Dulles' example when he faced the same question, puffed his pipe a moment, and answered flatly, 'No'—and was never the object of an investigative reporter's campaign to prove him false."

So, wrote Colby, "To protect my credibility, I felt it essential to return to that editorial board and correct my answer. . . . I also said that I was arranging to end arrangements with the five who remained, since they perhaps cast some question on the integrity of the American press, although I said I would continue to use the free-lance journalists."[7]

In reality, Colby had been less than candid. He did not reveal the elaborate restructuring of media assets that had enabled him to minimize the number of formal relationships with full-time staff. It was later discovered that the CIA had maintained ties with seventy-five to ninety American journalists, including executives, reporters, stringers, photographers, columnists, bureau clerks, and members of broadcast technical crews. Although many of them had been moved off of CIA contracts and payrolls, they continued their work under secret agreements.

In 1975, when Senator Frank Church's Committee on Intelligence Activities was formed, the agency's concern about revelations of its media connections led to new guidelines. In a letter to the committee dated October 21, 1975, Colby stated the following policy:

a. The Agency will continue its prohibition against placement of material in the American media. In certain instances, usually where the initiative is on the part of the media, CIA will occasionally provide factual non-attributable briefings to various elements of the media, but only in cases where we are sure that the senior editorial staff is aware of the source of the information provided.

b. As a general policy, the Agency will not make any clandestine use of staff employees of U.S. publications which have a substantial impact or influence on public opinion. This limitation includes cover use and any other activities which might be directed by CIA.

c. A thorough review should be made of CIA use of non-staff journalists; i.e., stringers and free-lancers, and also those individuals involved in journalistic activities who are in non-sensitive journalist-related positions, primarily for cover backstopping.[8]

Colby left the agency in January 1976, but his successor, George Bush, immediately addressed the CIA's policy on the media. On February 11, Bush issued a new policy directive:

Effective immediately, CIA will not enter into any paid or contractual relationship with any full-time or part-time news correspondent accredited by any U.S. news service, newspaper, periodical, radio or television network or station.

As soon as feasible, the Agency will bring existing relationships with individuals in these groups into conformity with this new policy. . . .

CIA recognizes that members of these groups may wish to provide information to the CIA on matters of foreign intelligence of interest to the U.S. Government. The CIA will continue to welcome information volunteered by such individuals.[9]

The CIA acknowledged that its new policy would terminate fewer than half of the fifty *admitted* relationships with journalists, and, of course, the "voluntary" services of newsmen were still welcomed.

When Stansfield Turner succeeded George Bush as head of the CIA in February 1977, he faced even greater congressional pressure than Colby and Bush had encountered. On November 30, 1977, he issued the media guidelines that form the core of current restraints:

1. *Policy.* The special status afforded the press under the Constitution necessitates a careful policy of self-restraint on the part of the Agency in regard to its relations with U.S. news media organizations and personnel. Accordingly, CIA will not:

   a. enter into any relationships with full-time or part-time journalists (including so-called "stringers") accredited by a U.S. news service, newspaper, periodical, radio, or television network or station, for the purpose of conducting any intelligence activities . . . ;

   b. without the specific, express approval of senior management of the organization concerned, enter into any relationships with non-journalist staff employees of any U.S. news media organization for the purpose of conducting any intelligence activities;

   c. use the name or facilities of any U.S. news media organization to provide cover for any Agency employees or activities.

2. *Limitations.*

   a. The policies set forth above are not designed to inhibit open relationships with journalists . . . which are entered into for reasons unrelated to such persons' affiliation with a particular news media organization. . . .

   b. In addition, CIA will not deny any person including full-time or part-time accredited journalists and stringers regardless of profession, the opportunity to furnish information which may be useful to his or her government. Therefore CIA will continue to permit unpaid relationships with journalists or other members of U.S. news media organizations who voluntarily maintain contact for the purpose of providing information on matters of foreign intelligence or foreign counterintelligence interest to the U.S. Government.

   c. Likewise, the Agency . . . will continue to maintain regular liaison with representatives of the news media.

   Exceptions. No exceptions to the policies and prohibitions stated above may be made except with the specific approval of the DCI [Director of Central Intelligence].[10]

The little-noticed ambiguity in the final line of Turner's guidelines would later become a major controversy. The use of the phrase "no exceptions . . . except . . ." left the door open for the DCI to use American journalists on his own authority, an option that was overlooked by the press for almost twenty years until John Deutch, CIA director under

In 1975, CIA director William Colby made public the CIA's first major guidelines limiting the agency's use of American journalists. Colby acknowledged that fewer than half of the admitted relationships with journalists would be terminated and the "voluntary" services of newspaper people would continue to be welcomed. Photo reproduced from the collections of the Library of Congress.

On November 30, 1977, CIA director Stansfield Turner issued the media guidelines that form the core of current restraints on the agency's use of journalists. Photo reproduced from the collections of the Library of Congress.

President Clinton, reasserted it before the Senate Intelligence Committee on July 17, 1996.

When Chairman Arlen Specter (R-Pa.) asked Deutch to present his understanding of the current restraints on CIA relationships with the media, Deutch said the CIA "was not to use journalists accredited to American news organizations [or] their parent organizations" and that their use for cover was also prohibited. Deutch said this policy had been in place for nineteen years but that he had recently reviewed it "to determine whether it was both appropriate and sufficiently circumscribed." His conclusion was disturbing.

"Mr. Chairman," he testified, "as the Director of Central Intelligence, I must be in a position to assure the President and the members of the National Security Council and this country that there will never come a time when the United States cannot ask a witting citizen to assist in combating an extreme threat to the Nation. So I, like all of my predecessors for the last 19 years, have arrived at the conclusion that the Agency should not be prohibited from considering the use of American journalists or clergy in exceptional circumstances. . . . I have therefore issued new policy guidelines which set out several specific tests that must be satisfied before the Director or Deputy Director may consider a waiver. . . . They are classified and I am available to discuss them in any detail the committee may wish, in closed session."[11]

The circumstances under which a waiver could be exercised remain classified to this day.

BACKGROUND: JOURNALIST-AGENTS DURING THE COLD WAR

Congressional investigations in 1976, 1977, and 1978 revealed that the CIA had recruited journalists at home and abroad and had sown confusion and distrust by having its agents pretend to be journalists as cover for their intelligence activities. As part of a 1977 investigation by the *New York Times*, one CIA official explained that such relationships were established with promises of "eternal confidentiality" and that the agency would continue to deny them "in perpetuity." Several former agency officers added that the CIA itself probably can never know how many American journalists have been on its payroll, because agency files are widely scattered and incomplete.[12]

The full scope of the agency's use of American editors, publishers, and reporters as intelligence agents may never be known, but what was revealed to Congress was enough to shock the most jaded media buff. Most of the verifiable details in this regard pertain to the period from the end of World War II through the mid-1970s, although the agency has made clear that its relationships with journalists, particularly freelance reporters and the foreign media, continue to this day. Since the 1970s, Congress has received general pronouncements from the CIA about its media policies, but no names or particulars have been given.

The history of press involvement in intelligence operations began with the Office of Strategic Services (OSS), the World War II predecessor to the CIA, and the use of the American media for intelligence purposes grew rapidly with the Cold War. The struggle with "international communism" was an ideological contest that required the media's assistance to an unprecedented degree. Frank Wisner, an OSS veteran, was brought into the government in 1948 to plan "black" operations (i.e., unattributed propaganda) against communist influence around the world. Wisner called his operation "my mighty Wurlitzer," a wondrous machine that exploited charitable foundations, labor unions, book publishers, the student movement, and, of course, the press.

During the 1970s information from CIA files was acquired revealing that the Agency had owned or subsidized more than 800 news organizations and individuals, including newspapers, news services, radio stations, periodicals, and other communications entities, both domestically and overseas. Another dozen foreign-based news organizations, though not financed by the CIA, were infiltrated by paid agents. More than 400 American journalists had maintained covert relationships with the agency. These were only those who were "tasked," that is, assigned particular duties or who were subject to some form of contractual control by the CIA. There was an even larger group of journalists who occasionally traded favors with CIA officers. During this period at least a dozen full-time CIA officers worked abroad as reporters or non-editorial employees of American-owned news organizations. More than 250 English-language books were financed or produced by the CIA, and nearly a dozen American publishing houses, many of them prominent names in the industry, published them.[13]

The agency preferred where possible to put its money into existing organizations rather than create its own. "If a concern is a growing concern," said one CIA official, "it's a better cover. The important thing is to have an editor or someone else who's receptive to your copy."[14]

CIA director Allen Dulles and cooperative media executives instituted a complex procedure for intelligence gathering. In addition to providing cover for CIA agents, American reporters returning from abroad were routinely "debriefed," at which time they shared their experiences, observations, and even their notebooks with agency personnel. Reporters returning from overseas were actually met at the docks by CIA officers. "There would be these guys from the CIA flashing ID cards and looking like they belonged at the Yale Club," recalled Hugh Morrow, a former reporter for the Saturday Evening Post. "It got to be so routine that you felt a little miffed if you weren't asked."[15]

In addition to accredited journalists the CIA made heavy use of free-lancers, who were paid by the agency under standard contracts. "Usually we dealt with stringers or people who worked for smaller newspapers—the hangers-on," recalled one former station chief.[16] Cooperative news organizations would often provide journalistic credentials for these stringers, some of whom filed news stories while others simply reported to the CIA.

The most serious aspect of CIA intrusion into the American media was its recruitment of legitimate, accredited members of news organizations. In addition to reporters the CIA recruited photographers, broadcast technical crews, network camera crews based abroad, and administrative personnel in foreign news bureaus. Some broadcast networks supplied the CIA with outtakes of news film and access to photo libraries, a service that the agency considered of extreme importance. The CIA also obtained carte blanche borrowing privileges at the photo libraries of dozens of American newspapers, magazines, and television outlets.

Journalist-agents were paid in various ways. Some received regular salaries and expenses. Others were placed on small retainers. Some were paid piece-rate on the basis of the information they provided. Others received only expense money for missions they undertook. The money was always paid in cash, and it was often laundered through a bank, a businessman, or, in those cases where the news organization was aware of the arrangement, through the publishers themselves. Sometimes the salaries paid by newspapers and broadcast networks were supplemented by payments from the CIA, in the form of retainers, travel expenses, or payment for specific services performed.

Reporters for major news organizations were sometimes offered amounts equal to their regular salaries. Wayne Phillips, a reporter for the *New York Times* during the 1950s, said he was offered $5,000 a year by the CIA if he would work for them overseas. A correspondent for *Time* magazine said he was offered a similar sum during the same period. Keyes Beech, then a correspondent for the *Chicago Daily News*, said he had been offered $12,000 a year "to make inquiries and deliver messages" as he covered Asia.[17]

Once a reporter had signed up with the CIA, he would be provided with training in the trade craft of espionage, including such things as the use of secret writing and how to conduct surveillance. A former CIA station chief described the training as "tailored to each case," but he added, "In no case did we try to make real spies out of the media people. It doesn't pay to give them the whole course." Some degree of training may have been provided as protection for the reporter, because the performance of espionage could be dangerous. In fact, Darriel Berrigan, a *New York Times* stringer in Bangkok who worked for the CIA, was murdered under mysterious circumstances in 1966.[18]

In at least one case, the CIA used an American reporter in an attempt to get another reporter to defect. During the armistice talks in Korea in 1953, Edward Hymoff, then a correspondent for the International News Service, was tasked by the CIA to offer $100,000 to Wilfred Burchett, an Australian journalist with ties to the North Korean communists. Hymoff said he warned the CIA that Burchett could not be won over, and that proved to be the case.[19]

Two journalists whose intelligence work is described in detail in CIA files were Jerry O'Leary of the *Washington Star* and Hal Hendrix of the *Miami News*. Hendrix, a Pulitzer prize winner who later became a high-level official for IT&T, provided the agency with detailed information about Cuban exiles in Miami. O'Leary was described as a valuable "asset" in Haiti and the Dominican Republic. A CIA official described O'Leary's work as assessing and spotting prospective agents, as well as reporting for the agency, but O'Leary denied that he was as heavily involved as Hendrix was. "Hal was really doing work for them," O'Leary told reporter Carl Bernstein in 1977. "I'm still with the *Star*. He ended up at IT[&]T."[20]

The American reporters who worked for the CIA performed a wide range of services, from simply reporting on what they heard or saw to more complex assignments: planting misinformation, helping recruit and handle foreign agents, hosting parties to bring together American agents and foreign spies, peddling "black propaganda" to foreign journalists, providing their hotel rooms or offices as "drops" for intelligence information, conveying instructions or funds to CIA-controlled members of foreign governments, and so on. Some reporters signed formal employment contracts, and many signed secrecy agreements pledging never to reveal their work with the agency. "The secrecy agreement was the sort of ritual that got you into the tabernacle," said a former assistant to the DCI.[21]

Whether the relationship was formal or informal, the reporters usually didn't give a second thought to their association with the CIA until years later when the ethical issues were more clearly drawn. At that point, many of them chose to deny their CIA connection. David Atlee Phillips, a former chief of clandestine services for the CIA and a former journalist, estimated that at least 200 journalists signed secrecy agreements or employment contracts with the CIA from the 1950s through the mid-1970s. Phillips, who was recruited by the CIA in 1950 while managing a small English-language newspaper in Chile, recalled that an agent approached him, asked for his assistance, but insisted that he sign a piece of paper before he could be told precisely what his work would be. "I didn't hesitate to sign," says Phillips, "and a lot of newsmen didn't hesitate over the next twenty years."[22] Columnist Joseph Alsop took the same position: "I'm proud they asked me and proud to have done it."[23]

Commentators and columnists were important assets for the CIA, and perhaps a dozen of them were revealed during the 1970s to have had agency connections that went beyond those maintained by reporters and sources. They were considered receptive to the agency's point of view and were counted on to provide a variety of undercover services. Three widely read columnists who functioned in this way were C. L. Sulzberger of the *New York Times* and Joseph Alsop and Stewart Alsop, whose columns appeared in the *Washington Post, New York Herald Tribune, Saturday Evening Post*, and *Newsweek*.[24]

Sulzberger and his uncle, who was then publisher of the *Times*, both signed secrecy agreements with the agency. "Young Cy Sulzberger had some uses," said one CIA official. "He was very eager, he loved to cooperate." One agency official described an incident in which Sulzberger, then the foreign affairs columnist for the *New York Times*, put his byline on a September 13, 1967, column that was in reality a verbatim briefing paper that the CIA had prepared for him.[25]

Stewart Alsop's CIA connection was even deeper than Sulzberger's. A high-level CIA official stated flatly, "Stew Alsop was a CIA agent." Alsop made particular use of his discussions with foreign government officials, acquiring information sought by the CIA, planting misinformation, and assessing opportunities for CIA recruitment. Joseph Alsop disputed the extent of his brother Stewart's connection with the CIA, saying, "I was closer to the Agency than Stew was, though Stew was very close. I dare say he did perform some tasks. He just did the correct thing as an American."[26]

The social aspect of these relationships ran deep. The founding fathers of the CIA were close personal friends of the Alsops. Joseph Alsop described former CIA deputy director Dick Bessell as his oldest friend from childhood. Given these personal connections, Alsop said he performed tasks for the CIA whenever he thought it was the right thing to do. He regarded it as his duty as a citizen. It would be misleading to suggest that the CIA relied on the initiative of individual journalists in forming its network of media spies. William Colby, DCI during the early 1970s, put the blame where it belonged: "Let's not pick on some poor reporters," he said. "Let's go to the managements. They were witting."[27]

The complicity of editors, publishers, and broadcast network executives was essential to the CIA's work with the media. When Allen Dulles moved from the OSS to become director of the CIA in 1953, he reached agreement with America's most prestigious publishers and editors, allowing him to use the media for recruitment of and cover for CIA agents. Whereas the working reporters and stringers were subject to direction from the agency, the CIA's relationship with news executives was much more social.

Among the media executives who most actively provided their ser-

During the 1950s, CIA director Allen Dulles, shown here with President Kennedy, reached agreement with America's most prestigious publishers and editors, allowing him to use the media for recruitment of and cover for CIA agents. Photo reproduced from the collections of the Library of Congress.

Senator Frank Church (D-Idaho) (left) played a major role in exposing the CIA's influence on the media. *New York Times* columnist C. L. Sulzberger (right) signed a secrecy agreement with the CIA and provided a variety of undercover services for the agency. Photo reproduced from the collections of the Library of Congress.

vices to the CIA were William Paley of the Columbia Broadcasting System (CBS), Henry Luce of Time, Inc., Arthur Sulzberger of the *New York Times*, Barry Bingham Sr. of the *Louisville Courier-Journal*, and James Copley of the Copley News Service. Other cooperating organizations included the American Broadcasting Company (ABC), the National Broadcasting Company (NBC), the Associated Press, United Press International, Reuters, Hearst Newspapers, Scripps Howard, *Newsweek*, the Mutual Broadcasting System, the *Miami Herald*, the *Saturday Evening Post*, and the *New York Herald Tribune*. A few executives, including Sulzberger of the *New York Times*, signed secrecy agreements, but such formality was rare.[28]

Of all the newspapers used by the CIA, the *Times* was probably its most valuable outlet. Between 1950 and 1966, about ten CIA employees were provided cover at the *Times*. The arrangements were approved by the paper's publisher, Arthur Hayes Sulzberger, as part of a general *Times* policy of providing assistance to the CIA. Sulzberger had particularly close ties to Allen Dulles. They reached an agreement in principle that the *Times* and the agency would help each other, but the actual arrangements were to be handled by subordinates. A high-level CIA official said, "They didn't want to know the specifics; they wanted plausible deniability."[29]

The *Christian Science Monitor* was another major newspaper that cooperated with the CIA from its home office. When Joseph Harrison became overseas editor of the *Monitor* in 1950, he discovered that his predecessor had frequently discussed stories with the CIA before running them. "I inherited the situation and I continued it," Harrison later said. "[E]verybody was doing it. They may deny it now. But they were doing it."[30] As for Harrison, he said he had been "happy to cooperate" with the CIA.[31]

Time and *Newsweek* magazines were both closely involved with the CIA. Sources within the agency and the U.S. Senate said that former foreign correspondents and stringers for both magazines signed written agreements with the CIA. Again, social relationships at the highest levels facilitated intelligence activities with prominent American magazines. Henry Luce, the founder of *Time* and *Life*, was good friends with Allen Dulles, and Luce readily allowed certain members of his staff to work for the agency. He also agreed to provide jobs and credentials to CIA agents who lacked journalistic experience.

During the 1950s and early 1960s, *Time*'s foreign correspondents attended regular "briefing" dinners held by the CIA, and Luce encouraged his correspondents to share information with the agency. Luce himself made it a practice to brief Dulles or other high-level agency officials when he returned from his frequent trips abroad. James Linen, former publisher of *Time*, said he was never sure which of his correspondents were working for the CIA, but he added, "I always assumed that some of them must have been."[32]

The CIA contracted the services of several foreign correspondents and stringers at *Newsweek* with the approval of senior editors at the magazine. *Newsweek*'s stringer in Rome during the 1950s made little effort to conceal the fact that he worked for the CIA. Malcolm Muir, *Newsweek*'s editor from 1937 until 1961, said, "[I]n those days the CIA kept pretty close touch with all responsible reporters. Whenever I heard something that I thought might be of interest to Allen Dulles, I'd call him up."[33]

Harry Kern, *Newsweek*'s foreign editor from 1945 until 1956, said, "When I went to Washington, I would talk to Foster or Allen Dulles about what was going on. . . . We thought it was admirable at the time."[34] Ernest Lindley, *Newsweek*'s Washington bureau chief during the 1940s and 1950s, said he regularly consulted with Dulles and other CIA officials before going abroad and briefed them upon his return. When *Newsweek* was purchased by the Washington Post Company in 1961, its new publisher, Philip L. Graham, continued the relationship with the CIA.[35]

The Copley Press and its subsidiary, the Copley News Service, were described by CIA officials as one the agency's most useful media outlets until the death of the chain's owner, James S. Copley, in 1973. Copley owned nine newspapers in California and Illinois, among them the *San Diego Union* and *Evening Tribune*. A report funded by a grant from the Fund for Investigative Journalism noted that at least twenty-three Copley News Service employees worked for the CIA. The report asserted that James Copley personally offered the use of his news service to then-president Eisenhower as "the eyes and ears . . . for our intelligence services" against the communist threat. Copley was also the guiding hand behind the CIA-funded Inter-American Press Association, made up primarily of right-wing Latin American newspaper editors. In 1976, one CIA official admitted, "The Agency's involvement with the Copley organization is so extensive that it's almost impossible to sort out."[36]

CIA files show similar arrangements with many other news organizations, including Scripps Howard Newspapers, Hearst Newspapers, Associated Press, United Press International, Reuters, and the Mutual Broadcasting System. One CIA official conceded that this was just a small part of the list.

The CIA has sometimes intervened directly with news organizations to shape the way the agency is described to the public. For example, the editors of the now-defunct *Colliers* magazine submitted an article on the CIA to the agency for censorship. The agency officer who read the manuscript noted a reference to the CIA's connections with two foreign corporations, links that were common knowledge abroad. *Colliers* killed the article.

In the months before the 1961 Bay of Pigs invasion of Cuba by CIA-trained exile forces, the agency was able to censor several stories about the training of the invasion force. One such article by David Kraslow of the *Miami Herald* was submitted to Allen Dulles, then head of the CIA, who said publication would not be in the national interest.

Broadcast journalism, like newspapers and magazines, was heavily infiltrated by the CIA. The Columbia Broadcasting System (CBS) was the agency's most valued network, with CBS president William Paley maintaining a close working and social relationship with Allen Dulles. Under Paley's direction CBS provided cover for CIA employees, including at least one prominent foreign correspondent and several stringers. Each year during the 1950s and early 1960s, CBS correspondents had private dinners and briefings with the CIA hierarchy.

Arrangements between the CIA and CBS were worked out by subordinates of Dulles and Paley. Sig Mickelson, president of CBS News between 1954 and 1961, was Paley's designated contact with the agency. Mickelson later became president of Radio Free Europe and Radio Liberty, both run by the CIA for many years.

In 1976 Richard Salant, then president of CBS News, ordered an in-home investigation of the network's CIA connection, and many details of the relationship were found in Mickelson's files. Among the information found by Salant's investigators was evidence that Frank Kearns, a CBS-TV reporter from 1958 to 1971, and Austin Goodrich, a CBS stringer, were undercover CIA employees. Mickelson later said, "When I moved into the job I was told by Paley that there was an ongoing relationship with the CIA. He introduced me to two agents who he said would keep in touch. I assumed this was a normal arrangement at the time."[37]

The CIA confirmed that several NBC correspondents undertook assignments for the agency during the 1950s and 1960s. When asked about such activity Richard Wald, president of NBC News during much of the 1970s, said, "It was a thing people did then."[38] Less is known about ABC's involvement with the CIA, but agency officials say ABC provided cover for operatives through the 1960s, always with the knowledge of network executives.[39]

The CIA was even more aggressive in directing its broadcast propaganda outside the United States, beginning with Radio Free Europe and Radio Liberty and extending to such relatively minor operations as Radio Free Asia, Free Cuba Radio, and Radio Swan, the latter intended as the main communication link for the Bay of Pigs invasion. Radio Swan's powerful signal could be heard over much of the western hemisphere, attracting potential advertisers that the CIA turned away.

Providing cover for CIA agents posing as journalists was an important service of many major news organizations. By appearing to be accredited news correspondents, CIA agents were able to achieve the kind of freedom of movement and access to intelligence that would have been impossible under other types of cover. The CIA went so far as to conduct formal training programs designed to teach its agents to be journalists, after which they were placed in major news organizations with the help of management. One prominent example was Robert Campbell, who was placed in a reporting job with the *Louisville Courier-Journal* in order to gain some newspaper experience before going abroad under journalistic cover. Executives at the *Courier-Journal* said they were unaware that Campbell worked for the CIA until he resigned from the paper.[40]

The CIA subsidized several American publications whose editors and publishers had fled Havana after Fidel Castro came to power. Recipients of these subsidies included *Avance, El Mundo, El Prensa Libre,* and *El Diario de las Americas.* The CIA also financed AIP, a radio news agency in Miami that sent programs to Latin America.[41]

A number of CIA agents posed as freelance authors as a way to cover their extensive intelligence work abroad. One such author/agent was Edward S. Hunter, who roamed Central Asia for years collecting information. Other CIA agents who worked abroad under cover as authors were Lee White, an employee of the agency's Middle Eastern Division, and Peter Matthiessen, who worked in Paris. Occasionally these author/agents would produce a successful book, and in one case such a book was actually reviewed in the *New York Times* by a CIA agent.[42]

THE FOREIGN PRESS

Numerous foreign-language newspapers and news services were financed and operated by the CIA from the end of World War II until the early 1970s. "We had at least one newspaper in every foreign capital at any given time," said one CIA officer, who added that if the agency did own or subsidize a paper, it placed paid agents on the staff to print any stories that were useful.[43] Among the foreign newspapers on which such agents were placed were *The South Pacific Mail, The Guyana Chronicle, The Haiti Sun, The Japan Times, The Nation* (Rangoon), *The Caracas Daily Journal,* and *The Bangkok Post.* Before the 1959 revolution in Cuba, the *Times of Havana* employed David Phillips as a columnist. He later became chief of the CIA's Western Hemisphere Division.[44]

Among the prominent foreign news agencies controlled by the CIA during this time were the West German news agency DENA, Agencia Orbe Latino Americano, and the Foreign News Service, which sold articles to as many as 300 newspapers around the world, including the *New York Times.* The CIA reportedly had agents within a number of other foreign news services, including LATIN in Latin America and the Ritzhaus organization in Scandinavia, and it also subsidized the international writers association known as PEN and the International Federation of Journalists.[45]

The Editors Press Service was a feature news service with clients throughout Latin America that, according to a CIA official, provided "cliché stories, news stories prepared by the agency or for the agency." One outright CIA proprietary was the Continental Press Service, headquartered in Washington and run by a CIA man named Fred Zusy. One of its major functions was to provide official-looking press credentials to agents seeking cover. Perhaps the most widely circulated of the CIA-owned news services was Forum World Features, located in London and ostensibly owned by John Hay Whitney, publisher of the *New York Herald Tribune*. According to CIA sources, Whitney was "witting" of the agency's control. Stories from Forum World Features were bought by countless newspapers around the world, including about thirty in the United States. By 1967 the news service had become perhaps the principal CIA media effort in the world.[46]

By 1950 the CIA had virtually unlimited funds with which to buy the services of newsmen working for newspapers around the world, including Reuters, Agence-France-Presse, Tass, and Hsinhua. These foreign journalists were used to float disinformation or misleading stories in virtually every capital of the world, and the stories planted there often found their way back to the American press to influence public opinion in ways that delighted American presidents and their intelligence agencies.

The Philippines was a typical case. Lt. Col. Edward G. Lansdale was sent to Manila as the head of CIA clandestine and paramilitary operations. As a former advertising man, Lansdale used market research and media deception to create a puppet candidate, Ramon Magsaysay, for the Philippine presidency. Lansdale ran his successful 1953 campaign, wrote his speeches, and used the CIA's paid editors and journalists to provide support for his programs and to attack unsympathetic journalists.[47]

From the Philippines, Lansdale moved on to Vietnam, where he conducted the same kind of covert media campaign that he had successfully overseen in the Philippines. (Lansdale's activities in Vietnam became so notorious that they were the basis for two semifictional books, *The Ugly American* and *The Quiet American*.)

During the 1950s and 1960s the CIA established numerous media-related front organizations in Europe, the principal one being the Congress for Cultural Freedom (CCF). The CCF operated in Western Europe, India, Australia, Japan, Africa, and numerous other countries, where it financed more than thirty periodicals. One CIA operative became an editor of the CCF's most important magazine, *Encounter*.

The CIA spent some $20 to $30 million a year in Italy during the 1950s and about $10 million annually during the 1960s. Much of it went to support magazines, book publishing, and other means of news and opinion manipulation, including planting news items in non-American media around the world and arranging for these stories to be reprinted in sympathetic Italian publications. *The Daily American* of Rome, Italy's leading English-language newspaper, was for much of the 1950s to the 1970s partly owned and/or managed by the CIA.[48]

During the 1960s the CIA dominated the press throughout much of Latin America, planting phony stories in cooperating newspapers. News items planted in one country would be picked up by other CIA stations in Latin America and disseminated through a CIA-owned news agency or radio station or through paid journalists. The CIA's media war against Cuba was among its more heavily financed activities. In addition to its foreign media empire, the CIA maintained anti-Castro news article factories in the United States, including subsidized Miami publications such as *Avance, El Mundo, La Prensa Libre, Bohemia,* and *El Diario de los Americas*. It also supported a radio news agency that produced programs sent free of charge to more than 100 stations in Latin America.

The CIA's most intensive media activities in Chile were intended to prevent the election of a Marxist president, Salvador Allende. Senate hearings in 1975 revealed that the CIA's media campaign made extensive use of the press, radio, films, pamphlets, posters, leaflets, direct mailings, paper streamers, and wall painting. Disinformation and "black propaganda"—material that purported to originate from another source—were used as well. "During the first week of intensive propaganda activity," said the Senate report, "a CIA-funded propaganda group produced twenty radio spots per day in Santiago and on 44 provincial stations; twelve-minute news broadcasts five times daily on three Santiago stations and 24 provincial outlets; thousands of cartoons, and much paid press advertising."[49]

Even after Allende's election victory the CIA generated, by its own count, over 700 articles, broadcasts, editorials, and similar items in the Latin American and European media. The post-election propaganda blitz came after the CIA and members of the Chilean army concluded that a military coup was necessary. It came on September 11, 1973, installing the notorious General Pinochet.

During the 1980s the Reagan administration's support for the Nicaraguan Contras occupied much of the CIA's energies. One of the more prominent civilian Contra leaders was Edgar Chamorro, an advertising executive who complained in his book *Packaging the Contras: A Case of CIA Disinformation* (1987) that he had been used as a figurehead for a CIA-controlled army. The CIA paid Chamorro $2,000 a month plus expenses, which included bribing Central American journalists and broadcasters to speak favorably of the Contras. "Approximately 15 Honduran journalists were on the CIA's payroll, and our influence was thereby extended to every major Honduran newspaper and radio and television station," said Chamorro.[50]

The CIA used broadcasting intensively in the psychological war against the Soviet Union and Eastern Europe. With powerful transmitters and often round-the-clock programming, the CIA funded Radio Liberty, Radio Free Russia, Radio Free Europe, and Radio in the American Sector. As cover, these stations were represented as private organizations funded by donations from corporations and the public. The CIA's funding and control were not revealed until 1967, after which congressional pressure led to open governmental financing of the stations.

The use of Soviet nationals in the West as CIA agents-journalists has been described by author William Blum as "a singular flop." Blum said the information reported was usually trivial and often fabricated. Many of the Russians who were recruited to work as newsmen for the various stations were later identified as members of Hitler's notorious Einsatzgruppen, which had rounded up and killed Jews in the Soviet Union during the early 1940s. Stanislaw Stankievich, who worked for Radio Liberty, had ordered the mass murder of Jews in Byelorussia, during which babies were buried alive with the dead. Such were the characters recruited by the CIA and represented as radio "journalists."[51]

THE END OF THE HONEYMOON: THE CHURCH COMMITTEE REVELATIONS

In his book *Secrecy and Democracy* (1985) Stansfield Turner, DCI during President Jimmy Carter's administration, described the problems he faced in dealing with the press during the 1970s: "Our media . . . had come to believe that they should have nothing to do with American intelligence," he wrote. "This was, however, a complete reversal from less than a decade before, when the CIA and the media cooperated closely. On foreign posts the CIA station chief and the bureau chief of a wire service or an American newspaper would usually be colleagues. . . . These relationships worked well for many years; then the roof fell in on both sides. . . . The touchstone for the media's turning its back on the CIA was the Church committee report in 1976."[52]

The committee that Turner decried was the Senate Select Committee to Study Government Operations with Respect to Intelligence Activities, chaired by Senator Frank Church (D-Idaho), whose name came to be associated with the committee and its work. Although its final report, issued on April 26, 1976, was circumscribed by CIA pressure and its effects on the CIA were limited and temporary, the Church Committee did mark the end of the honeymoon between the CIA and the media.

The Church committee described its work as "the only thorough investigation ever made of United States intelligence and its post–World War II emergence as a complex, sophisticated system of multiple agencies and extensive activities." The committee staff of 100, including 60 professionals, assisted the 11 members of the committee in an in-depth inquiry involving more than 800 interviews, over 250 executive hearings, and documentation in excess of 110,000 pages, covering spectacular issues such as assassination plots and poison pen letters. The inquiry into CIA relationships with journalists came almost as an afterthought, yet this program turned out to be the most sensitive of all the activities examined.

Despite its legal Senate mandate and the issuance of subpoenas, in no instance was the committee allowed to examine agency files on its own. Instead, complained the committee report, "[D]ocuments and evidence have been presented through the filter of the agency itself. Although the Senate inquiry was congressionally ordered, and although properly constituted committees under the Constitution have the right of full inquiry, the Central Intelligence Agency and other agencies of the executive branch have limited the Committee's access to the full record."[53]

Indeed, in some areas of the committee's investigation it was denied any form of access to files or documents, leading the committee to warn, "[T]here is a danger and an uncertainty which arises from accepting at face value the assertions of the agencies and departments which have in the past abused or exceeded their authority. . . . There must be a check: some means to ascertain whether the secrets being kept are, in fact, valid secrets."[54]

Despite its concern that the CIA was withholding information, the committee decided against questioning any of the reporters, editors, publishers, or broadcast executives whose relationships with the agency were described in CIA files. Former CIA directors Colby and Bush were able to convince the committee that even limited public disclosure of the agency's media activities would do irreparable damage to the nation's intelligence capabilities and to the reputations of hundreds of journalists. Colby is said to have warned of a "witch-hunt" whose victims would be reporters, editors, and publishers.

It was decided that the committee's investigation would be overseen by William Bader, a former CIA intelligence officer, and David Aaron, who later became deputy to Zbigniew Brzezinski, President Carter's national security adviser. Bader's first request for specific information about journalists was denied by the CIA on the grounds that there had been no abuse of authority and that current intelligence practices might be compromised. Only after committee members met with CIA director George Bush and complained about the denials did Bush agree to order a search of CIA files. Even then, Bush insisted that the committee could not have access to the raw files. Instead, the agency would condense the material into one-paragraph summaries describing the activities of individual journalists in the most general terms, with the names of journalists and their news organizations omitted.

By the time the CIA said it had completed searching its files, Bader had received over 400 summaries. Even then agency officials said it was impossible to produce all the files on the use of journalists, so they provided only a broad, representative picture. Nonetheless the summaries showed that the number of CIA relationships with journalists was far greater than the agency had ever suggested, and that their use was an intelligence tool of the highest magnitude. Of the more than 400 individuals summarized, between 200 and 250 were "working journalists"—reporters, editors, correspondents, photographers. The rest were nominally employed by book publishers, trade publications, and newsletters. A small number were foreign journalists, including those working as stringers for American publications.

Because the summaries were vague, sketchy, and incomplete, Bader told the agency that he wanted to see the full files on a hundred or so of the individuals summarized. The CIA flatly refused, declaring that it would provide no further information. The agency's intransigence forced a meeting at CIA headquarters in March 1976 at which Senator Church, vice-chairman John Tower, Bader, and William Miller, director of the committee staff, told CIA director Bush that without further information they could not fulfill their legal mandate to determine whether the CIA had exceeded its authority. The discussion was heated, but the agency continued to maintain that only the summaries of journalists, with names removed, would be provided to the committee.

Finally an agreement was reached allowing Bader and Miller to examine "sanitized" versions of the full files of twenty-five journalists selected from the summaries, but the names of journalists, news organizations, and associated CIA employees would be blacked out. Church and Tower would be allowed to examine the *unsanitized* versions of five of those twenty-five files, just to ensure that nothing but the names had been withheld. But the deal was contingent on the assurance that neither Bader, Miller, Tower, nor Church would reveal what they saw to other members of the Committee or staff.

From the twenty-five sanitized files, it became clear that from the 1950s through the early 1970s the CIA had concentrated on recruiting journalists in the most prominent media organizations, including four of the five largest newspapers, the broadcast networks, and the two major weekly news magazines. Because of their prominence, the journalists described could often be identified even though their names were withheld.

When Bader attempted to get information on the CIA's *current* relationships with journalists, he hit a stone wall. Bush not only refused to discuss such matters, but he urged the committee to curtail any further inquiries and to conceal its findings in the final report. One of the senators whom Bush lobbied later said that the CIA regarded its media relationships as "the highest, most sensitive covert program of all."

Some committee members and staff feared that the CIA had gained control of the inquiry. By the time the Church committee realized the extent and significance of the CIA's media program, it had squandered most of its time and resources. Not only was the committee forced to limit the extent of its inquiries, but much of its findings were hidden from the full membership of the committee, the Senate, and the public. This compartmentalization was motivated, in part, by the desire to avoid leaks of the explosive facts. The committee feared that the slightest sign of a leak would have led the CIA to cut the flow of sensitive information. "It was as if we were on trial—not the CIA," said one committee staffer.[55]

As the result of prolonged and elaborate negotiations with the CIA, the Church committee's final report obscured the most important discoveries of the investigation. No mention was made of the 400 summaries of journalists or the content of those summaries. By mentioning only some fifty recent CIA contacts with journalists, the impression was given that these represented the extent of the agency's dealings with the press. Director Colby's misleading public statements about the use of journalists were repeated without analysis or contradiction. The role of news executives in the use of their organizations by the CIA was given brief and superficial mention in the report, and the fact that the CIA continued to regard the press as an appropriate area for intelligence assistance went unmentioned. Despite such failings, the Church committee investigation irreversibly raised the consciousness of the public and the consciences of the press.

FEEDBACK, PLAYBACK, AND BLOWBACK: FALSE STORIES PLANTED ABROAD BECOME NEWS IN AMERICA

One former CIA official asserted that throughout the 1950s and 1960s it was "commonplace for things to appear in the U.S. press that had been picked up" from foreign publications in which the CIA had placed propaganda. Some foreign publishers were unaware of such propaganda, but more often they were what the agency calls "witting." One official said the agency preferred to give the propaganda "to somebody who knows what it is," but where that was not possible, "You gave it to anybody."[56]

Former agency officials said there was an "early warning system" to advise diplomats and key government officials to ignore news stories planted overseas by the CIA, but there was, and is, no such network for alerting the American media about foreign dispatches that were distorted or altogether false. There was no practical way, said these officials, to let the American public know which stories had been written by CIA agents. "We would not tell U.P.I. or A.P. headquarters in the U.S. when something was planted abroad," said one CIA official, who conceded that as a result such stories were likely to be carried over news wires in the United States.[57] Indeed, a number of former CIA officers admitted that there were attempts to propagandize the American public through "replay" of such stories.

In December 1977, when CIA director William Colby appeared before a House oversight subcommittee, he and Representative Bob Wilson (R-Calif.) discussed CIA guidelines concerning "feedback":

"Wouldn't any covert operators have to be very careful that they did not in fact give out false information that would find its way back to the U.S. press?" asked Wilson.

"[T]hat is a problem, what is called the feedback problem, of being printed abroad and then being used here," answered Colby, who then attempted to reassure Wilson that if the false story produced the desired effect, it was no longer a lie. "Maybe it started as just an idea and maybe as just a story, but if it becomes a major fact thanks to the kinds of support it got, then, it is a real fact."

"How, then, can you protect against the feedback of that kind of slant?" asked subcommittee chairman Les Aspin (D-Wis.).

"[I]f it really became a big story with no foundation at all," said Colby, "you would have a problem. I think the post mortems of some of the coups that have occurred around the world have indicated that the propaganda quotient of it was very high. . . . [Y]ou can argue about whether we should have done it or not in each case, but the fact is that in that case you did produce a result, . . . even though it started as an exaggeration."

"In other words," said Aspin, "If you do the job well, the story becomes true."

"Yes, sure," said Colby.[58]

Following Colby's testimony, a panel of journalists addressed the subcommittee and expressed their concern about the feedback of CIA disinformation abroad. Freelance journalist Tad Szulc disputed Colby's claim that such feedback was a minimal problem. "I don't think it is minimal," he said. "[T]he potential is there, feedback, if the *New York Times* or a wire service picks up a story from an authoritative newspaper in India or in France, and this turns out to be a deep CIA plant, this is played back in the United States, has an impact on your decisions in Congress, has an impact on public opinion, then I think it becomes a very pernicious and dangerous thing."

Another journalist, Ward Just, said the only way to avoid CIA feedback from abroad was to restrict the agency's ability to plant such stories. "I have roughly the same feelings about the foreign media as I do about our own," said Just. "I think they [the CIA] ought to keep their hands off . . . the media there as well as here. . . . I can't, as a writer, approve of the Central Intelligence Agency suborning other writers. I don't care where they work. . . . [T]hat we should truck around the world . . . hiring journalists who are writing for foreign publications is . . . an outrage."[59]

Stuart Loory of the *Chicago Sun-Times* said, "The danger of blowback is you feed propaganda to a foreign journalist and the first thing you know you are reading it in the *Chicago Sun-Times*. . . . I think there are extremely ethical and moral problems involved in polluting the world's information network."

Eugene Patterson of the *St. Petersburg Times* declared, "On the one hand, our Government and our press stand for a belief in expression free of Government influence everywhere. On the other, the intelligence agency of the U.S. Government reserves the right to subvert journalists anywhere abroad. . . . Not even Americans can be sure of the news fed back to them from abroad if it is planted there to mislead others. Why should this Nation mislead anybody with calculated untruths, abroad or at home?"

Gilbert Cranberg, editor of the *Des Moines Register-Tribune*, seemed to summarize the views of all the journalists: "The CIA should be required to quit planting false and misleading stories abroad, not just to protect Americans from propaganda fallout, but to protect all readers from misinformation. This government should not deliberately deceive foreign readers any more than it should deceive its own people.[60]

THE MORNING AFTER: COLD WAR JOURNALISTS REFLECT ON THEIR INTELLIGENCE BINGE

During the 1970s, when the story of the media's intelligence activities began to hit the public fan, the response of news organizations was predictable. First came denial, in the form of silence. In late 1974 Stuart Loory, a former White House reporter for the *Los Angeles Times*, wrote a thoughtful article in the *Columbia Journalism Review* in which he decried the unwillingness of newsmen to pursue the story of the CIA's use and infiltration of the American news business. He noted the contrast between that silence and the aggressive exposure of ethical tangles in nonjournalistic institutions.[61]

Along with official silence came bureaucratic suspicion. Many news organizations now feared that their ranks were full of secret CIA operatives. Officials of the *New York Times* and the *Washington Star-News* went to CIA director Colby to ask for information about their staff members. Colby met with James Reston of the *Times* and assured him that no staff members or stringers at the paper were currently in the agency's employ. No such assurance was given to the *Star-News*.

Colby told Katharine Graham, publisher of the *Washington Post*, that none of the *Post*'s full-time staff members were on the CIA payroll, but he would not discuss stringers. *Time, Newsweek,* and *U.S. News and World Report* were given similar personal assurances by Colby, but, again, Colby explicitly refused to discuss stringers. When United Press International (UPI) and CBS attempted to contact Colby, they could not get beyond the CIA's press representative.

William Small, then CBS's Washington bureau chief, recalls, "They refused to discuss the matter at all. I asked to talk to Colby and was told that I could not. . . . He did not return my call. I wrote him a letter. He did not answer it."[62] Ronald Cohen, UPI's Washington news editor, was treated in a similar fashion.

None of the news executives who succeeded in speaking with Colby bothered to ask him whether their staff had worked for the CIA *in the past.* In addition, because the inquiring news executives did not compare notes with each other, they did not realize that the CIA was responding selectively to their inquiries.

Meanwhile, individual journalists began their own soul-searching. Their attitudes were mixed. Most of those who had worked for the CIA refused to publicly admit it. Some of the privileged old-timers, insiders such as Joseph Alsop and Stewart Alsop, who profited professionally from their relationship with the CIA, expressed pride at having been trusted by the most powerful political figures in the nation's government. These journalists were a product of a news business that needed the cooperation of the CIA as much as it needed them, fostering what Stuart Loory recognized as a love-hate relationship that blurred ethical considerations.

Back in 1974, Loory concluded, "There is little question that if even one American overseas carrying a press card is a paid informer for the CIA, then all Americans with those credentials are suspect. We . . . congratulate ourselves for our independence. Now we know that some of that independence has, with the stealth required of clandestine operations, been taken from us—or given away."[63]

When the House Select Committee on Intelligence interviewed journalists during its 1977–1978 hearings, Loory was among them. He called for a full airing of past relationships between the CIA and the press, including names, dates, places, and duties. "There have been reports that even some of the most distinguished American journalists have at times disseminated CIA propaganda, sometimes knowingly," said Loory. "If this is so, it makes a mockery of the historic arm's-length relationship between the press and the Government of the United States. The news business in this country just cannot function properly if it is to become a handmaiden of the Government, if its reporters are to moonlight clandestinely for Government agencies, if its dispatches are to be polluted unwittingly, or wittingly, with untruths or slants that alibi for the Government."

Loory was unwilling to accept the CIA's claim that it had not compromised the independence of the American press. "I think there is a need to determine the extent to which the CIA . . . functioned as a propaganda machine aimed largely at affecting public opinion in the United States," testified Loory. "Frankly, I do not believe that the primary purpose of the Agency's propaganda effort was always only to support U.S. policies overseas. I think that it also worked to create a favorable climate at home for the enactment of foreign policy."[64]

The other journalists testifying during the 1977–1978 hearings took roughly the same position as Loory. Joseph Fromm, deputy editor of *U.S. News and World Report*, told the committee that journalists should share with the CIA only that information which they would feel free to publish. Such information should not be provided for pay, except to the journalist's publication. Fromm concluded: "[A] journalist's relationship with the CIA . . . should be guided by four principles: No pay, no tasking, no violation of confidence, and no conscious reporting of disinformation."

Herman Nickel, member of the Board of Editors for *Fortune* magazine, was even more explicit: "It is emphatically not the function of journalists to gather information for their government, except in the sense that government officials can buy newspapers and magazines . . . like anyone else. Anyone who allows himself or others to be used in this fashion does serious danger to the cause of an independent press. If the impression were to get around that many, or even only a few, American journalists allowed themselves to be used in this fashion, it would seriously undermine the effectiveness, access, and credibility of all correspondents for American media abroad.

"Publishers and editors who allow the CIA access to their files, or allow an intelligence service to use their news service as a cover for intelligence operations in my view do a grave disservice to our profession. . . . A reporter who moonlights for the CIA or any other intelligence service because of the lure of money in my view prostitutes himself. But appeals to patriotism . . . , not to mention appeals to the vanity of people who revel in being picked by the government for an important secret mission, should be resisted just as hard. . . . Our patriotic duty as journalists is to keep our independence, for if we don't, we can't properly fulfil our constitutionally recognized function in a free society."[65]

Clayton Kirkpatrick, editor of the conservative *Chicago Tribune*, did not hesitate to condemn the CIA's media policies. "The CIA has been guilty of practices that reflect unfavorably upon the organization, upon the United States generally, and upon the free news media of the world. . . . The credibility of American news media is damaged when evidence is produced . . . that reporters, editors, and publishers are used to support and promote governmental policy. . . . I strongly urge . . . that the CIA extend its commitment to avoid recruiting American journalists to a broader commitment to avoid recruiting all journalists, foreign as well as American."[66]

THE MODERN VIEW: JOURNALISTS IN THE 1990s

Almost twenty years after journalists had expressed their concern about the CIA to the U.S. House of Representatives, a new group of press representatives was called before the Senate to testify on the need for clearer guidelines on the CIA's use of journalists. In May 1996 the House had overwhelmingly passed an intelligence authorization bill containing a provision, called the Richardson amendment, that would have established statutory limits on the CIA's use of journalists. The House measure, approved by a vote of 417 to 6, would have prevented the CIA from using any American news correspondent "as an agent or asset for the purpose of collecting intelligence" but also would have allowed the president to waive the restriction if "it is necessary to address the overriding national security interest of the United States." In addition to the presidential waiver, the bill would have allowed voluntary work for the CIA by any journalist "who is aware that the cooperation is being provided to an element of the United States intelligence community."[67] The bill would have imposed no restrictions on the use of CIA agents posing as journalists or on the use of foreign journalists as spies.

On July 17, 1996, the Senate Select Committee on Intelligence held hearings in anticipation of a similar Senate bill at which a number of prominent journalists testified. Terry Anderson, a journalist who had been held hostage by terrorists in Lebanon from March 1985 to December 1991 because they suspected him of being a CIA agent, said that the CIA's employment of journalists represented not only a threat to the independence of the American media but a physical threat to the safety of members of the American press.

"Both as personal experience and in my duties as the Director of the Committee to Protect Journalists, I know that journalists are put in danger by the perception that they are connected to intelligence agencies," said Anderson. "We all know that in much of the world, the CIA is viewed with great suspicion and distaste. . . . If we are making rules for anyone, part of the consideration has to be the behavior of the people to whom the rules will apply. If they are generally orderly, obedient, and respectful of rules, then we can afford to make the rules somewhat less tightly and provide for exceptions and interpretation. If they, on the other hand, have shown themselves to be disrespectful of rules and are of a tendency to stretch exceptions, then we have to make the rules con-

siderably stricter and apply them more forcefully. With all due respect
...I would suggest that there is sufficient evidence on the part of the
CIA to put them in the second category rather than the first." Anderson
concluded, "[T]he best thing that we can do, I think, is try to repair the
damage by a greater prohibition, without exceptions."[68]

Ted Koppel, anchor of the popular ABC News show *Nightline*, testified
next.

"I am unalterably and categorically opposed to the notion of the CIA
having the legal option of using journalism as a cover for its officers or
agents," declared Koppel. "Having said that, there are circumstances under which the Agency has, under what it perceives to be the greater
national interest, broken American laws in the past, and I have no doubt
that it will continue under such circumstances to do so in the future.
Pragmatism demands that we accept that as a fact of life. ... It does not
require, however, that Congress sanction such illegal behavior with its
own benediction or that it facilitate the process by changing the laws."

Committee chairman Arlen Specter interjected, "Well, we prize ourselves very, very highly of being a nation of laws, and laws that cannot
be violated even by the President."

Koppel responded, "With all due respect, sir, we also have precedent
for the intelligence agencies of the United States routinely violating laws
and simply assuming that they won't be held to account. All too frequently, I am afraid, they are quite right."[69]

Mort Zuckerman, chairman and editor-in-chief of *U.S. News and World
Report*, chairman of the *Atlantic Monthly*, and chairman and copublisher
of the *New York Daily News*, was also unequivocal in his opposition to
CIA manipulation of the media. "[W]hatever gains may be justified and
whatever grounds may be used to justify intelligence work by the press
in whatever form this may take, it seems to me that these gains must
still be assessed in the context of what they do to the press as an institution of a free society. The central role of journalism is that of a constitutional check on government and not as an instrument of government.
... Any association, it seems to me, with a government agency, or particularly with intelligence services, undermines the credibility and the
greater good done by independent journalists. Untainted journalism today is likely to do more good for America ... than anything that the
occasional journalist acting as an intelligence agent might accomplish.

"So I would share in the conclusion that these prohibitions must be,
if anything, increased and made more absolute. ... It is not enough ...
to say that if an individual consents, that is, if he is witting, that he
therefore should be available as a resource or asset for the intelligence
services. Because the effects of this individual's decision go way beyond
what this individual may or may not be involved with. I think it affects

the role of the press, it affects the security of the press, it affects the integrity of the press, it affects the credibility of the press."[70]

The only journalist testifying on the side of the CIA was Kenneth L. Adelman, not a journalist at all but a former Reagan administration official working as a syndicated columnist. Adelman proclaimed, "My experience in government has been that the CIA is, if anything these days, because of the revelations of the 70s, too timid and too cautious, rather than too bold." Noting the low esteem in which the public holds the media, Adelman concluded, "So maybe Ted Koppel's profession would be helped and not tainted by associating with the CIA."[71]

The Senate ultimately seemed more swayed by the flippant remarks of Kenneth Adelman than by the earnest advice of the assembled journalists. No legislation to control the CIA's media relationships was passed, and as the twenty-first century begins the agency continues to function under regulations that allow the unlimited recruitment of foreign journalists, the unlimited use of "voluntary" press relationships, and secret criteria under which the DCI may "waive" all agency regulations regarding the media.

Specific details on the CIA's current relationships with journalists, at home and abroad, will, of course, be hidden from the public for many years, perhaps forever. But the prominent loophole in the CIA's media guidelines allowing, indeed encouraging, the use of foreign journalists makes it likely that the agency is, at the very least, heavily involved in overseas media. Unofficial accounts of such involvement circulated during the 1990s, particularly from the volatile Balkan nations with which the United States has forged an intrusive love-hate relationship.

In Bosnia and Kosovo, currently administered as American-led NATO protectorates, all media are tightly controlled by NATO, and the CIA's influence is common knowledge. In Croatia, America's client state in the Balkans, CIA involvement in local media is quietly acknowledged. Even within archenemy Serbia, the massive American aid to the "independent press" is assumed to be CIA-tainted.

As the public concern about spies in the media declines and charges of new CIA involvement with the press surface, one is reminded of the prediction offered by a senior CIA official in 1977, at the height of the agency's press scandals. "The pendulum will swing, and someday we'll be recruiting journalists again," said the official, who chose to remain anonymous. "I will have no problem recruiting. I see a lot of them, and I know they're ripe for the plucking."[72]

NOTES

1. Suzan Revah, "Deja Scoop: Journalists and the CIA," *American Journalism Review* (April 1996), p. 10.

2. Ibid.

3. "CIA Policy Allows Agents to Enlist, Pose as Journalists," *New Media and the Law* (spring 1996), p. 4.

4. Jane E. Kirtley, Executive Director, Reporters Committee for Freedom of the Press, letter to John M. Deutch, Director of Central Intelligence, April 24, 1996. Part of press release by Reporters Committee for Freedom of the Press.

5. *Foreign and Military Intelligence Activities of the United States*, Final Report of the Select Committee to Study Governmental Operations with Respect to Intelligence Activities, U.S. Senate, April 26, 1976 (Washington, D.C.: U.S. GPO, 1976), Book I, p. 194.

6. Carl Bernstein, "The CIA and the Media," *Rolling Stone* (October 20, 1977), p. 65.

7. William Colby, *Honorable Men: My Life in the CIA* (New York: Simon & Schuster, 1978), p. 377.

8. *Foreign and Military Intelligence Activities of the United States*, Final Report, April 26, 1976, pp. 196–97.

9. Ibid.

10. *The CIA and the Media*, Hearings of the Subcommittee on Oversight of the Permanent Select Committee on Intelligence, U.S. House of Representatives, 95th Cong., 1st and 2nd Sess., December 27–29, 1977, January 4–5 and April 20, 1978 (Washington, D.C.: U.S. GPO, 1978), pp. 331–34.

11. *CIA's Use of Journalists and Clergy in Intelligence Operations*, Hearing before the Select Committee on Intelligence of the U.S. Senate, 104th Cong., 2d Sess., July 17, 1996 (Washington, D.C.: U.S. GPO, 1996), pp. 6–7.

12. John M. Crewdson, "The CIA's 3-Decade Effort to Mold the World's Views," *New York Times* (December 25, 1977), 1.

13. Ibid., 1, 12.

14. John M. Crewdson, "Worldwide Propaganda Network Built by the C.I.A.," *New York Times* (December 26, 1977), 37.

15. Cited in Bernstein, "The CIA and the Media," p. 58.

16. Stuart H. Loory, "The CIA's Use of the Press: A 'Mighty Wurlitzer,' " *Columbia Journalism Review* (September/October 1974), p. 14.

17. John M. Crewdson, "C.I.A. Established Many Links to Journalists in U.S. and Abroad," *New York Times* (December 27, 1977), p. 40.

18. Ibid.

19. Bernstein, "The CIA and the Media," p. 59.

20. Ibid.

21. Ibid., p. 56.

22. Ibid., p. 57.

23. Ibid.

24. Ibid., p. 59.

25. Ibid.

26. Ibid., pp. 59–60.

27. Ibid., p. 58.

28. Bernstein, "The CIA and the Media," pp. 57, 60.

29. Ibid., p. 60.

30. Joseph Harrison cited in Loory, "The CIA's Use of the Press," pp. 14–15.

31. Cited in Crewdson, "C.I.A. Established Many Links to Journalists in U.S. and Abroad," p. 40.

32. Ibid.

33. Bernstein, "The CIA and the Media," p. 63.

34. Ibid.

35. Ibid.

36. Ibid., p. 64.

37. Ibid., pp. 61–62.

38. Ibid., pp. 62, 64.

39. Ibid., p. 64.

40. Ibid.

41. Crewdson, "Worldwide Propaganda Network Built by the C.I.A.," p. 37.

42. Ibid.

43. Ibid.

44. Ibid.

45. William Blum, *Killing Hope: U.S. Military and CIA Interventions since World War II* (Monroe, Maine: Common Courage Press, 1986), p. 104.

46. Crewdson, "Worldwide Propaganda Network Built by the C.I.A.," p. 37.

47. Blum, *Killing Hope*, pp. 42–43.

48. Crewdson, "Worldwide Propaganda Network Built by the C.I.A.," p. 37.

49. *Covert Action in Chile, 1963–1973*, Staff Report of the Select Committee to Study Governmental Operations with Respect to Intelligence Activities, U.S. Senate, December 18, 1975 (Washington, D.C.: U.S. GPO), pp. 8, 15–16.

50. Edgar Chamorro, written affidavit, September 5, 1985, in John Stauber and Sheldon Rampton, *Toxic Sludge Is Good for You: Lies, Damn Lies and the Public Relations Industry* (Monroe, Maine: Common Courage Press, 1995), p. 160.

51. Blum, *Killing Hope*, p. 118.

52. Stansfield Turner, *Secrecy and Democracy: The CIA in Transition* (Boston: Houghton Mifflin, 1985), pp. 100–101.

53. *Foreign and Military Intelligence Activities of the United States*, Final Report, pp. 1–2, 7–8.

54. Ibid., p. 8.

55. Ibid., p. 67.

56. Crewdson, "The CIA's 3-Decade Effort to Mold the World's Views," p. 12.

57. Ibid.

58. *The CIA and the Media*, pp. 24–25, 28.

59. Ibid., pp. 130–34.

60. Ibid., pp. 206–7, 243, 250.

61. Cited in Loory, "The CIA's Use of the Press," p. 11.

62. Ibid.

63. Ibid., pp. 17–18.

64. *The CIA and the Media*, pp. 197–98.

65. Ibid., pp. 98–102.

66. Ibid., p. 242.

67. "Spies and the Media," *The News Media and the Law* (summer 1996), p. 12.

68. *CIA's Use of Journalists and Clergy in Intelligence Operations*, pp. 15–17, 22.

69. Ibid.

70. Ibid., pp. 19–20, 25.

71. Ibid.

72. Cited in Crewdson, "CIA Established Many Links to Journalists in U.S. and Abroad," p. 40.

CHAPTER 4

Press Controls in Time of War

AMERICAN WARTIME CENSORSHIP: FROM THE REVOLUTIONARY WAR TO KOREA

In 1917 Senator Hiram Johnson uttered the oft-quoted insight, "The first casualty when war comes is truth." Ten years later Norman Thomas, America's venerable socialist spokesman, extended that characterization of war, saying "its first casualties are liberty and truth."[1] Both comments are true today and, indeed, have ever been so. Among the disturbing side effects of war is the seemingly unavoidable role that the press has played as its handmaiden. Whether through formal military press controls, self-censorship, or the editorial policies of its publishers, the press can usually be counted on to sound the drumbeat for war long before the first bullet has been fired and long after the last bomb has been dropped.

As the twentieth century was approaching its conclusion, political satirist Mark Russell put together a mock history of the modern world in a single thirty-minute comedy show on public television. In his introduction, Russell explained the secret of condensing a thousand years of human history into a half-hour. "How did we do it? We left out the wars."[2] There is some serious insight here.

Author Michael Linfield has pointed out that the approach of war brings a panoply of restrictions on expression, restrictions that extend well beyond the end of hostilities. He notes that it has generally taken ten to fifteen years after the formal end of war for the "war era" and its accompanying restrictions to end. For example, the "wartime" restrictions of World War I lasted from approximately 1914 to 1925; World War II restrictions from 1939 to 1950; Korean War restrictions from 1950 until 1960; Vietnam War restrictions from the mid-1960s until the late 1970s; and the Persian Gulf War and Balkan Wars restrictions from 1990 to the present. In short, says Linfield, "wartime" was America's norm, not its exception, during the twentieth century.[3] This makes the practice of wartime press controls all the more controversial.

During America's revolutionary war era, the publication of Royalist materials was prohibited and major opposition editors were arrested and their newspapers closed. There was no substantial military censorship during the War of 1812 or the Mexican War (1846–1848), and comprehensive military censorship was not seen in the United States until the Civil War era. Initially the Union government proposed a voluntary system of newspaper censorship, but it was soon made compulsory. Information transmitted by telegraph was closely supervised and censored, and newspapers that printed inappropriate military information were suspended and their editors jailed. Union general William T. Sherman discouraged any communication with reporters, claiming that the Confederacy obtained more intelligence from Northern newspapers than through espionage.

During the Spanish-American War (1898), the navy exercised complete censorship control over cable communications. Similar naval censorship was imposed in 1914 at Vera Cruz following the U.S. intervention there, but it was the American entrance into World War I in 1917 that truly marked the beginning of systematic military censorship. A new propaganda and censorship agency, the Committee on Public Information, was created to check on the content of all printed material and motion pictures and to recommend the removal of anything objectionable. Parallel bureaus were also created within the U.S. Postal Service, Justice Department, War Department, and State Department. Telegraph messages were intercepted and seized, and motion pictures showing unpatriotic subjects were censored. Overseas, the American press censor in France was replaced by a committee of army officers and former journalists commissioned as reserve officers. During the entire period of American involvement in World War I, the government prohibited publication of any photographs of American dead.

Throughout World War I, government and press worked together to create a political hysteria that produced laws such as the Espionage Act of 1917 and the Sedition Act of 1918, which punished disloyal expression or criticism of the American government by up to twenty years in prison and a $10,000 fine. Under these laws, subversive newspapers were banned from the mails and pre-approval of all foreign language papers was required.

In 1941, when Japan's attack on Pearl Harbor brought the United States into World War II, the U.S. Navy formally requested that the media cease publishing military-related information without specific naval authorization. Both the army and navy soon introduced broad press controls, and FBI director J. Edgar Hoover was given temporary censorship authority over all news and telecommunications traffic. On December 18, 1941, pursuant to the War Powers Act, President Roosevelt created a new Office of Censorship headed by Byron Price.

The Office of Censorship provided "voluntary" guidelines, called the Code of Wartime Practices, for domestic news censorship. One part of the code stipulated that no press accounts of new or secret weapons or experiments would be allowed. Atomic secrecy would later become an important part of the policy. A note was sent to all American editors stating that nothing could be printed or broadcast about experiments on atom smashing, atomic energy, atomic fission, or any of their equivalents. Also prohibited were stories on the military use of radioactive materials, heavy water, cyclotrons, or information about the following elements or their compounds: polonium, uranium, ytterbium, hafnium, protactinium, radium, rhenium, thorium, and deuterium.

Even fiction was subject to the Office of Censorship. An already published detective novel, *The Last Secret*, contained no actual atomic information, but the army was concerned with a brief reference to atomic energy in the first chapter. As a result the Office of Censorship rebuked the novel's publisher, Dial Press, in a letter stating that "when fiction incorporates factual information dealing with restricted subjects, it can give information on to the enemy as readily as any other form of published material."[4]

Perhaps the most bizarre example of censorship during World War II occurred on April 14, 1945, when the nationally syndicated comic strip "Superman" showed the Man of Steel among a group of guests in a university physics lab being addressed by an arrogant professor. "Gentlemen—the strange object before you is the cyclotron—popularly known as an 'atom smasher,' " says the professor. "Are you still prepared to face this test, Mr. Superman?"

The Man of Steel answers calmly, "Why not?"

Superman's friends are horrified, and one shouts, "No, Superman, wait! Even you can't do it! You'll be bombarded with electrons at a speed of 100 million miles per hour and charged with three million volts! It's madness!"

The Office of Censorship wrote to the newspaper syndicate that distributed the comic strip, saying that although the office was not usually in the business of censoring comics, any discussion of atomic energy should be discouraged for the duration of the war. The Superman comic strip was promptly rewritten to remove any future mention of atom smashing.[5]

The censorship of visual images was more significant and sophisticated during World War II than it had ever been before. As in World War I, photographs of American dead were prohibited, though late in the war the public was allowed to see selected images. Under no circumstances were images of America's "emotionally wounded" to be displayed, and the War Department's Bureau of Public Relations insisted on "complete silence" about "psychoneurotic" casualties.[6]

The Code of Wartime Practices required that all news reports be submitted in duplicate, one copy to public relations and one copy to the censors. This process often delayed stories filed by reporters for a week or more, but there were no delays imposed on "official" military press releases. Because they were processed immediately, the official releases reached the home front well in advance of the actual news.

The Office of War Information (OWI), created in 1942 as America's propaganda agency and liaison between the government and the press, had the job of portraying America's war effort in the most positive light. But the reluctance of government agencies and the military to provide accurate and timely information to the public caused constant friction between the OWI and the press.

Military censorship overseas was particularly severe. In the Pacific theater, General Douglas MacArthur and Admiral Ernest J. King exercised almost dictatorial censorship. MacArthur was known for his use of censorship for "image building," and the navy had the habit of withholding bad news until it could be matched by stories of combat successes.

Press censorship in the European theater followed somewhat different procedures. By the time American troops arrived in Great Britain in January 1942, a system of joint British/American censorship had already been created. The U.S. military censorship group in London was located with the British censors at the Ministry of Information. The censors actually went ashore with the landing troops in order to monitor the war correspondents.

In North Africa the American censors seemed more concerned about blocking political news than military information. This was because the U.S. State Department opposed General Charles de Gaulle's French government in exile, supporting the more cooperative General Henri Geraud. As a result, American officials censored all political news out of North Africa until an arrangement was negotiated between de Gaulle and Geraud.

As the end of the war approached, a Joint Press Censorship Group composed of American, British, and Canadian officers was created. By D-Day there were over 500 combat correspondents in England, and many of them accompanied the Normandy invasion. Press reports from bridgeheads ashore were routed to censorship units behind the lines by courier, radio, or even carrier pigeon.

Although the Office of Censorship was disbanded shortly after the end of World War II, much of the bureaucracy of secrecy remained in place and was even strengthened as the Cold War set in. American entrance into a shooting war in Korea in 1949 brought a formal reactivation of the World War II restraints on the press. A voluntary gentleman's agreement between the military and the press was attempted, but when stories about South Korean corruption and inferior American military equipment were published, field press censorship was reimposed. When some news stories continued to get through the field censors, Tokyo headquarters introduced a censorship review of the censors themselves. On January 6, 1953, the Far East Command created a Joint Field Censorship Group composed of military censors from the U.S. Army, Navy, and Air Force. The chief field press censor who headed the group imposed censorship in all United Nations and East Asian commands in a rigid and political manner.

VIETNAM, GRENADA, AND PANAMA

After the Korean War each of the armed services assumed its own information-security planning, but by 1964, when American military involvement in Vietnam was reaching a significant level, the Pentagon once more introduced a centralized and nominally "voluntary" censorship code. The apparently airtight controls belied the fact that reporters were free to fly into, out of, and around Vietnam on civilian planes. Thus a reporter whose story was censored could simply fly out of Vietnam and file it elsewhere. Once outside of military jurisdiction, the only punishment for such acts was the loss of Department of Defense (DOD) press accreditation.

Because reporters in Vietnam traveled with combat units, unescorted by censors, their observations often contradicted the "official" military briefings. As a result, reporters came to ignore the propaganda from higher military authority, basing their stories instead on information provided by lower-ranking field officers. The stark images presented by the press led the already disenchanted American public to oppose the war. Indeed, General William Westmoreland characterized the conflict in Vietnam as the first war in history lost in the columns of the *New York Times*.

The Pentagon's view of the press has led it to impose increasingly harsh censorship on all post-Vietnam conflicts. This was first evident in the brief 1983 invasion of the tiny island of Grenada, during which the press was kept in total isolation. Whereas journalists covering the Vietnam War were afforded substantial freedom of movement in the field, the press covering Grenada could not arrange independent access to the area of conflict. Those who tried to reach the island of Grenada by way of chartered boats were intercepted by the U.S. military and held on a navy ship.

The brief military action in Grenada went without a hitch, and the American public learned only what was told to an isolated press by the military. After the unparalleled public relations success in Grenada, the Pentagon sought to formalize the new press rules by appointing Brigadier General Winant Sidle to prepare guidelines for future military press coverage. Sidle, who had served as the military's chief of public affairs in Vietnam, recommended the creation of a "pool system" of controlled and supervised press access to military action. That recommendation was implemented in 1984 when the Department of Defense Media Pool was created.

The first opportunity to implement the new pool system came in 1989, when United States forces invaded Panama to capture and depose Panamanian dictator Manuel Noriega. The official press-pool plane was delayed for five hours in order to keep reporters out of Panama City when U.S. troops arrived. When reporters were finally allowed into the city, military escorts barred them from first-hand observation of combat areas. To this day a shroud of mystery surrounds the Panama invasion, with even the number of casualties a matter of ongoing dispute. But to the Pentagon, the Panama invasion, like Grenada before it, was both a military and a public relations success. The press pool system worked like a charm, and it would come to full flower during the Persian Gulf War.

THE PERSIAN GULF WAR: OPERATION DESERT STORM

During the Persian Gulf War the system of press pools prevented independent reporting by rigidly supervising the small groups of reporters allowed to observe the war. These segregated press pools were then allowed to pass on their information to the full contingent of reporters. In addition to the restraints of the pool system, all journalists were subject to traditional DOD restrictions on the kinds of information that could be reported, including details of future operations, data on troop strengths or locations, information about downed or missing airplanes or ships, and information about operational weaknesses in the allied forces.

The new system of press controls also included a review process by which stories filed by pool reporters were censored by military officials prior to release. For the first time in memory, Americans saw messages like "Cleared by U.S. Military" or "Cleared by Israeli Censors" or "Cleared by Iraqi Censors" on their television screens or in their newspapers.

The pool system was unpopular with the press, the public, and even Congress. In 1991 Sydney Schanberg, associate editor and columnist for *Newsday*, testified about the pool system before a U.S. Senate committee: "The purpose of the government's system," said Schanberg, "is to control and manipulate information, to sanitize and clean it up so that the war will sound more like a choir boy's picnic than the grungy thing that it is."[7]

In early 1991 a group of magazines, newspapers, radio stations, and individual writers actually sued the Pentagon over the pool system, challenging its restrictions on coverage of the Persian Gulf War. A similar suit was brought by the French news service Agence France-Presse. The American suit sought an injunction against hindering press coverage of U.S. combat forces or prohibiting the press from areas where U.S. forces were deployed unless legitimate security reasons could be demonstrated. Before the court could consider the merits of the case, Iraq withdrew from Kuwait and the United States ended hostilities. In the absence of hostilities the case was declared moot and the suit was dismissed, but there remained general concern among the press that the pool system had been inappropriately used by the government to control the news and shape American political opinion about the war.

The most visible hand behind the Persian Gulf War's press controls was Pete Williams, assistant secretary of defense for public affairs. Needless to say, Williams thought the pool system had been a great success. Indeed, he claimed that it had produced "the best war coverage" in U.S. history. Reporters saw it differently. Stanley Cloud, *Time* magazine's Washington bureau chief, wrote an op-ed article for the *New York Times* in which he stated that "Mr. Williams could not have been more wrong. Desert Storm was certainly the *worst*-covered major U.S. conflict in this century."[8]

Even some military men were embarrassed by the Persian Gulf War press coverage. Colonel David Hackworth, who served twenty-five years in the U.S. Army and later reported on the Gulf War for *Newsweek*, said that when the Vietnam War ended, military leaders such as General Westmoreland blamed the press for their own inefficiency. He said Colin Powell and Norman Schwarzkopf, chairman of the Joint Chiefs of Staff and commander of the invasion of Iraq during the Gulf War, respectively, were "little captains" then, but they learned their lesson from Westmoreland. "When they had their own war out in the desert, they said never again," said Hackworth. "We had kind of a dry run for the desert in Panama where the press was greatly controlled; or even before that in Grenada. . . . They learned that we can kind of keep the press hostage and we can report the war as we want to, and that is not the American way."[9]

Hackworth described the physical nature of the military's press censorship. "I've had a little bit of experience knocking around battlefields," he said, "and I've never had more weapons pointed at me, I've never been more abusively treated than I was in the desert as a result of being a reporter. And when you examined what happened to reporters, they were detained, they were interrogated, they were arrested—by the U.S. military."[10]

The major print, radio, and TV news organizations wrote to Secretary of Defense Dick Cheney complaining that there was virtually no coverage of the Gulf ground war until it was over. Another letter from news executives said the pool system was used in the Persian Gulf War not to facilitate news coverage but to control it.

Many media critics have said the press itself was irresponsible in passively accepting the military restrictions on reporting. Hackworth claimed that the press censored itself and took an uncritical pro-war position because "if an editorial appeared in a newspaper that was opposed to the war or offered caution or offered criticism toward the military or told the truth, the people became hostile, advertisers freaked-out and jerked their advertisement. And what the media is all about is about money, so that's why the press rolled over and sang the military song, which is very, very threatening."[11]

Ironically, it was not America's battlefield commanders that promoted the press restrictions. "They wanted to tell their story," said Hackworth. "I've had commanders say to me, 'Look, we'll tell you what's happening. Don't identify me. And if my commander comes, you just got here and you're just leaving.' And they were very, very open, very supportive and most of them were very angry, as was articulated by one young soldier to me, 'Why am I out here . . . fighting for democracy, fighting for freedom and my own press is suppressed?' "[12]

After the end of the Persian Gulf War, a group of news organizations appointed five senior reporters to begin negotiating with Pete Williams in an effort to regain the press freedoms that had been lost. After eight months of discussions, a statement of nine principles was issued to cover future combat reporting. Primary among these principles was the understanding that pools would not be the standard method of covering military action, though they could be used in the early phase of a conflict, or in remote areas, or during highly classified special operations. The journalists who negotiated the nine principles admitted that they had no guarantees that the Pentagon would not impose the same heavy-handed controls on information that had been used in the Persian Gulf War. Indeed, the Pentagon insisted that it would retain the option of imposing security reviews on news reports.

Just two years later, during the Pentagon's 1994 planning for an invasion of Haiti, it became clear that military censorship was as onerous as ever. White House and Pentagon officials requested that the television networks observe an eight-hour broadcasting blackout during the invasion, and reporters in Haiti were to be restricted to their hotels until further notice. These restrictions were never actually imposed, because the invasion was canceled after successful negotiations with the Haitian junta, but the *New York Times* commented, "It shows that the news-management policies that took root in the Reagan-Bush years and reached their full propagandistic flower during Operation Desert Storm are still in place at the Pentagon."[13]

THE BALKAN WARS

The quality and independence of press coverage of America's wars have been deteriorating since the Vietnam War era. As we have seen, journalists generally considered the Persian Gulf War to be the worst-covered major conflict in American history. Unfortunately, the coverage of the Balkan Wars of the 1990s set a new and shameful standard from which wartime journalism may never recover.

The causes of this latest journalistic collapse are fourfold. One, the press has become addicted to the use of public relations firms as news sources (see Chapter 2). Two, the "Tabloid Decade" (see Chapter 5) has enabled the press to segue seamlessly from Monica Lewinsky to Slobodan Milosevic, producing yet another caricature at the expense of news. And the two more recent burdens that the press now wears around its neck are, three, an unprecedented new system of Pentagon secrecy, and four, the rise of "the journalism of attachment."

Pentagon Secrecy

The Pentagon's new system of information control began in the mid-1990s during the Bosnian conflict, but it reached full flower during the 1999 war against Serbia in Kosovo. At that time the Pentagon announced that not only would government control of information during the Kosovo war be tighter than in *any* previous American conflict, but in all likelihood the press would *never* see a return to even the abominable standards of the Persian Gulf War.[14] The Pentagon's new information controls were described on April 6, 1999, by Assistant Secretary of Defense for Public Affairs Kenneth Bacon, himself a former editor and reporter for the *Wall Street Journal*.

"We have adopted a more restrictive policy than in the past," said Bacon on public television's *NewsHour With Jim Lehrer*. "And I think I should be very clear on that. The reason is that this battle in particular, and I think modern times in general, have changed the dynamics of information released for warfare." Bacon gave four reasons for the new secrecy requirements. First, he claimed that an "alliance war" such as the NATO campaign in Kosovo made operational security difficult to maintain. Second, he said, "We now live in an era where information is made available instantly to the enemy. We know that they watch television. We know that they are on the Internet. We know that they have cell phones. . . . So we want to give the enemy as little information as we can in order to help them with their own defenses against the attacks." Third, he complained of the competitive media age in which journalists must get on the air as soon as possible with details of the war. Finally, he said that the press is much less restrained in the use of operational information today than it used to be.

Military correspondent George Wilson asked Bacon how a post-audit of air strikes—what the bombs hit or didn't hit, who was involved, how many sorties were flown—could compromise security. Bacon responded, "We have different operational security restraints today than we used to have." Because the Yugoslav government can analyze media reports, said Bacon, "we've just decided to give them as little information as possible. That does mean being more tight with information we give to the press, but we've done this purely for operational reasons."[15]

When Wilson asked how the press was to know that the Pentagon was giving out truthful information, Bacon answered simply, "That's a good question." Bacon admitted that there had been a "sea change" in Pentagon information control that began with the August 1998 bombing of alleged terrorist camps in Afghanistan and a pharmaceutical plant in Khartoum. At that time, Bacon simply refused to discuss those actions with the press. That total silence has now been extended to all subsequent Pentagon activity. Bacon denied personal responsibility for the sea change, saying that General Henry Shelton (chairman of the Joint Chiefs of Staff) and Defense Secretary William Cohen insisted that "there ought to be less operational detail discussed in public and less . . . printed in public, and they have set out to try to make that happen." Bacon said the war against Yugoslavia was "the biggest example of the new policy."[16]

Bacon's claim that an "alliance war" required unprecedented press controls contained a measure of truth. Information access during NATO's bombing of Kosovo and the rest of Serbia was reduced to its lowest common denominator, as the censorship proclivities of nineteen NATO members were compounded to produce an absurd news blackout more severe than that imposed by the beleaguered Serbian media. Indeed, an increasing amount of American and European television footage of the war was coming from Serbian TV, and because much of this included disturbing images of bombing damage in Belgrade, NATO announced an unusual policy.

At NATO's April 8, 1999, news conference, a BBC reporter asked NATO's military spokesperson, David Wilbey, "Can you confirm reports that NATO will now be striking television and radio transmitters, antennae, etc. [in Serbia]?"

"Serb radio and TV is an instrument of propaganda and repression," answered Wilbey. "It is therefore a legitimate target in this campaign. If

President Milosevic would provide equal time for Western news broadcasts in its programmes without censorship three hours a day between noon and 1800 and three hours a day between 1800 and midnight, then his TV could become an acceptable instrument of public information."

The assembled journalists were dumbfounded. "Can we take it that that reply should be seen as either a threat or a promise that you will be bombing the television transmitters unless they allow three hours of Western television?" asked the BBC reporter.

"I think you can take it as a public statement, a public announcement," said Wilbey.[17]

Indeed, NATO forces immediately began intensive bombing of all media facilities in Serbia. Broadcast studios were destroyed, killing numerous journalists in the process. The state radio and television network, RTS, was hit particularly hard, and an April 23 attack on RTS studios in Belgrade killed at least eleven people.

NATO spokesperson Jamie Shea insisted, "RTS is not media. It's full of government employees who are paid to produce propaganda and lies. . . . And therefore, we see that as a military target."[18]

Outraged news organizations around the world protested the bombing of media targets as a threat to journalists of all nationalities and a violation of the 1949 Geneva Convention protecting civilians in time of war. Robert Leavitt, associate director of the Center for War, Peace, and the News Media, gave two reasons why NATO was not justified in targeting Serbian radio and television. "The first is that this is really a deliberate targeting of civilians, which is questionable in any circumstance," said Leavitt. "This is not a military target, no matter what NATO says. The second is that it really creates a very dangerous precedent with regard to freedom of the press. Once we start defining journalists as legitimate targets, it becomes very hard for us to criticize any other attacks on media. . . . There are many governments around the world who are very happy now that NATO has said it's legitimate to target journalists. And they will be doing that in the future."[19]

On May 7, 1999, NATO forces bombed the Chinese embassy in Belgrade. Among the twenty-four casualties were three deaths, all of them journalists. The United States blamed the attack on faulty maps. The *Observer* (London) and Copenhagen's *Politiken* reported that "according to senior U.S. and European military sources," the Chinese embassy had been targeted because it was serving as a rebroadcast station for the Yugoslav army.[20]

The Journalism of Attachment

During the Kosovo conflict, NATO and the Pentagon effectively made war on the media, at home and abroad, but press coverage of the conflict was further degraded by journalists themselves. Official secrecy was exacerbated by the spread of a journalistic practice that may be more dangerous than government censorship. The remnants of a once proud tradition of aggressive, objective war reporting have frequently been replaced by a sentimentalism that is vulnerable to manipulation.

The new approach to covering the news became evident in the early 1990s, but it was not given a name until 1997, when Martin Bell, a prominent television reporter, embraced the new style and called it "journalism of attachment." Bell wrote, "By this I mean a journalism that cares as well as knows; that is aware of its responsibilities; and will not stand neutrally between good and evil, right and wrong, the victim and the oppressor."[21]

A number of veteran journalists have recognized the pernicious effects of the journalism of attachment. Christopher Dunkley wrote, "The worrying thing about 'the journalism of attachment' is that it is being preached—and worse, practiced—by hard news reporters." Dunkley noted that the war in Bosnia "has done most to inspire the journalism of attachment, with one side demonized, the other sides sanctified, and the public in other countries often encouraged to believe that Serbs alone were responsible for atrocities and all other parties were blameless." Dunkley was concerned with the growing tendency of reporters to reflect their emotional involvement in their reporting. "From there it is only a step," said Dunkley, "and perhaps not a conscious one, to the selection and manipulation of the facts to favour one side."[22]

For example, the BBC's Nik Gowing characterized the one-sided anti-Serb reporting in Bosnia as "a secret shame" for the journalistic community. "I think there is a cancer now which is affecting journalism," said Gowing. "[I]t is the unspoken issue of partiality and bias in foreign reporting. There is something rather taboo . . . to talk about this in media circles, partly because to do so would undermine the perceived integrity and objectivity of correspondents who report from battle zones."[23]

Mick Hume, editor of *LM* magazine, said, "The Journalism of Attachment uses other people's wars and crises as a twisted sort of therapy, through which foreign reporters can discover some sense of purpose— first for themselves and then for their audience back home. It turns the life and death struggles of others into private battlegrounds where journalists who have lost faith in the old values of their profession can fight for their souls." In this process, "the war reporter emerges not as journalist but as combatant, not as news broadcaster but as the news itself, a singularly moral figure on a self-appointed mission to save the world. . . . But at what price for journalistic standards? Or for those unfortunate enough to be turned into cannon fodder for the media people's personal crusades?"[24]

Hume contrasts the crusading journalists of the past, whose aim was to expose the faults in their own societies, with the new breed of "attached" journalists who search for signs of evil in other people's back-yards. "Wherever there is trouble these journalists demand more political and military intervention, on the grounds that 'something must be done . . . ,' " wrote Hume. "They are apparently oblivious to the lesson of history which the best of the old campaigning journalists had grasped; that whatever 'something' the Great Powers do around the world, it is likely to be at the expense of freedom and justice."[25]

Some very influential journalists have embraced the journalism of attachment in covering the Balkan War, often merging their reporting with official government policies. CNN's Christiane Amanpour is a prominent example. In 1996 she told an audience of journalists that neutrality was not acceptable in places such as Bosnia, because "[w]hen you are neutral, you can become an accomplice."[26]

Amanpour made no apology for ignoring the causes and complexities of the conflicts she covers. "I am not a political reporter," she said. "I am not a diplomatic reporter. I do wars; I do crises. I don't do politics."[27]

Some of Amanpour's colleagues have had trouble accepting her personalized journalism. "I have winced at some of what she's done, at what used to be called advocacy journalism," wrote Stephen Kinzer of the *New York Times*. "She was sitting in Belgrade when that [Sarajevo] market massacre happened, and she went on the air to say that the Serbs had probably done it. There was no way she could have known that."[28] Indeed, a subsequent UN report identified the Bosnian Muslims as the source of the massacre.[29]

Amanpour's cheerleading for the Clinton administration's military intervention in the Balkans was noted with concern by her peers, but there was little open criticism until she joined the official family by marrying James Rubin, the State Department's high-profile spokesperson. Stella Jatras of the *Washington Times* said there was "something unhealthy" about having Amanpour and Rubin cover the same "breaking news" story. "Ms. Amanpour, who never ceased to present a one-sided CNN perspective throughout the Bosnian war, is now doing the same with her one-sided anti-Serb CNN perspective of the civil war now raging in Kosovo," wrote Jatras. "At the same time, Mr. Rubin is touting the anti-Serb position from the State Department. . . . Is CNN running the State Department, or vice versa? There is clearly a conflict here." Jatras called for Rubin to step down as State Department spokesperson. "How can there be any semblance of journalistic impartiality with such a relationship between a 'news' agency and the government?" she wrote.[30]

Journalist and columnist Alexander Cockburn complained, "Christiane Amanpour, CNN's leading foreign correspondent, and a woman whose reports about the fate of Kosovan refugees did much to fan public appetite for NATO's war, is literally and figuratively in bed with the spokesman for the State Department and a leading propagandist for

NATO during that war, husband Jamie Rubin. If CNN truly wanted to maintain the appearance of objectivity, it would have taken Amanpour off the story."[31]

On public television's *NewsHour With Jim Lehrer*, Amanpour recently admitted that the relationship between government and press "is now almost exclusively adversarial or party line." Without characterizing her own reporting, she explained, "It's two extremes, if you like. . . . By that, I mean to say that the military is now able and does more and more demand certain very, very rigorous conditions from journalists in order to be able to cover their operations. You either have to join what some of my colleagues have called the 'propaganda machine,' or you don't go and cover at all." When *NewsHour* moderator Terence Smith asked Amanpour how the military was able to impose its propaganda machine on individual reporters, she responded, "By basically putting the ring through our nose and telling us this is how you will cover the news. . . . [I]t was almost perfected in the Gulf War with the pool system, with the very rigorous conditions that were put on journalists."[32]

Morley Safer, veteran reporter and coeditor of *60 Minutes*, was quick to point out that the military propaganda had been foisted on the American public "with the compliance of Christiane's network [CNN]."[33]

Recent revelations suggest an even more ominous connection between CNN and the U.S. military. On February 21, 2000, an article by Abe de Vries in the reputable Dutch newspaper *Trouw* revealed that military personnel from the U.S. Army's 4th Psychological Operations Group (PSYOPS) worked for CNN during NATO's Kosovo war.[34] The same 4th Army PSYOPS Group had staffed President Reagan's Office of Public Diplomacy (OPD) during the 1980s, planting propaganda in the U.S. media supporting Reagan's Central American policies. (See Chapter 2.) The *Trouw* story reported on a military symposium held in Arlington, Virginia, in February 2000 at which Colonel Christopher St. John, commander of the 4th PSYOPS Group, called for "greater cooperation between the armed forces and media giants." St. John told the symposium that PSYOPS personnel had worked for CNN for several weeks and "helped in the production of some news stories for the network."[35] He concluded that "the cooperation with CNN was a textbook example of the kind of ties the American army wants to have with the media."[36]

Major Thomas Collins of the U.S. Army Information Service confirmed that "PSYOPS personnel, soldiers and officers have been working in CNN's headquarters in Atlanta through our program 'Training with Industry.' They worked as regular employees of CNN. Conceivably they would have worked on stories during the Kosovo war. They helped in the production of news."[37]

CNN corroborated the hiring of two PSYOPS personnel in television, two in radio, and one in satellite operations. "I found it astonishing," de

Vries told journalist Alexander Cockburn. "[T]hese kinds of close ties with the army are, in my view, completely unacceptable for any serious news organization. Maybe even more astonishing is the complete silence about the story from the big media."[38]

Journalist de Vries was concerned with CNN's loss of independence. "Did the military learn from the TV people how to hold viewers' attention? Or did the PsyOps people teach CNN how to help the U.S. government garner political support?" he asked. "The U.S. Army leadership appears to have concluded that new and more aggressive measures in psychological warfare are needed. Not only do the PsyOps people want to spread handpicked 'information' and keep other news quiet, the army also wants to control the Internet, to wage electronic warfare against disobedient media, and to control commercial satellites."[39]

The watchdog media publication *Fairness and Accuracy in Reporting* wrote, "What makes the CNN story especially troubling is the fact that the network allowed the army's covert propagandists to work in its headquarters, where they learned the ins and outs of CNN's operations. . . . Did the network allow the military to conduct an intelligence-gathering mission against CNN itself?"[40]

The Picture That Fooled the World

German journalist Thomas Deichmann has cited a particular case of media coverage in which the journalism of attachment may have allowed a misinterpreted photograph to irreversibly distort world opinion about the Bosnian war.[41] After unconfirmed press reports of Serb-run "concentration camps" in Bosnia, a British team from Independent Television News (ITN) visited the Trnopolje refugee camp on August 5, 1992. A single shot from their footage, a closeup showing an emaciated Muslim man behind barbed wire, was presented as "proof" of the existence of Serb-run, Nazi-style concentration camps in Bosnia. The heavily cropped picture was shown in newspapers and on television the following day, giving rise to the image of the Serbs as the Nazis of the Balkans. Only years later, after the ITN pictures had precipitated U.S. military intervention in Bosnia, did the true story of Trnopolje emerge.

In May 1992, at the height of the Bosnian civil war, Serbian units captured the town of Trnopolje, causing many Muslim inhabitants to take refuge in the town's school, community center, and the open area behind both buildings. There the reporters shot the pictures that would have worldwide impact. The most striking was that of an emaciated man, Fikret Alic, standing shirtless in a group of Muslims behind what appeared to be a barbed wire fence.

The image of Alic behind barbed wire told its own story. In England, the August 7 *Daily Mail* ran the picture under the headline "The Proof," while the *Daily Mirror* captioned the photograph "Belsen '92." Some

William Westmoreland, the U.S. Army chief of staff during the Vietnam War, characterized that conflict as the first war in history that had been lost in the columns of the *New York Times*. That view, accepted throughout the military, led to extreme controls during subsequent wars. Photo reproduced from the collections of the Library of Congress.

In May 1992, at the height of the Bosnian civil war, a British television crew captured the image of an emaciated Bosnian Muslim named Fikret Alic. What later came to be known as "The Picture That Fooled the World" encouraged NATO intervention in the Balkans. Photo made from "Judgement" video-tape, courtesy of Jared Israel.

newspapers actually added concentration camp watchtowers to the picture to make sure that the implication was clear. In the United States, ABC-TV News introduced a report about the camps with the comment: "Faces and bodies that hint at atrocities of the past. But this is not history, this is Bosnia. Pictures from the camps: A glimpse into genocide."[42]

In an article entitled "How Media Misinformation Led to Bosnian Intervention," George Kenney, former State Department desk officer for Yugoslavia, told how ITN's pictures of the Trnopolje camp precipitated war. "The first turning point, that led straightaway to the introduction of Western troops," said Kenney, "coincided with ITN's broadcast of images of what was widely assumed to be a concentration camp, at the Bosnian Serb-run Trnopolje refugee collection center in August 1992." Kenney explained that ITN's coverage produced a wave of sanctions against the Bosnian Serbs from international organizations, followed by the threat of military force. Roused by the barbed wire picture, the British government made 1,800 soldiers available for deployment in Bosnia, and Bill Clinton requested military action against the Serbs during his electoral campaign.[43]

The ITN report on Trnopolje was a perfect example of the journalism of attachment, as video journalists aggressively sought to enlist public support for one side of a civil war. Four and a half years after the ITN pictures were shot, Thomas Deichmann, a journalist for the German magazine *LM*, discovered the true nature of the "Picture That Fooled the World." He and his wife were looking at the picture when she observed that the barbed wire appeared to be nailed from the inside, the "prisoner's" side, something quite out of the ordinary. After studying the ITN outtakes and those of an accompanying camera crew, Deichmann visited Trnopolje and interviewed former guards and civilians from the area. He was soon able to prove that Alic and the other men in the picture were not encircled by barbed wire.

"There was no barbed-wire fence surrounding the Trnopolje refugee and transit camp," wrote Deichmann. "The barbed wire was only around a small compound next to the camp, which had been erected before the war to protect agricultural products.... Penny Marshall and her [ITN] team got their famous pictures by filming the camp and the Bosnian Muslims from *inside* this compound, shooting through the compound fence at people who were actually standing *outside* the area fenced in with barbed wire." Deichmann concluded, "The unedited ITN rushes I obtained show clearly from where the famous shot was taken. Also the Tribunal in the Hague and the ICRC confirmed that there was no barbed wire around the camp."[44]

Indeed, when viewing the video outtakes from local TV crews who accompanied ITN to Trnopolje, one notices immediately that the "barbed wire" through which the ITN pictures were taken was mostly thin chicken wire, with barbed wire only at the very top. It is also clear that the assembled refugees are not confined behind wire of any kind. It is the camera crew that has located itself behind a short stretch of wire fence in order to shoot pictures of the Muslims in the open field beyond. The film shows that ITN journalist Penny Marshall initially selected a refugee who spoke English and asked his name. "My name is Mehmet," he answered.

Marshall then asked about the circumstances at the camp, and the following conversation took place.

Mehmet: I think it's very quiet. Nothing wrong, but very hot.

Marshall: Do you sleep outside?

Mehmet: No, no, inside. [Points to building in background]

Marshall: Do they treat you badly?

Mehmet: No, no, very kind.

Marshall: Very kind?

Mehmet: Very kind, very kind.

Marshall: How did you come here? Are you a fighter?

Mehmet: In a bus. With the bus.

Marshall: Are you a fighter?

Mehmet: No, no.

Marshall: Do you feel safe here?

Mehmet: I think it's very safe, but it's very hot. Other things are fine.

Marshall: This man is very thin. [Motions to the thin Muslim man whose photo would soon be seen around the world as evidence of a Serbian concentration camp.]

Mehmet: I think all people are not the same.

[A male questioner off camera intervenes and asks if Mehmet is a prisoner of war.]

Mehmet: No, no. We are in a refugee camp, not prisoners.

[The male questioner asks if Mehmet could get on a bus and go to the nearby town of Banja Luka.]

Mehmet: It depends on the civil government.

Marshall: You cannot leave here?

Mehmet: Not now, not now.

[Male voice off camera asks again whether Mehmet is a prisoner.]

Mehmet: It's not a prison. It's a refugee camp.[45]

Clearly, neither the function of the Trnopolje camp nor the events surrounding the filming of the emaciated Muslim were accurately presented in the media. Perhaps with the best of intentions, journalists around the world had manipulated the ITN footage to mislead the public about the nature of a Balkan civil war. What came to be known as The Picture That Fooled the World precipitated a disastrous escalation of military conflict in the Balkans that proceeds apace.

Thomas Deichmann has warned of a trend in which journalists take sides in conflicts and adopt a moral mission rather than doing their traditional job as war reporters. "This trend has brought forth a new code of conduct regarding what can and cannot be said," he said. "The moral agenda of journalists has created an orthodoxy that no one is allowed to challenge. If you do so you not only risk becoming a target of smear campaigns, you are silenced.[46]

NOTES

1. Michael Linfield, *Freedom under Fire: U.S. Civil Liberties in Times of War* (Boston: South End Press, 1990), p. 1.

2. Mark Russell, "Comedy Special," WETA/PBS, December 19, 1999.

3. Linfield, *Freedom under Fire*, p. 5.

4. Patrick S. Washburn, "The Office of Censorship's Attempt to Control Press Coverage of the Atomic Bomb during World War II," Association for Education in Journalism and Mass Communication, July 2–5, 1988, ERIC document ED295201, p. 8.

5. "Superman," *Washington Post* (April 14, 1945), 7B.

6. Herbert N. Foerstel, *Free Expression and Censorship in America: An Encyclopedia* (Westport Conn.: Greenwood Press, 1997), p. 139.

7. Cited in Steve Daley, "Journalists Getting Only a Piece of the Story, Lawmakers Told," *Chicago Tribune* (February 21, 1991), p. 5.

8. Stanley W. Cloud, "Covering the Next War," *New York Times* (August 4, 1992), A19.

9. "The Media in the Iraq War," *America's Defense Monitor*, PBS series produced by the Center for Defense Information, August 11, 1991, pp. 4–5 of transcript.

10. Ibid., p. 6.

11. Ibid., p. 13.

12. Ibid., p. 15.

13. "Military Censorship Lives," *New York Times* (September 21, 1994), A22.

14. "The Pentagon and the Press," Online NewsHour, April 6, 1999, pp. 3–4, www.pbs.org/newshour.

15. Ibid.

16. Ibid.

17. NATO press conference, April 8, 1999, pp. 6–7. www.nato.int/docu/speech/1999/s990408a.

18. "Off the Air," Online NewsHour, May 4, 1999, pp. 2–3, www.pbs.org/newshour.

19. Ibid.

20. Joel Bleifuss, "A Tragic Mistake?" *In These Times* (December 12, 1999), p. 1, web.lexis-nexis.com/universe.

21. Martin Bell, "TV News: How Far Should We Go?" *British Journalism Review*, vol. 8, no. 1 (1997), p. 7.

22. Christopher Dunkley, "Whose News Is It Anyway?" *Financial Times* (September 20, 1997), p. viii.

23. Cited in Eleanor Randolph, "Journalists Find Little Neutrality over Objective Reporting," *Los Angeles Times* (April 22, 1997), A5.

24. Mick Hume, *Whose War Is It Anyway? The Dangers of the Journalism of Attachment* (London: BM InformInc, 1997), pp. 5, 18.

25. Ibid., p. 23.

26. Cited in Randolph, "Journalists Find Little Neutrality over Objective Reporting," A5.

27. Cited in Sandra Harris, "On Top of a Troubled World," *High Life* (June 1997), p. 14.

28. Cited in Stella Jatras, "Odd Alliance at State, CNN?" *Washington Times* (March 14, 1999), B5.

29. Florence Levinsohn, *Belgrade: Among the Serbs* (Chicago: Ivan R. Dec, 1994), p. 314.

30. Jatras, "Odd Alliance at State, CNN?," B.5.

31. Alexander Cockburn, "Inside CNN and Psyops," *Counterpunch* (March 26, 2000), p. 5, www.counterpunch.org.

32. "Covering the War," Online NewsHour, April 20, 2000, pp. 3–4, www.pbs.org/newshour.

33. Ibid., p. 4.

34. Abe de Vries, "U.S. Army 'PsyOps' Specialists Worked for CNN," *Trouw* (February 21, 2000), pp. 1–2, translation on www.emperors-clothes.com.

35. Cockburn, "Inside CNN and Psyops," pp. 3–4.

36. Abe de Vries, "The American Army Loves CNN," *Trouw* (February 21, 2000), p. 2, translation on www.emperors-clothes.com.

37. De Vries, "U.S. Army 'PsyOps' Specialists Worked for CNN," pp. 1–2.

38. Cockburn, "Inside CNN and Psyops," p. 4.

39. De Vries, "U.S. Army" 'PsyOps' Specialists Worked for CNN," pp. 1–2.

40. "Action Alert," FAIR: Fairness and Accuracy in Reporting (March 27, 2000), p. 1, www.fair.org.

41. Thomas Deichmann, "Misinformation: TV Coverage of a Bosnian Camp," *Covert Action Quarterly* (fall 1998), pp. 52–54.

42. Ibid., p. 52.

43. George Kenney, "How Media Misinformation Led to Bosnian Intervention," Serbian Unity Congress (April 1997), http://www.suc.org/politics.

44. Deichmann, "Misinformation: TV Coverage of a Bosnian Camp," p. 54.

45. Jared Israel and Peter Makara, eds., *Judgement (Presuda)* (New York: Emperors Clothes, 2000), film, www.emperors-clothes.com.

46. Ibid.

CHAPTER 5

The Growing Influence
of Tabloid Journalism

THE ORIGIN OF THE TABLOIDS

On June 26, 1919, two days before the signing of the Treaty of Versailles
that brought an end to World War I, the *New York Illustrated Daily News*
burst upon the scene, marking the formal beginning of tabloid journalism. "At first glance," wrote author Simon Bessie, "one might almost
have mistaken it for a magazine, so little did it resemble the customary
American newspaper. Its page was barely more than half the size of the
traditional newspaper page and, with the exception of a single headline
and some small type, it was covered entirely with pictures. The style was
. . . called 'tabloid' because of its smallness and its concise presentation
of the news."[1]

Within two years the *Daily News* had become the best-selling newspaper in New York City, and by 1938 its circulation had reached,
1,750,000 on weekdays and 3,250,000 on Sundays, far exceeding the sales
of any other daily newspaper in the entire country. In response to this
success story, "tabloids" sprang up in cities and towns around the nation.

The tabloids had many critics. Journalist S. T. Moore considered them
"an unhealthy blot on the fourth estate—they carry all the news that
isn't fit to print." Publicist Aben Kandel said, "they reduce the highest
ideals of the newspaper to the process of fastening a camera lens to every
boudoir keyhole." In comparing the tabloid press with nineteenth-
century newspapers, venerable critic Oswald Garrison Villard said, "no

journalist of the 90's [1890s] ever sank to quite such depths of vulgarity, sensationalism and degeneracy as do the tabloids in New York today.'"[2]

By the mid-1920s the tabloids were regarded as a menace that would disrupt the home, ruin the morals of youth, and precipitate crime and perversion. Yet despite the opposition of the middle and upper classes, the tabloids flourished and the mainstream press followed in their path. "In their selection of stories, all newspapers came to adopt the values of the tabloid," wrote Simon Bessie. "Attention was concentrated upon sex, crime, sport and sentiment. . . . Devotion to features became so intense that 'the side shows threatened to swallow the main tent.' "[3]

In 1927 the *New Republic* warned that "the tabloid is a genuine menace, and publishers are right in watching its development with some apprehension." The *New Republic* was particularly concerned about the "moral effect" of the tabloids on mainstream journalism, and it complained, "[W]e find today, that even papers which seem safely beyond the reach of tabloid competition are alarmed by their mushroom growth and tend to imitate many of their most undesirable characteristics. It is not really true that there is a Gresham's Law of journalism by which the baser metal drives out the true coinage, but since the publishers seem to believe this is the case, we get, temporarily at least, the same gravely undesirable results."[4]

In 1938 Simon Bessie confirmed the permanence of the tabloids: "Although less than twenty years have passed since its appearance in America, the tabloid has become an important, established part of the national scene. The original stigma persists but a true reading of the legend would show that the tabloids are 'legitimate heirs of the fourth estate.' "[5]

THE MODERN TABLOIDS

On Wednesday evening, January 20, 1999, former president George Bush returned to Capitol Hill, then the scene of President Clinton's ongoing impeachment trial, for an informal address to U.S. senators. A major focus of his remarks concerned diminished press standards, particularly in the coverage of the White House sex scandal. "I worry, too, about sleaze, about excessive intrusion into private lives. I worry about once great news organizations that seem to resort to tabloid journalism, giving us sensationalism at best, and smut at worst."[6]

On TV's *NewsHour With Jim Lehrer*, journalism professor Todd Gitlin was asked, "Is President Bush on to something here? . . . Are the mainstream news organizations following the tabloids?"

"Absolutely," answered Gitlin. "The tabloids have even complained that some of the mainstream news organizations have used terms that they in their respectability wouldn't dare use. It's a pleasure to agree with former President Bush on this."[7]

There is no end in sight. The media seems happy to declare itself guilty as charged. David Kamp, writing in *Vanity Fair* magazine, called the 1990s "the tabloid decade." Peter Carlson, reviewing Kamp's article for the *Washington Post*, declared the 1990s to be "The Decade of Dishing Dirty Laundry."

"You're skeptical," Carlson says to the reader. "You're thinking, *Hey Buddy, this is America, every decade is a tabloid decade.*"

Then he runs through some of the names that made the news in the 1990s: Joey Buttafuoco, John Wayne Bobbitt, Tonya Harding, O. J., the Menendez brothers, Heidi Fleiss, JonBenet Ramsey, Anna Nicole Smith, Hugh Grant. And the "fun couples" of the decade: Woody and Mia, Clarence and Anita, Chuck and Di, Chuck and Camilla, Di and Dodi, Bill and Gennifer, Bill and Paula, Bill and Monica.

Carlson concludes, "It's a decade characterized by Mike Tyson's ear-biting, Marv Albert's back-biting, Dick Morris's toe-sucking, Monica Lewinsky's . . . well, you get the idea. Kamp is right: This *is* the Tabloid Decade. . . . It's not just the plethora of cheesy characters and sleazy deeds . . . it's the unprecedented way that the media, high and low, have publicized every seedy detail of their tawdry shenanigans."[8]

Kamp dates the official beginning of the Tabloid Decade as July 21, 1991, when a *New York Post* headline announced the arrest of kiddy-TV star Paul Reubens for masturbating in an X-rated movie theater: "OH, PEE-WEE!" squealed the front-page headline, followed by, "Exposed: 1st Photo of Kids' Star in Custody." From that moment on, only the most infantile vulgarity was good enough for the press.

"The tabloidification of American life—of the news, of the culture, yea, of human behavior—is such a sweeping phenomenon that it can't be dismissed as merely a jokey footnote to the history of the 1990s," wrote Kamp. "Rather, it's the very hallmark of our times."[9]

Virtually every American would agree that the modern press has increasingly adopted the standards of the tabloids. What tabloids? Eighty years after the appearance of the *New York Illustrated Daily News*, what tabloid publications are exercising such a pernicious influence on the mainstream press? The most laughably extreme, and therefore least harmful, of these publications are the so-called supermarket tabloids, the sensational Hollywood-oriented weekly magazines that are prominently displayed at the check-out counters of most supermarkets. The *National Enquirer* and the *Star* are two of the more popular of such magazines.

The January 19, 1999, issue of the *National Enquirer* featured a full-color cover of Monica Lewinsky under the headline, "Monica's Revenge." On the same date, the *Star* displayed a cover of Princess Diana headed, "Princess Diana's Secret Life." The February 2 issues of both magazines continued the drum beat. The *Enquirer*'s cover blared, "Lewinsky: I'm Having a Baby." The *Star*'s cover invited the reader to savor

"Di's Touching, Secret Love Letters." All these stories featured photos of the two women, who had been recent favorites of the magazines. The content was superficial and sensational, with little concern for accuracy.

Maintstream magazines have taken the tabloid path as well. The February 1999 issue of *Redbook* featured a cover story, "I Made Love to Harrison Ford (and My Husband Didn't Care)." That same month, *Harper's Bazaar* featured a story on the 1980s tabloid icon Sydney Biddle Barrows ("the Mayflower Madam"), including a full-page photo of her face-lift, with its surgical scar and caked blood. Even the conservative *National Review* displayed a naked blonde on its cover with the headline, "Is Sex Still Sexy?"

Given the proud history of American newspapers, their tabloid transformation has been the most shocking of all. It is probably neither fair nor appropriate to compare the *New York Times* to the *National Enquirer*, though the *Times*, like most major newspapers, pursued the Princess Diana and the Monica stories to an excessive degree and sensationalized those stories over what seemed like an interminable period. When critics complain of the tabloidification of the press, they usually refer to the standards of the magazine-style newspapers typified by Rupert Murdoch's *New York Post*.

John Terenzio, formerly executive producer of the tabloid TV show *A Current Affair*, believes the tabloid transformation of the mainstream media has been completed. "I would argue that at this point I would eliminate the word 'tabloid' from our vocubulary—it doesn't mean anything anymore," said Terenzio.[10]

Cult film director John Waters, an avid reader of supermarket tabloids like the *National Enquirer*, the *Star*, and the *Globe*, says these publications have been outflanked by the mainstream press. "My sense," he says, "is that they *hate* the Monica [Lewinsky] story, because they've been robbed of it. They feel gypped. It should be theirs, and it's everyone's."[11] Indeed, during the first six months of 1998 when the most intense coverage of the Lewinsky story occured, the three major supermarket tabloids suffered dramatic declines in circulation as the broader press claimed their stories. The media fixation on domestic scandal has done more than corrupt the taste of the press. It has driven out serious news coverage, particularly on international affairs.

Ironically, the tabloid press shares two seemingly contradictory characteristics. It is out of control on matters of taste and privacy while being under the thumb of government on foreign affairs. This translates into vulgar sensationalism in domestic coverage and inflammatory chauvinism in international coverage. The *New York Post* typically devotes less than a single page to foreign affairs out of its approximately 50 to 90 pages. That page usually consists of an inflammatory story about a recently designated international pariah.

The mainstream press and broadcast media have moved shockingly close to this tabloid approach. Domestic scandal, sex, and violence dominate the front pages, with international news relegated to warmed-over State Department pronouncements and xenophobic editorials. The process of choosing lead stories was recently described by Dan Rather: "The companion to 'If it bleeds, it leads,' is 'If you lead with a foreign story, you lose.' The Hollywoodization of the news is deep and abiding."[12]

Author William Greider has noted that "the contentious variety of the free press has been transformed into a voice of dull sameness, a voice that speaks in narrow alignment with the governing authorities more often than it does in popular opposition." As a former editor at the *Washington Post*, he expressed particular disappointment with the transformation of that newspaper. "In effect, it made peace with power—the rival elites in both government and business," says Greider. "[T]he *Post* has become a much more reliable partner in the governing constellation. Its reporters routinely defer to authority by accepting the official versions of what is true."[13]

The invasive and personalized treatment of public figures is part of the modern image of tabloid journalism, and it applies to both domestic and foreign personalities. Both are forms of what is called attack journalism, but there is a difference. Personal attacks on American politicians are a distorted remnant of the independent, often adversarial posture that characterized the press in generations past. On the other hand, when it comes to foreign affairs, tabloid journalism makes no pretense of independence. Its selective attacks on designated foreign leaders or "pariah states" are little more than Pentagon or State Department press releases, rewritten to make them even more inflammatory.

Marvin Kalb, former broadcaster and current director of the Shorenstein Center on the Press, Politics, and Public Policy, has characterized this media approach as the "new news." Kalb explained, "The new news is the news that so many Americans now simply don't trust, that they feel is populated by journalists who hype stories, who sensationalize stories, who are no longer interested in public service stories, but bottom line kind of stories. . . . [E]ach news program at a network has to be a profit center, or else it is simply dropped. . . . [T]he new news robs the American people of information that they ought to have and cheapens the product itself."[14]

THE NEWS AS ENTERTAINMENT

"Entertainment, politics, and entertainment *about* politics all come across the same box," wrote Kurt Anderson recently. "It has become kind of low comedy, perfect for nothing but late-night jokes."[15]

The question that begs asking is whether politics, and "news" gener-ally, has descended to entertainment fare, or whether that is simply the tabloid take on all public matters. President Clinton certainly exploited, and therefore encouraged, this trend by playing the saxophone on the *Arsenio Hall Show*, indulging in personal small talk on *Larry King Live*, describing his underwear to students on MTV, and trading barbs with talk-radio host Don Imus. Indeed, White House aide Paul Begala peri-odically called Imus and asked to be on the show. Given the vulgar and venomous treatment of Clinton on the show, Begala was often asked why he would want to be on it. "I can give you 10 million reasons—his 10 million listeners," said Begala. "I get more feedback from being on 'Imus' than from any other media appearance."[16]

Given Clinton's continued high public opinion ratings throughout sev-eral years of scandal, one might conclude that he effectively tamed the tabloid beast, but he and his family have paid a heavy personal price. In 1998, according to the Center for Media and Public Affairs, the four major late-night TV variety shows told 1,712 jokes about President Clin-ton, compared with just 338 in 1995.

The media's increasingly coarse treatment of public figures may not in itself be anything more than a reflection of popular discourse, but there is a growing indication that such tabloid communication is becom-ing the way by which the media *informs* the public. In a 1996 Pew Re-search Center poll, one-quarter of those surveyed identified the late-night TV comedians as their source of information about the presidential cam-paign. That figure rose to 40 percent for those under age 30.

Frequently these entertainment/news commentaries present false sto-ries, either through carelessness or by intent. Jay Leno devoted several nights of monologue to what was later found to be a false story about a supposed Clinton "love child" fathered with a prostitute. Leno joked, "I mean, who do you believe, a hooker or President Clinton? For most Americans that's a tough call."

Ironically it was a tabloid newspaper, the *New York Post*, that Leno used as his source for the story, but it was a supermarket tabloid, the *Star*, that published DNA tests on the teenager showing that she was not Clinton's child. Leno apologized on the air. "I waited until it was in a reasonably legitimate paper, like the *New York Post*," said Leno. "I don't regret it."[17]

Other examples of the mainstream media carrying phony tabloid sto-ries abound. In January 1999, American Family Radio, a conservative network run by the Reverend Donald Wildmon, ran a story saying that James Carville, President Clinton's friend and adviser, had assaulted his wife, Mary Matalin, while wielding an oversize hunting knife and firing a semiautomatic pistol. The story said Carville then spent the night in a Montgomery County jail.

The network, which reaches twenty-five states, claimed that it got the story from the "Montgomery County Ledger," a nonexistent newspaper. Marvin Sanders, general manager of American Family Radio, said the Carville story, which it also posted on its Web site, was "very well written, very detailed, very newsy." But the gaping holes in the story soon forced Sanders to issue a retraction. For one thing, the incident was described as occurring at Carville's home in Rockville, Maryland, whereas Carville lives in Virginia. According to the story, the incident occurred on Monday, January 18, but Carville was in Nashville and Phoenix on that day. The story cites Rockville police lieutenant Bobby Masters, but there is no such person.[18]

The story was picked up by newspapers as far away as Boston and Phoenix. Upon hearing of the phony story, former Republican senator and presidential candidate Bob Dole was prompted to issue an unsolicited statement. "[T]he journalistic hoax is an example of the 'politics of personal destruction' that needs to be condemned in the strongest possible terms," said Dole. "I was saddened to learn that one or more minor news outlets reported this totally fictitious story as fact, thereby adding to the pain, concern and confusion already inflicted upon James, Mary [and] their children."[19]

Shortly after the story broke, a reporter from the *National Enquirer* knocked on the door of Carville's Virginia farmhouse, asking if the charges against him were true. Carville invited the reporter in and introduced him to his tabloid competition, a *New York Times* reporter who was already there investigating another political story.[20]

The pressure for mainstream news organizations to indulge in more tabloid subjects has been accompanied by an increased use of "feature stories" by newspapers and "magazine shows" by the TV networks. Award-winning journalist Charles Levendosky has noted, "What used to be proud, hard-news newspapers—like the *Atlanta Constitution*, the *Los Angeles Times* and the *Chicago Tribune*—are turning flabby as they have begun running feature pieces on their front pages as well as in the middle of the paper. . . . Feature news stories are a part of a trend to trivialize the news. And this is perhaps one of the most dangerous trends in the American media. When newspapers and TV networks spend weeks and reporter resources following sex scandals instead of tracking the impact of poverty or the likely impact of congressional legislation, the people lose—all the people."[21]

Television news has been similarly trivialized by the proliferation of "magazine shows," the hottest programming growth sector among the broadcast networks. They are now carried six nights out of seven each week and are the most watched television news shows. Network producers have discovered that news magazine shows, with their much lower costs, can be a greater money-maker than the traditional entertainment shows. For example, NBC's *Dateline* magazine show accounts for about 20 percent of all NBC profits. But to be competitive the magazine shows must, first and foremost, be entertaining.

Don Hewitt, executive producer of CBS's *60 Minutes*, has stated, "The networks have gone out of the entertainment business, which they were once very serious about and did very well, into the news business that they're not very serious about and they don't do very well."[22] Dan Rather also has expressed concern over the proliferation of TV magazine shows: "As the field gets more and more crowded, the temptation increases to dumb it down and sleaze it up in order to get an audience, and therein lies the danger."[23]

Joan Konner, an award-winning television producer and publisher of the *Columbia Journalism Review*, wonders whether the many news magazine shows are "entertaining news" or "newsy entertainment." She has made a distinction between public interest journalism and entertainment journalism. "[M]ore of the news magazines are at the entertainment end today than at the level of public interest journalism," said Konner. "They seem very focused on the personal story that really has no larger significance, . . . and I find it exploitive, manipulative, voyeuristic. I don't think that it's a form of journalism that serves the wider public interest."[24]

THE CLINTON-LEWINSKY AFFAIR: THE ULTIMATE TABLOID STORY

Throughout 1998 and early 1999, the story of President Clinton's sexual affair with a 21-year-old White House intern dominated the news media. According to the Center for Media and Public Affairs, as of December 15, 1998, the three broadcast networks had presented 1,502 stories on the scandal. The crisis in Iraq produced one thousand fewer stories. *Nightline*, a respected news program anchored by Ted Koppel, devoted fifteen programs in a row to Monica Lewinsky, driving out news that Koppel would normally have covered.

A striking demonstration of the dominance of tabloid priorities over serious coverage of international news occurred on January 26, 1998, the day that Monica Lewinsky's name first surfaced. Virtually the entire international press corps was in Havana at that time, covering the pope's historic visit to communist Cuba. The moment Lewinsky's name appeared on the wires, the representatives of the major American news services fled Havana like lemmings, leaving coverage of the pope's visit to the foreign press.

Journalism professor Todd Gitlin saw this press fixation on the Clinton-Lewinsky scandal as the pinnacle of modern tabloid journalism, whereby profit-minded media executives encourage a pack mentality among reporters. "[F]rom the moment that the network anchors left Havana more than a year ago, left the story of Cuba and the Pope to run away with this galloping story, it's been very hard to find journalists who would simply say no," complained Gitlin.[25]

From that point on, the Lewinsky story saturated the media to an extent that soon exceeded the appetite of the American public. By November 1998 a poll by *New York* magazine revealed that 50 percent of those surveyed believed that the media's coverage of Lewinsky was "somewhat" or "very" irresponsible. Forty-seven percent said the public's high ratings of President Clinton were "sending a message that they are tired of the story." Forty-eight percent said they were no longer paying attention to the story, and 43 percent said they didn't want to hear any more.[26]

The media was slow in recognizing the public's growing distaste for the Lewinsky story, but some journalists eventually caught on. Keith Olbermann, who anchored MSNBC-TV's "White House in Crisis" and "The Big Show," quit that station in November 1998 after concluding that he didn't want to spend another night talking about Monica Lewinsky. "It became quite a strain," he said. "There's no way to rationalize this or get around it. The media in its entirety, we amplified this. We served as a megaphone for the whole process."[27]

As the Clinton-Lewinsky saga dragged into its final stage, the impeachment of the president, independent prosecutor Kenneth Starr claimed that the president's "high crimes and misdemeanors" had nothing to do with sex. Rather, they concerned lying and covering up that sex. But Starr's report to Congress, on which the impeachment was to be based, described the shocking sexual activities of the president in explicit detail, leading the press to continue its focus on such sensational tidbits.

Journalists and political leaders around the world were confused and embarrassed at America's tabloid priorities. At home, journalists were stunned. "The press is sullied. No Woodward and Bernstein. No heroes here," said ABC's Sam Donaldson. "We come out tarnished, and the public hates us."[28]

Foreign journalists were particularly disturbed by the behavior of their American counterparts. Gustavo Gorriti, a Latin American investigative reporter who recently won the International Press Freedom Award, was asked what he thought about the American media's obsession with Monica Lewinsky. "[I]t is a depressing sight," said Gorriti, who acknowledged that most Latin American journalists had been heavily influenced by earlier investigative reporters in the United States. "[T]o see the evolution, or shall we say the involution, of this great journalistic tradition, getting totally bogged down in that miserable case, and in all the triviality of that—losing perspective of what is the business of news to get into show business is somehow depressing. . . . I am sure that in the future this whole Lewinsky-Starr era will be seen as a sort of journalistic abomination."[29]

Does this suggest a post-Monica return to noble press traditions? Marvin Kalb, former diplomatic correspondent for CBS and NBC, is doubtful. "I see no incentives that would drive journalism in a different direction," said Kalb. "Quite the contrary. . . . The reputation of news organizations had begun to suffer well before Monica came aboard. But the lines have dipped more precipitously with the scramble of traditional news organizations to hold off the challenge of these news outlets, cable talk programs, 24-hour news, the Internet."[30]

Indeed, even after the Senate voted against removing the president from office for his dalliance with Monica Lewinsky, she was still able to command $660,000 and 75 percent of the distribution sales for an interview with British TV. Then, on March 3, 1999, came a two-hour interview with Barbara Walters on ABC-TV. The next day her book, *Monica's Story*, was released. By the end of the tabloid decade, Monica had signed on as the official spokeswoman for the diet company Jenny Craig, Inc. As the new millennium began, Monica, claiming she had lost 31 pounds on the company's diet plan, was appearing regularly in TV commercials.

Explicit Language Becomes Common

One measurable effect of the Clinton-Lewinsky scandal on the media was the increased use of explicit sexual language. Perhaps the most significant breakthrough came on September 12, 1998, when the *New York Times* printed the word "fuck" in its pages for the first time as part of the Linda Tripp–Monica Lewinsky tape transcripts. But more significant and pervasive was the migration of words about sex organs and sex practices from newspapers' health and medicine pages to the Washington beat.

In 1998 the single most prolific source of dirty words in the press was independent counsel Kenneth Starr's report to Congress, which described at great length the sexual details of the Clinton-Lewinsky affair. Even the report's footnotes documented activities such as the use of a cigar as a sex toy. Starr's report was major news, but initially some reporters tried to tip-toe through its scatological contents, using euphemisms or code words to avoid sexual terms. The semen on Lewinsky's dress was called "residue," "DNA," "bodily fluids," or President Clinton's "essence." CBS's Bob Schieffer referred to oral sex as "sex of a kind." He later admitted, "I don't know why in the world I came up with that phrase."[31]

But as the sensational details of the Lewinsky story came to dominate the news, reporters became quite comfortable with the language of sex. For example, a database search by *USA Today*[32] produced the following

Monica Lewinsky (top left) and Kenneth Starr (top right) were President Bill Clinton's paramour and prosecutor, respectively, in the tabloid story of the decade. Former senator and Republican presidential candidate Bob Dole (bottom) became a tabloid figure when he began making television ads touting a product that had cured his "erectile dysfunction." Photos of Monica Lewinsky and Kenneth Starr courtesy of Uniphoto Stock Photography. Photo of Bob Dole reproduced from the collections of the Library of Congress.

count for the use of the words "semen" and "oral sex" in newspapers between 1993 and 1998:

Semen	1993	1994	1995	1996	1997	1998
New York Times	35	56	50	50	44	91
Washington Post	35	26	29	24	55	118
Los Angeles Times	34	47	48	37	54	98
Chicago Tribune	57	64	64	36	39	88
Dallas Morning News	27	24	21	24	23	66
Cleveland Plain Dealer	22	28	14	16	32	60
Atlanta Journal-Constitution	13	17	19	12	34	40
USA Today	12	17	16	10	13	33
Oral Sex	1993	1994	1995	1996	1997	1998
New York Times	60	39	36	34	65	167
Washington Post	66	73	48	39	89	248
Los Angeles Times	72	66	45	39	67	182
Chicago Tribune	6	46	66	45	49	125
Dallas Morning News	53	41	30	27	101	146
Cleveland Plain Dealer	64	39	36	27	59	96
Atlanta Journal-Constitution	44	63	46	34	67	111
USA Today	31	23	32	16	54	135

Dick Wald, ABC's senior vice-president for editorial quality, believes that the Clinton-Lewinsky affair will force the news media to draw a line on the use of explicit language. "What has happened in the past year has caught everyone with the sense that we've gone too far," said Wald in 1998, but there is no indication that the spiral of explicit language has peaked.[33] *Washington Post* columnist Tony Kornheiser summed up the popular sentiment concerning sexual language in the press: "I never want to hear the phrase 'semen-stained' again (Unless it's a new shade of Duron paint)." Kornheiser noted that even as the explicit press coverage of President Clinton's sexual goings-on began to wane, former presidential candidate Bob Dole began appearing on television doing commercials for Viagra, claiming that it cured erectile dysfunction.[34]

INVADING PERSONAL PRIVACY

Perhaps the most common tabloid characteristic adopted by the mainstream media during the 1990s was the aggressive intrusion on the private lives of public figures. The intense media coverage of Princess Diana's turbulent personal life and tragic death in 1997 were a direct spillover from the supermarket tabloids and their intrusive, paparazzi-style photo features. The broader press sought to mask its sensationalism with a holier-than-thou attack on the tabloids, but its coverage of Princess Diana was almost indistinguishable from that of the supermarket press.

In generations past, the private lives and sexual affairs of American political figures, particularly presidents, were not considered "news" by the mainstream media. This policy was not the result of a traditional newsroom judgment. It was simply a "gentleman's agreement" between media executives and politicians that the sexual escapades of the politically powerful would not be revealed by the press. The erosion of this understanding was completed in 1987, when five *Miami Herald* reporters staked out the Washington town house of Senator Gary Hart (D-Colo.), a prominent presidential candidate, to expose his affair with Donna Rice. The resulting story forced Hart out of the presidential race.

This milestone in the march toward tabloid journalism was in part a function of the public's increasing acceptance of explicit sexual material in magazines, motion pictures, and the broadcast media, but it also marked a change in the balance of power between the nation's media and its political structure. Reporters and politicians had traditionally maintained a symbiotic relationship. Without access to political figures, reporters were denied stories. Without media coverage, politicians were denied name recognition. But as political campaigns became media events, pure and simple, politicians became increasingly dependent on the media and ultimately became its creatures. In this unequal relationship, a gentleman's agreement was impossible. Any aspect of a public figure's life that would sell newspapers was fair game.

The Clinton presidency represented the logical extension of this new relationship. In 1992 Gennifer Flowers sold the story of her alleged affair with presidential candidate Bill Clinton to the supermarket tabloid *Star*. The mainstream media picked up the story and carried it from there. After Paula Jones accused Clinton of sexual harassment in 1994, the *Washington Post* became the first major newspaper to feature the story. The story of Clinton's sexual relationship with Monica Lewinsky first appeared in the online tabloid magazine the *Drudge Report*, but it took just three days for the story to break in the *Washington Post*, in the *Los Angeles Times*, and on ABC. Unlike Gary Hart, Clinton survived the tabloid blitz and triumphed. Indeed, as the Clinton sex scandals deepened, the media coverage sent his ratings soaring.

During the 1990s Clinton was not the only politician whose sex life was exposed in the media. In the summer of 1992 the *New York Post* carried a front-page story of an alleged affair by President George Bush with a longtime aide. In 1998, after *Vanity Fair* announced plans for an article revealing that Representative Dan Burton (R-Ind.) had fathered a son out of wedlock, the *Indianapolis Star and News* published the story of Burton's "love child." That same year, the *Idaho Statesman* disclosed that Representative Helen Chenoweth (R-Idaho) had carried on a relationship with a married man. And as House Judiciary Committee chairman Henry Hyde (R-Ill.) was about to convene impeachment proceedings against President Clinton, the online magazine *Salon* reported the story of Hyde's extramarital affair thirty years previously. "There's virtually no zone of privacy left for any public official," commented Sanford Ungar, dean of American University's School of Communication. "And there are many co-conspirators in creating that situation—politicians themselves, the media, the Internet."[35]

Howard Kurtz, media reporter for the *Washington Post*, said, "[T]he old limits on what was fair game for aggressive journalists have been all but obliterated. There are simply too many pathways—front door, back door, basement drainpipes—for sleaze to drip its way into the mainstream media."[36]

There were still more lines for the media to cross, new subjects that even the tabloid media felt uncomfortable scrutinizing. Just as the vulgar media fixation on Monica Lewinsky was winding down, the press began a brief fling with an unlikely spinoff from Monicagate: President Clinton's daughter, Chelsea. In November 1998, when the *National Enquirer*, the *Star*, and the *New York Post* published stories about Chelsea's personal struggle to deal with the Lewinsky scandal, the White House dismissed them as the work of mere "tabloids." But on February 5, 1999, *People* magazine, a glossy weekly with a circulation of 3.2 million, published a cover story on Chelsea, describing her anger at her father's infidelity and telling of her breakup with her boyfriend at Stanford University.

The White House issued an unusual statement from Bill and Hillary Clinton:

"We deeply regret and are profoundly saddened by the decision of *People* magazine to print a cover story featuring our daughter, Chelsea. For over six years the media has understood and respected the unique situation facing Chelsea as she grows up in the spotlight focused on her parents. Other than in public situations where she is an integral part of our family, we have been very grateful for the media's restraint in allowing Chelsea the privacy that any young person needs and deserves.

Unfortunately, despite personal appeals with respect to her privacy and her security from her parents, *People* magazine has chosen to run the story. We can only hope that the media will continue its policy of restraint with respect to our daughter."

Carol Wallace, *People*'s managing editor, issued the following statement to justify the story: "Chelsea is nearly 19 years old and a poised young adult. We feel that because she is an eyewitness to the family drama and historical events unfolding around her, that she is a valid journalistic subject."[37]

Some in the mainstream press were uneasy with this latest tabloid encroachment on privacy. *Washington Post* columnist E. J. Dionne Jr. rejected Wallace's justification for the story. "Is Chelsea to be blamed for the fact that she's 'poised'?" he asked. "If she weren't 'poised,' would there have been no story? Does she have to answer for her father's problems because she's reached the ripe age of 'nearly 19 years old?' To say she has been 'an eyewitness to the family drama and historical events' makes her seem like Mike McCurry or Dick Morris. She wasn't hired to work in the White House." Dionne concluded, "[T]hanks to *People* magazine, we're reminded that some rules are simple. One is: Lay off politicians' kids."[38]

Elizabeth Drew, a long-time White House reporter, said on TV's *NewsHour With Jim Lehrer*, "One of the very few civilized arrangements that's been going on in Washington for the last decade . . . has been the press' acceptance of the Clintons' plea to just let her grow up. . . . *People* says she's now 19, but . . . there's almost a prurient interest now in how the family crisis has affected . . . Chelsea. I think she can do without that."[39]

Gene Gibbon, former White House correspondent for Reuters and current managing editor for the Internet publication *Stateline*, responded to Drew in typical tabloid fashion: "Fame creates risk," he said. "As long as there are mentally unstable people who are magnetized by it, that's going to be the case. Chelsea is better equipped than most people to handle that."[40]

Larry Flynt: Investigative Pornographer

Larry Flynt, publisher of the pornographic magazine *Hustler*, made his revelations of the sex lives of politicians the media's most sensational intrusion on personal privacy. On Sunday, October 4, 1998, readers of the *Washington Post* were surprised to come across the following full-page ad in the main section of the newspaper:

Larry Flynt and Hustler Magazine Announce a Cash Offer of Up To $1 Million
Have you had an adulterous sexual encounter with a current member of the United States Congress or a high-ranking government official?

Can you provide documentary evidence of illicit sexual relations with a Congressman, Senator or other prominent officeholder?

Larry Flynt and HUSTLER Magazine will pay you up to $1 million if we choose to publish your verified story and use your material.

The ad provided a "hotline" phone number and an e-mail address, and it concluded with the note: "All calls and correspondence will be kept strictly confidential."[41]

Flynt, who had paid $85,000 for the *Post* ad, was recently dubbed an "investigative pornographer" by the *Post* and a "pornalist" by Pulitzer Prize-winning columnist William Safire. Flynt said he was only hoping to demonstrate the hypocrisy of sanctimonious politicians who were attempting to hound President Clinton out of office because of his sexual escapades.

On the Sunday the ad appeared, about 2,000 people tried to call *Hustler*. Many more were to follow. Most of the callers simply congratulated Flynt for exposing the sexual hypocrites. A smaller number complained of Flynt's gutter tactics. At least 250 of the callers claimed knowledge of sexual affairs by members of Congress. "I just wanted to expose hypocrisy," said Flynt. "If these guys are going after the president, they shouldn't have any skeletons in their closet. This is only the beginning."[42] On December 17, 1998, Representative Bob Livingston (R-La.), the incoming House Speaker (the replacement for Newt Gingrich), resigned from the House when he learned that Flynt was about to reveal his adulterous behavior. In his resignation speech, Livingston admitted that he had "on occasion strayed from my marriage."[43]

Washington reporters quickly got into the act and tried to scoop *Hustler* by learning the names of Livingston's paramours. "We've been tabloid-launderers for years," admitted *Time* columnist Margaret Carlson. "Now we're Flynt-launderers. Maybe we're reaching the point where we're so sickened by all this that we stop."[44]

Flynt's campaign to expose adulterers in Congress apparently caused the press and the public to reassess their attitude toward privacy. A January 1999 *Washington Post* survey found that 40 percent of the people questioned approved of Flynt's efforts, and nearly half said that news organizations should report the names of members of Congress who are found by Flynt to have had affairs. Republican National Committee spokesperson Clifford May called the poll results "disturbing" and accused journalists of "a striking deterioration of standards from the time the press didn't want to cover the Gennifer Flowers story because it was published in a tabloid newspaper."[45]

When Flynt scheduled a live news conference on C-SPAN to reveal embarrassing information about Representative Robert Barr (R-Ga.), Republican national chairman Jim Nicholson sent a fax to C-SPAN chairman Brian Lamb: "Giving Larry Flynt this platform will, in effect, bridge what had been the considerable gap between your news organization on the one hand, and the worst tabloid and pornographic publications on the other."[46]

Eric Effron, writing in *Brill's Content*, noted the efforts of "real" journalists to distinguish themselves from Flynt. "Journalists, I guess, know real journalism when they see it," wrote Effron. "But the public can be excused for not being sure where the line between respectable and despicable is drawn anymore. It was tough enough when the boundaries separating news and entertainment got fuzzy. Now news has blurred with entertainment's lowliest offspring, pornography. . . . [T]he establishment press is too fearful of the competition to ignore many of the same stories on which the more fringe outlets thrive. So yes, there's a blur, and citizens themselves must now take on the role of discerning consumers of information." Effron asked, "Did Flynt drag us further into the mud . . . or did he simply jump into the mudbath in which we were already swimming? Who disappointed us more, Flynt, for running an advertisement in the *Washington Post* in which he offered to pay for information about philandering politicians, or the *Post*, which ran the ad and became an estimated $85,000 richer as a result?"[47]

Washington Post columnist Richard Cohen had trouble distinguishing Flynt from his colleagues. "[T]hose of us who condemn Flynt, we national media types who would never stoop to such journalism, ought to pause for a moment and wonder if Flynt is not following . . . the path we establishment journalists have already blazed."[48]

What finally soured the media on Flynt was his announcement that he "would start investigating the private sex lives of media personalities." Flynt warned, "All the media moguls better watch out."[49] Apparently that was too much.

THE TABLOID WAR

What better story to finish out the Tabloid Decade than a tabloid war in Kosovo—a war waged by the nineteen wealthiest powers in the world against tiny, bankrupt Yugoslavia, a nation that even before the devastating NATO bombardment had an economy 20 percent smaller than Idaho's; a "humanitarian" war against a nation that represents no threat to its neighbors; a war that all combatants acknowledge did not serve their national interests; a war whose public support seemed to depend on the personal credibility of Bill Clinton; a war with no news, only pictures.

Conservative columnist George Will noted, "The United States is disastrously conducting a war without having been attacked, or an ally having been attacked or any other emergency that would preclude a debate."[50] The closest the United States came to holding a political debate on the war occurred on April 28, 1999, when a House resolution to support the ongoing NATO air campaign against Yugoslavia failed on a 213–213 tie vote. No matter. The bombing only intensified.

The Kosovo conflict was a secessionist war initiated by the Kosovo Liberation Army (KLA), a local mafia that built its power through drug running, prostitution, and extortion. That the terrorist KLA should become the darling of the "liberal" media is one of the ironies of the Tabloid Decade. At a Washington rally organized by former Democratic representative Joseph DioGuardi (N.Y.), Senator Joseph Lieberman (D-Conn.) said the "United States of America and the Kosovo Liberation Army stand for the same human values and principles. . . . Fighting for the KLA is fighting for human rights and American values."[51]

Liberal members of Congress quickly lined up to support the tabloid war, as thirty-five House and Senate Democrats who *opposed* the 1991 Persian Gulf War now *supported* the Kosovo war. Columnist Robert Novak asked, "How is it possible for a rational person to vote against force to guarantee the nation's access to Middle Eastern oil and to vote for force to restore autonomy to a small Serbian province? Because this is a liberal war." Novak explained that liberal war "rejects the doctrine of national interest" and is "motivated by sentiment rather than calculation."[52] Such wars provide ample fodder for the tabloid press.

Within the print media, the *Washington Post* led the drum beat for war, spinning a tabloid tale of a new holocaust in the Serbian province of Kosovo, perpetrated by the new Hitler, Slobodan Milosevic, president of Yugoslavia and Serbia, its largest republic. No matter that these parallels were contradicted by the facts: Milosevic came to power through elections, not a putsch; Serbia represented no threat to any of its neighbors; and casualties in the Kosovo conflict prior to NATO bombing had been the lowest in any civil war in modern history. President Clinton, seeking a defining event on which to end his tarnished administration, surfed the tabloid waves into a brutal, purposeless war. It was another great story that flowed seamlessly from the Lewinsky scandal.

"In Monicagate, the surreality was merely silly," wrote columnist Charles Krauthammer. "In Kosovo it is serious. . . . Attack the enemy where the lighting is best—nice big shiny buildings in downtown Belgrade: They make for good video."[53]

Newspaper and television analysis of the war consisted of little more than captions on pictures of wailing refugees. MSNBC, the cable news station that had earlier been known as "all Monica all the time," segued seamlessly into the demon Milosevic. Media critic Howard Kurtz wrote, "[T]he shift from Monica to Milosevic has given an unmistakable boost to the Microsoft-NBC cable venture, which was struggling with an identity crisis after gorging itself on the Lewinsky scandal."[54]

With the end of Monicagate MSNBC's ratings had slipped, but during the first month of NATO's bombing of Yugoslavia its ratings rose 103 percent. Indeed, April 3, 1999, was the eighth most watched day in MSNBC's history. The top seven involved either the Lewinsky scandal or the death of Princess Diana. Erik Sorenson, MSNBC's vice president, proudly proclaimed that 97 percent of its programming was now being devoted to the Balkan War.[55]

One staffer said of MSNBC: "They don't care what the big story is— it could be JonBenet Ramsey, the war, the president—as long as it's something they can build a soap opera around." NBC News president Andrew Lack suggested that the intense tabloid coverage of the war was playing even better than did the Lewinsky affair: "Sometimes that approach is going to look great, like in Kosovo, and sometimes, after a long, 16-month saga with the president, it's going to look not so great."[56]

Even with the end of the war in Kosovo, the media attempted to maintain the tabloid story, but events on the ground made it awkward. The "humanitarian war" had become a murderous peace. Throughout Kosovo, Serbs, Gypsies, Goranis, even ethnic Albanians suspected of being loyal to Yugoslavia were murdered by heavily armed KLA gangs. Ethnic Serbs were systematically "ethnically cleansed" from this Serbian province while international peacekeepers looked on in horror. The good guys and bad guys had changed places, and the press, apparently concluding that events in Kosovo no longer matched the tabloid script, relegated the story to the back pages.

CONCLUSION

The realities of twenty-first century media confirm Simon Bessie's declaration over sixty years ago that the tabloid press was the legitimate heir of the fourth estate. It remains the whipping boy of the "mainstream" press, which has nonetheless embraced all of its most vulgar characteristics. The weakness of tabloid journalism is also its strength: popular appeal instead of elitist pretension. The often invoked phrase "the marketplace of ideas" draws a parallel between journalism and commerce. If we believe that good products will inevitably drive out bad products in a free capitalist market, why will not good journalism drive out bad journalism in that same market? We can criticize the product of tabloid journalism, but how can we criticize the right of the public, the customer, to decide what to read? As always, however, one warning must be heeded: *caveat emptor*—buyer beware!

NOTES

1. Simon Michael Bessie, *Jazz Journalism: The Story of the Tabloid Newspapers* (New York: E. P. Dutton, 1938), p. 16.

2. Ibid., p. 19.

3. Ibid., p. 232.

4. "Who Reads the Tabloids," *The New Republic* (May 25, 1927), p. 7.

5. Bessie, *Jazz Journalism*, p. 25.

6. "George Bush," excerpts from a January 20, 1999, speech by former president Bush, Online Newshour, January 21, 1999, p. 2, www.pbs.org/newshour.

7. "Lowering the Bar?" Online Newshour, February 3, 1999, p. 2, www.pbs.org/newshour.

8. Peter Carlson, "The Decade of Dishing Dirty Laundry," *Washington Post* (February 2, 1999), C2.

9. David Kamp, "The Tabloid Decade," *Vanity Fair* (January 1999), p. 66.

10. Ibid., p. 70.

11. Ibid.

12. Cited in "Fear, Money, and the News," *Brill's Content* (October 1998), p. 116.

13. William Greider, *Who Will Tell the People: The Betrayal of American Democracy* (New York: Simon & Schuster, 1992), pp. 288, 298.

14. "Cited in A Changing Industry," Online NewsHour, November 6, 1998, pp. 1, 4, www.pbs.org/newshour.

15. Cited in Howard Kurtz, "Americans Wait for the Punch Line on Impeachment," *Washington Post* (January 26, 1999), A6.

16. Ibid.

17. Ibid., A1.

18. Howard Kurtz, "Carville Hoax Retracted," *Washington Post* (January 22, 1999), C7.

19. Cited in Howard Kurtz, "Hooray for Larry Flynt?" *Washington Post* (January 25, 1999), C4.

20. Ibid.

21. Charles Levendosky, "Can the Marketplace Protect Free Speech?" in *War, Lies and Videotape: How Media Monopoly Stifles Truth* ed. Lenora Foerstel (New York: International Action Center, 2000), p. 261.

22. "News Magazines," Online NewsHour, January 13, 1999, pp. 1–4, www.pbs.org/newshour.

23. Ibid.

24. Ibid.

25. "Lowering the Bar?" Online NewsHour, p. 2, www.pbs.org/newshour.

26. Cited in Howard Kurtz, "Not in It for the Sport," *Washington Post* (November 16, 1998), C1.

27. Ibid.

28. Cited in Howard Kurtz, "For the Press, a Lot of Ink over the Dam," *Washington Post* (February 13, 1999), C7.

29. "Rewarding Courage," Online NewsHour, November 25, 1998, p. 5, www.pbs.org/newshour.

30. Cited in "Scandal's Damage Is Wide If Not Deep," *Washington Post* (February 11, 1999), A16.

31. Cited in "For Mature Audiences Only," *USA Today* (December 31, 1998), p. 3A.

32. Ibid.

33. Ibid.

34. Cited in Tony Kornheiser, "Down, Bob, Down," *Washington Post* (February 28, 1999), F1.

35. Howard Kurtz, "Larry Flynt and the Barers of Bad News," *Washington Post* (December 20, 1998), F3.

36. Ibid.

37. Cited in Howard Kurtz, "People Magazine Goes Ahead with Article on Chelsea," *Washington Post* (February 5, 1999), C2.

38. E. J. Dionne Jr., "Drawing the Line at Chelsea," *Washington Post* (February 8, 1999), A18.

39. "Other People's Business?" Online NewsHour, February 5, 1999, pp. 3–5, www.pbs.org/newshour.

40. Ibid.

41. Paid advertisement, *Washington Post* (October 4, 1998), A11.

42. Cited in Howard Kurtz, "Larry Flynt, Investigative Pornographer," *Washington Post* (December 19, 1999), C5.

43. Cited in Joel Achenbach, "On the Hill, They Still Swear It's Not about Sex," *Washington Post* (December 19, 1999), C1.

44. Cited in Kurtz, "Larry Flynt, Investigative Pornographer," C5.

45. Cited in Howard Kurtz, "Hooray for Larry Flynt?" *Washington Post* (January 25, 1999), C1, 4.

46. Cited in Howard Kurtz, "Airing on the Side of Caution," *Washington Post* (January 13, 1999), C7.

47. Eric Effron, "The Big Blur," *Brill's Content* (March 1999), pp. 42–43.

48. Richard Cohen, "Dirt Bag Journalism," *Washington Post* (January 14, 1999), A27.

49. Cited in Howard Kurtz, "No Rest for the Scandal-Weary," *Washington Post* (March 1, 1999), C9.

50. George Will, "Our MIA Congress," *Washington Post* (April 29, 1999), A33.

51. Cited in "Marchers Strut Support for Independent Kosovo," *Washington Post* (April 28, 1999), B3.

52. Robert D. Novak, "Multiple Kosovos," *Washington Post* (April 29, 1999), A33.

53. Charles Krauthammer, "Fighting to Feel Righteous," *Washington Post* (April 23, 1999), A37.

54. Howard Kurtz, "NBC's News Machine Marches to War," *Washington Post* (April 21, 1999), C2.

55. Ibid.

56. Ibid.

The Paparazzi: Feeding the Public's Appetite for Celebrities

THE ORIGINS OF THE PAPARAZZI

One of the characteristics of modern journalism is its increasing reliance on photographs. Initially photos were used to add visual interest to text. Today's press, influenced by the tabloids, often uses the text as little more than explication for the photos. For the print journalist the traditional process of developing a story on an individual was relatively unintrusive, relying on background research and interviews. Photographs are inherently more personal, and unlike interviews they can easily be taken without the approval of the subject. Seen in this context, the emergence of aggressive press photographers, known today as the "paparazzi," was inevitable.

The early stages of this phenomenon were apparent in the late 1920s when Charles Lindbergh, an instant celebrity after his epic flight across the Atlantic, had to flee a pursuing press corps. When Lindbergh secretly married Anne Morrow, the couple hid in the back seat of a friend's car. A week later they were spotted on their honeymoon aboard a small yacht, at which time they were buzzed by a seaplane with a photographer leaning out of the window. The worst was yet to come.

In 1932, when the Lindberghs' young son was kidnapped and murdered, photographers entered the morgue, broke open the child's coffin, and photographed the mangled corpse. No major newspaper was willing to publish the photographs, but prints were sold for $5 each on the streets of New Jersey, where the Lindberghs lived. Photographers continued to pursue Lindbergh's family, and one actually forced a car carrying his second son to nursery school off the road.

The modern term "paparazzi" derives from Federico Fellini's 1959 film *La Dolce Vita*, in which a rapacious photographer pursuing European celebrities was called Paparazzo, an Italian word that literally means "flashbulb popping gnat." The paparazzi in Europe were regarded by Americans as a comic cultural phenomenon until the death of Princess Di caused many people to brand them as killers.

IN PURSUIT OF PRINCESS DIANA

On August 31, 1997, Diana, Princess of Wales, died in car crash in a Paris tunnel. Also killed were Diana's companion, Mohammed (Dodi) al-Fayed, and the car's driver. At the time of her death the 36-year-old princess was vacationing with Mr. al-Fayed, the wealthy son of the owner of Harrods, Britain's largest department store. Her charm, good looks, and highly publicized squabbles with the royal family had already made her a tabloid figure in Europe and the United States. Her 1981 wedding to Charles, Prince of Wales, heir to the British throne, had been watched on TV by millions, and her 1996 divorce was covered even more heavily by the press. Adding to Diana's tabloid image were her publicized struggles with bulimia and reported attempts at suicide.

Photographers in England followed Diana in unprecedented numbers. For example, in 1975 on a tour by Queen Elizabeth there were ten photographers in her party. In 1983 on a tour by Diana there were thirty, and by 1990 the number had swelled to one hundred. Because only about twelve newspapers in England send photographers on such tours, the majority were freelance paparazzi.

Diana's violent death in Paris put her on the front page of every American and European newspaper and demonized the paparazzi in the process. At the scene of the accident, a spokesman for the Prefecture of Police said, "The car was being chased by photographers on motorcycles, which could have caused the accident."[1] Nine photographers were detained for questioning and then arrested. Among them was Jacques Lanagevin, a French photojournalist who had won awards for his coverage of the 1989 Tienanmen Square massacre in Beijing. The credentials of the photographers did not matter. They were all "paparazzi." Graffiti on a wall near the crash site said: PAPARAZZI, ASSASSIN.

A spokesperson for the royal family expressed anger over Princess Diana's death, saying the accident was predictable because photographers relentlessly pursued the princess wherever she went. Diana's brother said, "I always believed the press would kill her in the end." Even British foreign minister Robin Cook blamed the press for Diana's death, warning, "Serious questions will have to be asked whether the aggressive intrusion into her privacy has contributed to this tragedy."[2]

British newspapers suggested that a crackdown on the press was imminent. "If the newspapers in this country do not exercise self-restraint . . . in response to the present wave of revulsion, Parliament could impose dangerous restrictions on media freedom," warned the *Daily Mail*.[3]

Americans also responded with outrage over the paparazzi's apparently predatory behavior, and the U.S. Congress joined in the call for legislation to restrain the press from stalking celebrities.

But were the paparazzi really responsible for Diana's death? No sooner had the press made that assumption than the news emerged that her driver, an employee of al-Fayed's father, had been drunk on that fateful night. In fact, his blood alcohol level had been triple the legal limit. And he had been driving at triple the speed limit. The princess, Dodi, and the driver were not wearing seat belts. The only survivor, Trevor Rees-Jones, Diana's bodyguard, was belted in.

Bill Thompson of Knight-Ridder Newspapers wrote, "The paparazzi were armed with cameras, not AK-47s. Even if they had managed to ditch their camera-wielding tormentors, Diana and Dodi surely would have found another battalion of photographers lurking just down the road. Yes, the death-by-photographer theory makes a great story, and it gives frustrated celebrities an excuse to vent their anger at the dreaded paparazzi. But the plain truth is, Princess Diana wasn't killed by photographers. She was killed by a drunken driver. It can happen to anyone."[4]

Despite such occasional expressions of objectivity, much of the press continued to blame the paparazzi. Finally, in late 1999, the Paris prosecutor's office made an official recommendation to dismiss all charges against the nine photographers and a photo-agency motorcyclist who had been under investigation since Princess Diana's automobile accident in 1997. The prosecutor's office said its "meticulous and exhaustive investigations" had produced no grounds for bringing criminal charges. The office concluded, "The investigation did not in fact allow any direct causal link to be established between the conduct of the people placed under investigation and the loss of control of the vehicle by the driver, which appears to be the determining cause of the accident."[5]

Goskin Sipahioglu, the owner of Sipa, one of the photographic agencies involved, said, "The photographers were unjustly accused of being responsible for Diana's death. The paparazzi are not responsible. When something like this happens, the duty of any journalist or photographer is to try to be on the scene as soon as possible. It's not a crime; it's the job."[6]

On September 3, 1999, French judges dismissed all charges against the nine photographers and a press motorcyclist. The magistrates concluded that the accident was caused not by the photographers' pursuit but by the car's drunken driver. Although the judges said the behavior of the photographers raised ethical and moral questions, it did not "constitute in this case a violation of the penal code." In particular, the judges said the photographers "did not resort to ruse or violence."[7]

REPORTERS CLAIM THE HIGH GROUND—
PHOTOGRAPHERS CHARGE HYPOCRISY

In the wake of Princess Diana's death, newspaper and TV reporters were quick to distance themselves from the paparazzi. "One has to draw one's own line as to taste and respect," said television personality Barbara Walters. "I'm not being holier-than-thou, but there's a very big difference between people on motorcycles looking in bedroom windows and real journalists doing their jobs in a responsible way."[8]

Other media critics questioned whether people like Barbara Walters, who bask in the glow of celebrities, can really fault the photographers who pursue those same popular figures. "Simply put," commented Michael Gross, "paparazzi photographs and aggressive tactics are indispensable for any publication that aspires to cover celebrities. And photographs by some of the very same 'jackals' who were arrested at the scene of the car crash have been published by *Time, Newsweek, Forbes, Business Week, USA Today*, and even the *New York Times*."[9]

Carol Wallace, the editor of *People* magazine, compared Diana's death chase with the helicopter pursuit of O. J. Simpson's Ford Bronco on June 17, 1994. "It was riveting," she said. "Was it intrusive? You can't have rules that apply to all situations. . . . If you're a magazine covering celebrity news and you write about people getting arrested or passing out on heroin, that's intrusive, but it's also news."[10]

Some have suggested that the frenzied media coverage of Diana's death simply represents media grieving for the loss of a major source of profit. Indeed, her image was worth millions. Even before her sensational death, *People* magazine had put Diana on its cover forty-four times, and *Time* and *Newsweek* seven times each.

It should be kept in mind that media coverage of celebrities is not secretly mapped in editorial rooms. It is negotiated with publicists who function as the marketing arm of the entertainment industry and attempt to manufacture the public image of their clients. Hollywood has targeted the paparazzi because they are largely beyond the control of press agents. Publicists for Hollywood stars such as Tom Cruise have sought to control the press, even to the point of making journalists sign contracts limiting their questions and their publications as a prerequisite for access.

The resultant artificial scarcity, according to Michael Gross, creates the very frenzy on the part of outsiders that Hollywood claims to deplore. But most of all, it is the public appetite for the paparazzi's product that fuels their behavior. "The public is insatiable for more graphic, private, intimate, invasive photos," said Gross. "They wouldn't be published if the public didn't want them."[11]

Yet the press is uncomfortable in satisfying that public hunger. After the death of Princess Di, even the tabloids in England were contrite. London's *Daily Star* wrote, "In the midst of the grief there is anger and the need to blame someone—the paparazzi, the media who buy their photographs and in doing so encourage their relentless pursuit of the famous. It would be hollow hypocrisy for the media to try to wash its hands of Diana's death."[12]

British photojournalist Ray Bellisario has pointed out that the mainstream British press pays incredibly high sums of money for the right to print "exclusive, blatantly intrusive photographs and stories," and he has asked, "[I]s it surprising that anyone from paparazzos to royal servants will do cartwheels to meet the demand?"[13]

Miguel Arana is a self-confessed paparazzo. "Sometimes what we do is completely useless, for example photographing famous people," he admits. "Yet lots of times, when a big news story hits the headlines . . . it's because there's a photojournalist or journalist behind it, pursuing the story." Arana says there are two types of news photographers. One is what he calls "cowboys," young people who buy a cheap camera and try to make some quick money taking pictures. "They have no idea how to do it; they don't know the rules," he says. The other type, says Arana, are the professional press photographers, *all* of whom have worked as paparazzi at one time or another. He says all newspapers used to have four or five staff photographers, but in an effort to save money "they sacked everybody." Now all those press photographers are freelance.

Arana claims that much of the stigma associated with the paparazzi derives from the text and context within which bad reporters use their photographs. "I could believe that 90% of what appears in the newspapers may be complete rubbish, but the photographs do not lie," he says. "We have no control over what stories get written. All we do is provide the images and they don't lie."[14]

TAKING THE PAPARAZZI TO COURT

As we have seen, the paparazzi and the entertainment industry can't live with each other and can't live without each other. And because Hollywood is the world's entertainment center, it was inevitable that the focus of the ambivalent relationship should come to reside in tinsel town.

Even before Princess Diana's death, there had been confrontations, some of them violent, between the paparazzi and Hollywood stars. Some of these disputes ended up in court.

In 1985 actor Alec Baldwin stood trial for assaulting a photographer who tried to videotape his wife, actress Kim Basinger, who was bringing their three-day-old baby home from the hospital. Baldwin said, "There's a difference between being in legitimate forums where press and photographers are supposed to be, and being stalked. We make ourselves available, and we go to places where we're going to encounter the press. We're as nice as can be and we do what people expect. But with this guy coming after the baby. . . . Just think about it: He was waiting for us in front of our house. He was not wearing any press credentials. The guy came over. He was very odd-looking, and he continued to insist on photographing us, even after I said very nicely, 'Don't do it.' I went to push the camera out of his hand, and I inadvertently hit him in the face. He says I punched him."[15]

In 1995 actor Woody Harrelson was involved in a highly publicized scuffle with the paparazzi that resulted in a court judgment against him. Harrelson was traveling with his young daughter when a group of paparazzi descended on them at the airport. Harrelson recalls, "I said, yeah, you can take pictures of me, but please don't take any pictures of my daughter. They kept doing it for ten, fifteen minutes. They would not stop. They would not relent." Harrelson took matters into his own hands, tackling one of the photographers. "Did I cross the line on a moral basis?" asks Harrelson. "No. They didn't have a right to take those pictures. I get convicted of violating their rights. . . . These guys violated my family, the most sacred thing to me."[16]

Perhaps the most prominent of the court cases involving paparazzi and Hollywood celebrities occurred in 1997, when two photographers were charged with misdemeanor battery and false imprisonment for using their cars to box in *Terminator* star Arnold Schwarzenegger and his celebrity wife, Maria Shriver. The two photographers, Giles Harrison and Andrew O'Brien, were trying to get the first photos of Schwarzenegger after his heart surgery, in which a faulty aortic valve was replaced.

Harrison was charged with reckless driving and false imprisonment, and O'Brien was charged with four counts of false imprisonment. O'Brien was also charged with battery, because he allegedly shoved two people who tried to help Schwarzenegger and Shriver during the incident.

Police said the Hollywood couple encountered the two photographers when they were trying to drop off their son at school. Harrison allegedly pulled his car in front of Schwarzenegger's car, and O'Brien then drove alongside to box them in. Having trapped Schwarzenegger and Shriver, the photographers then took their pictures. Police recovered some, but not all, of the pictures when they arrested Harrison and O'Brien.

The trial began on January 30, 1998, and the presiding judge found Harrison and O'Brien guilty of all charges. Harrison was sentenced to 90 days in jail and O'Brien received 60 days. Superior Court judge Robert Altman said the photographers had created a dangerous situation by their aggressive behavior. Still, he emphasized that his sentence was not to be interpreted as an anti-paparazzi move. "There may be a problem when celebrities feel they cannot go outside their houses," said Altman, "but I don't think this is the place to debate this issue. Any type of car chase is simply life-threatening to those involved."[17]

LEGISLATION AGAINST THE PAPARAZZI

The flurry of American legislative remedies proposed in the wake of Princess Diana's death could all be traced to California, the home of the entertainment industry. State legislation preceded federal bills, with two bills announced in the California Senate on September 2, 1997, as it observed a moment of silence in honor of the princess.

State senator Charles Calderon (D-Whittier) offered a bill that would require photographers to stay at least 15 feet from their subjects, if so requested. "The public and legitimate media should no longer tolerate the tactics of a business that thrives on lies, scandal, speculation and death," said Calderon. He said his bill would send a "message to paparazzi and tabloids who buy the photos that we will not tolerate harassment, spectacle or endangerment of people's lives."[18]

Senator Tom Hayden (D-Los Angeles) is another California legislator who advocates restrictions on picture-taking in his celebrity-rich city. He seeks to change California's anti-stalking law to prohibit "invasive technology" such as zoom lenses, and he would set heavy fines to cut the profits of freelance photographers who break state laws in chasing the rich and famous. Hayden was something of a celebrity himself before his divorce from actress Jane Fonda. His spokesperson, Stephanie Rubin, has said, "Tom clearly has his own experiences. He's been hounded by the paparazzi."[19]

The Hayden legislation would create a cause of action for knowing and willful behavior that, in the judgment of a reasonable person, threatens, intimidates, harasses, or causes alarm, harm, or the potential of harm to the person of media interest. The Calderon legislation would make it an invasion of privacy to intrude, harass, assault, batter, falsely imprison, stalk, or solicit with the intent to obtain information about or photographs of a person.

A number of First Amendment experts were quick to suggest that both the Calderon and Hayden bills were overbroad and vague and would probably not pass constitutional muster. Roger Myers, a media lawyer, said the bills "propose to criminalize routine newsgathering." Douglas Mirrell, a board member of the ACLU of Southern California, called the proposals a "sledgehammer approach to legislation." He concluded, "This is an irrational response to a nonproblem."[20] Finally, in 1998, the California legislature enacted SB1796, a bill criminalizing the tactics of what Governor Pete Wilson called the "stalkerazzi." First Amendment advocates were appalled. ACLU spokesperson Mirrell warned, "Under the California legislation, all individuals who take photographs, whether they're paparazzi or members of the mainstream media, if they use a telephoto lens to take a close-up photo of a celebrity, those individuals are now guilty of violating the law."[21]

The U.S. Congress—led, of course, by members representing California—was quick to follow with similar federal proposals. The most prominent came from Representative Sonny Bono (R-Calif.), himself a full-fledged celebrity because of his previous career in the music industry when he was part of the singing duo Sonny and Cher. Bono's bill, titled the Protection from Personal Intrusion Act (H.R.2448), criminalized "harassing" any person within the United States or any U.S. citizen outside the United States. Bono said he introduced the bill in response to the auto accident that took the life of Princess Diana and her companions.

The term "harass" was defined to mean persistently physically following or chasing a victim "for the purpose of capturing by a camera or sound recording instrument of any type a visual image, sound recording, or other physical impression of the victim for profit in or affecting interstate or foreign commerce." Penalties would include a minimum of twenty years in prison if death were to result, a minimum of five years in prison if bodily injury were to result, and not more than one year in prison if neither death nor bodily injury were to result. These penalties would apply "in circumstances where the victim has a reasonable expectation of privacy and has taken reasonable steps to insure that privacy."[22]

H.R.2448 found little support among media lawyers, who felt that phrases such as "reasonable expectation of privacy" were unconstitutionally vague. "Due process protections require that a person be able to predict what it is that violates the law," said First Amendment scholar Floyd Abrams.[23]

First Amendment problems were also anticipated in H.R.2448 because it targeted photographers, exempting obsessed individuals who follow celebrities. Media lawyers noted that threats posed by aggressive photographers could be addressed by trespass and assault laws and anti-stalking statutes already in existence in all fifty states. "In the United States, the open public spaces are reserved for freedom of expression, both for speaking and gathering information," said Rodney Smolla, a

Prominent aviator Charles Lindbergh was one of the first celebrities to endure predatory press photographers. When his son was kidnapped and murdered, photographers entered the morgue, broke open the child's coffin, and photographed the mangled corpse. Photo reproduced from the collections of the Library of Congress.

Representative Sonny Bono (R-Calif.), a full-fledged celebrity from his *Sonny and Cher* days, introduced the Protection from Personal Intrusion Act in an effort to curb the intrusive behavior of the "paparazzi." Photo courtesy of Uniphoto Stock Photography.

prominent First Amendment author and professor of law at William and Mary Law School.[24]

The Stars Trek to Washington

When Sonny Bono died in a skiing accident in 1998, his anti-paparazzi bill (H.R.2448) quickly lost steam, but a companion bill (H.R.3224) introduced by Representative Elton Gallegly (R-Calif.) soon put the paparazzi back in the congressional spotlight. On May 21, 1998, a delegation of Hollywood celebrities entertained the House Judiciary Committee with tales of invasion of privacy at the hands of the paparazzi.

Chairman Henry Hyde (R-Ill.) introduced the celebrity hearings. "Last year, a stunned America heard the news of Princess Diana's untimely death," he began solemnly. "Early reports laid blame for the accident that caused her death on photographers, whose reckless pursuit through a Paris tunnel caused her car to career out of control. . . . The role of the media in the Princess' death has now been disputed, but the controversy over its conduct continues." Chairman Hyde acknowledged that it was Sonny Bono who had brought the committee together for the hearings. "It was Sonny who first took up this issue as his cause and who convinced me that it was a subject worth pursuing," said Hyde. "Fortunately for him, and for us, Elton Gallegly was there to step into the void left by his death." Hyde concluded sternly, "Freedom of the press as guaranteed by the First Amendment is a fundamental cornerstone of our democracy, but it does not confer a license to engage in criminal conduct in the interest of securing news. When in the guise of getting a story, the press puts someone at risk of death or serious injury, the First Amendment is no shield."[25]

The first witness was Michael J. Fox, star of TV sitcoms and motion picture hits such as *Back to the Future*. Fox complained of "the intrusive, harassing and mercenary tactics of tabloid photographers," and he strongly disputed the argument that "some sort of Faustian bargain has been struck whereby 'public' figures are fair game, any time, any place, including within the confines of their own homes." Fox said the tactics of the paparazzi were often cruel, destructive, and criminal. "They have chased me on foot and in my car, yelled obscene comments at my entire family, and literally staked out my home, on a 24 hour basis, in hopes of capturing that one photograph that will win them the bounty," he said. "For years, we have spotted photographers around the edge of our personal property and trailing us in the streets and parks with high-powered lenses, taking pictures of private moments and of our children, who have no concept of what it means to be a 'public figure.' . . . I have seen freelance photographers intentionally frighten children of celebrities (including my own) in order to provoke a distressed reaction. Such a shot can inspire fantastic copy." Fox concluded his testimony by stating, "It is clear that the legislation dealing with both persistent chasing and intrusion into private property with long-lens cameras is needed."[26]

Following Michael J. Fox came Paul Reiser, comedian and star of the hit sitcom *Mad About You*. Reiser said it was not his desire to enact a law "to help fancy celebrities enjoy their fancy lives in their big fancy homes." Instead, he said, we need to protect "the famous and the not famous from the invasive and very often dangerous tactics of some—not all—but some photographers and news gatherers."

Reiser had his own set of horror stories. "My experience with these invasions of privacy started a few years ago with the birth of my son," he said. "When my wife went into labor several weeks prematurely, someone at the hospital apparently decided this was news-worthy and passed the information on to the press. Within hours we were told that the hospital began receiving calls from imposters posing as relatives and concerned friends, trying to unearth juicy tidbits about our infant's condition, and that several intruders were spotted in the halls outside and around the intensive care unit with cameras, trying to steal a picture of our newborn child.

"Simply because our son had—against our wishes—become a news item, he was, suddenly, photo worthy. And our lives changed. Cars began to follow us on our daily errands. Strangers with video cameras camped outside our home. One resourceful photographer gained access to a house down the street from us and with a telescopic lens was able to get a photo of my son in the privacy of our backyard."

Reiser said a line had been crossed in the way news was gathered and the code of civility and decency had vanished. "I realize it's not possible to legislate civility and manners," he said. "But I do believe that the time has come to take the first step in that direction and send forth the message that there is still a distinction to be made between public and private. That even in the pursuit of news or human interest stories, there is a point where harassment, trespassing and physical endangerment are not only unacceptable but should be punishable by law."[27]

Reiser, like Fox, concluded by offering his support for the proposed legislation.

The Judiciary Committee also heard from the public relations industry, as Dick Guttman, a thirty-year PR man for the entertainment industry, introduced the committee to the new term, "stalkerazzi."

Guttman surprised the committee when he said, "Paparazzi are a legitimate part of the Hollywood publicity mill. They don't hunt down celebrities like prey to steal private moments or to provoke ugly ones. ... Stalkerazzi are tabloid predators who conduct guerilla warfare through acts of pursuit and provocation rather than acts of news gathering. They hunt a personality's reaction under duress. Intrusive pursuit by stalkerazzi impacts the emotional, family and career well-being of celebrities. It endangers their safety. None of us wishes to be hounded, and the absolute surrender of privacy and dignity is not the mandatory trade-off for fame."

Guttman also noted that the bills under consideration criminalized certain aggressive behavior by photographers but did not censor the *products* of that behavior. "Even in a worst case Princess Diana–type tragedy," he said, "the right of media to publish or broadcast the resulting photos or videos or audio material will be protected. Hopefully, this law would foster an awareness that would influence media self-evaluation and make less attractive the product of these stalkerazzi."[28]

Richard Masur, president of the Screen Actors Guild, summarized the celebrity testimony and told the Judiciary Committee that the intrusiveness of modern technology made legislative control of the paparazzi essential. "We believe that Congress must now translate . . . traditional privacy protection into a form that takes into account these technological advances, and create a new cause of action for technological invasion of privacy or constructive trespass," said Masur. "This would create a tort against anyone who would invade one's privacy by making a sound or visual recording of a personal or familial activity, through the use of an audio or visual enhancement device, for commercial purposes." Masur admitted that the proposed legislation represented a new legal concept, but he insisted that it was grounded in traditional trespass, eavesdropping, and peeping statutes. "We realize that we are asking that the balance between the individual's right to privacy and the press' right under the First Amendment be adjusted, in order to accommodate current and future technologies," he said.[29]

Of course, there were witnesses before the Judiciary Committee whose opposition to such First Amendment "adjustments" contrasted with the celebrity testimony. Paul McMasters, former president of the Society of Professional Journalists and current head of the Freedom Forum, said the proposed legislation "would unwisely add problematic new categories of criminal and civil actions as well as new penalties against journalists who ran afoul of these restrictions while exercising their rights under the First Amendment. . . . For these reasons and more, enacting a new federal law regulating the news media would be unnecessary, unwise, and unconstitutional."

McMasters brought a bit of sober reflection to the celebrity-sated committee members. "We urge you to keep in mind that while the focus of these deliberations is on the plight of Hollywood stars, the fact is that this legislation goes far beyond what is needed for their protection and creates a situation that allows public figures to dictate the way they are portrayed to the public," he said. "What's more, this proposal substitutes the uninformed and self-interested opinions of newsmakers, prosecutors, and the courts for the informed editorial judgment of editors and news directors. The First Amendment is a constitutional contract between the government and the people; it is not a movie script. When Hollywood calls for a rewrite, we respectfully urge you to remember that the first six words of the First Amendment counsel the utmost restraint when it comes to making laws that restrict freedom of speech and the press."[30]

The McMasters testimony was endorsed by the American Society of Newspaper Editors, the Magazine Publishers of America, the Newspaper Association of America, the National Newspaper Association, the National Press Photographers Association, the Radio-Television News Directors Association, the Reporters Committee for Freedom of the Press, and the Society of Professional Journalists.

David Lutman, president of the National Press Photographers Association, told the Judiciary Committee, "Under the proposed bill, journalists are accorded less legal rights than other citizens, as journalists face criminal and civil sanctions for engaging in the same type of conduct that any other citizen can freely engage in."[31]

Paul Tash, executive editor of the *St. Petersburg Times*, said the American Society of Newspaper Editors, whose Freedom of Information Committee he chairs, vigorously opposes the proposed bill. "We know the sponsors want to protect movie stars and other celebrities from the unblinking and voracious attention of the tabloid press," he said. "The sponsors may think they are aiming only at the so-called paparazzi, but they will surely hit the rest of us too.... This bill is unnecessary, and it reaches way beyond the ultimately narrow problem it purports to address. It might keep a few celebrity photos out of print and off the air, but it would also keep the public from seeing some characters who prefer to stay in the shadows."[32]

Barbara Cochran, president of the Radio-Television News Directors Association, testified, "[I]n attempting to curb the excesses of the so-called 'paparazzi,' the proposed legislation would without a doubt unduly restrict and punish the important and protected newsgathering activities of mainstream news organizations. Moreover, the proposed legislation is overbroad, unnecessary, unconstitutional, and would have a debilitating impact on the ability of reporters and videographers to bring news stories to the American public."[33]

Dr. Robert Richards, director of the Pennsylvania Center for the First Amendment, told the committee, "We must ask ourselves then why it is necessary to create a new federal law that, for all intents and purposes, singles out a particular group for punishment? These bills would not apply, for instance, to an ordinary fan who zealously pursues a celebrity for personal amusement.... In summary, while very little is gained in terms of protecting individuals from the harmful behavior of the paparazzi, much can be lost in terms of the freedom the press enjoys (and the public benefits from) in the United States."[34]

A FINAL ATTEMPT TO HANDCUFF THE PAPARAZZI

Perhaps in response to the virtually unanimous legal opinions that the earlier anti-paparazzi bills were unconstitutional, two heavyweights from the Senate, Dianne Feinstein (D-Calif.) and Orrin Hatch (R-Utah), employed constitutional law professors to help create a bill that would pass constitutional muster. The new bill, called the Personal Privacy Protection Act, would apply criminal penalties for a narrowly defined form of "harassment" and provide civil action against certain kinds of trespass.

When she introduced the bill on May 20, 1998, Senator Feinstein said, "In crafting this legislation, we worked with some of the most renowned constitutional scholars and First Amendment advocates in the nation, including Erwin Chemerinsky of the University of Southern California Law School, Cass Sunstein of the Chicago School of Law, and Lawrence Lessig of Harvard Law School. We took the approach of plugging loopholes in existing, long-recognized laws prohibiting harassment and trespassing, rather than creating new provisions out of whole cloth, in order to craft a constitutional bill that fully respects First Amendment and other constitutional rights. . . . The constitutional scholars concurred unanimously that this legislation is narrowly drafted to withstand constitutional challenge on First Amendment, federalism, or any other grounds."[35]

Professor Chemerinsky explained, "There's no constitutional right to reckless endangerment, and there's no constitutional right to trespass. This [bill] doesn't do anything to offend the First Amendment." He said that under the new bill, violators of the criminal endangerment provision would have to be shown to be persistently and physically following or chasing a person, causing a reasonable fear of bodily injury. Similarly, he said, the civil trespassing provision was scaled back to apply only to "personal or familial activity" on private property that could not be otherwise observed.[36]

Feinstein insisted that her bill would not intrude on press rights. "Freedom of the press is the bedrock of American democracy," she said. "But there is something wrong when a person cannot visit a loved one in the hospital, walk their child to school, or be secure in the privacy of their own home without being dangerously chased, provoked, or trespassed upon by photographers trying to capture pictures of them to sell to the tabloids."[37]

In a press conference with Screen Actors Guild president Richard Masur and members of the Guild, Feinstein said, "Just because a person makes their living on television or in some other public arena should not mean they forfeit all rights to personal privacy. There is a line between legitimate news gathering and invasion of privacy; between snapping a picture of someone in a public place and chasing them to the point where they fear for their safety. Unfortunately, that line is crossed more and more frequently today by an increasingly aggressive cadre of fortune-seekers with cameras." Feinstein said she and Senator Barbara Boxer (D-Calif.) began developing the current legislation after meeting with members of the Screen Actors Guild. She noted that the tragic death of Princess Diana "brought the seriousness of the problem home with a blunt force that stunned the world."[38]

The harassment provision of Feinstein's bill prohibits persistently following or chasing people in order to photograph, film, or record them for commercial purposes in a manner which causes them to have a reasonable fear of bodily injury. The bill establishes a penalty of up to one year in prison for such harassment and at least five years in prison if the "harassment" actually causes serious bodily injury. If such actions cause a death, the penalty is at least twenty years in prison. Civil action may also be taken by the victim of harassment, including recovery of compensatory damages, punitive damages, and injunctive and declaratory relief.

Victims of trespass/personal intrusion may institute a civil action under the Feinstein bill if the paparazzi have (1) trespassed, or (2) used "visual or auditory enhancement devices" to capture recordings for commercial purposes that they otherwise could not have captured without trespassing. The bill does not criminalize trespass, and it limits remedy for trespass to civil action by either the property owner or the person photographed.

Both the harassment and trespass provisions of the Feinstein bill apply only to a photographer or person directly involved in the activity, not the publisher of the resulting film or photograph.

Neither the Feinstein bill nor any of its predecessors appear likely to pass. At the end of the year 2000, all remained buried in committee. For the time being, neither Congress nor the media seem anxious to resume their exaggerated rhetoric about the hordes of paparazzi descending on celebrities. Perhaps the recent court judgments on the Princess Di tragedy have had a calming effect.

PRESS RIGHTS VERSUS PERSONAL PRIVACY: CURRENT OPINIONS

The most recent flurry of paparazzi activity occurred after the July 1999 death of John F. Kennedy Jr. and his wife and sister-in-law in a plane crash. At the July 23 memorial service in New York there were hundreds of paparazzi, and to the dismay of the Kennedy family, many of the photographers followed family members to their homes. On the day after the memorial service one paparazzi photographer, Laura Cavanaugh, caught Caroline Kennedy Schlossberg, her husband, and two of her children, all grim-faced, leaving their New York apartment.

"I just got lucky," said Cavanaugh. "I was only there for five minutes, and out came Caroline and the kids." Cavanaugh said she sold her photos to *People* magazine for "about $1,000" and to other foreign magazines for lesser amounts. Did she have any qualms about pursuing the family, including the 6-year-old son and the 9- and 11-year-old daughters? "No," said Cavanaugh. "They didn't duck or yell at me to stop."[39]

Journalist and publisher Steven Brill was sufficiently concerned about such paparazzi behavior to conduct a survey of public and media attitudes toward privacy. The week after the Kennedy memorial service, Brill faxed a questionnaire to members of print and broadcast news organizations, asking if they would be willing, in the light of the coverage of the Kennedy tragedy, to observe two voluntary restrictions on media intrusions into personal privacy. Briefly paraphrased, those restrictions would commit press organizations to voluntarily:

1. Withhold publication of photographs or video images of children under age 14 without the permission of the children and one of their parents or a guardian and avoid posting reporters or photographers outside their homes without their permission. Children in show business or who accompany their politician-parents to campaign functions are excepted.

2. Withhold publication of current photographs or video images of family members who have lost a loved one within one week following the death and avoid posting reporters or photographers outside their homes, at the funeral, etc., without their permission. If a funeral or memorial service is deemed to be "newsworthy," the news organization may post photographers outside the location (or inside if given permission) unless explicitly asked not to do so by the family, in which case they "should place great weight on that request."

   Addendum: As with any general policy, there could arise "special circumstances" that would cause the news organization to make exceptions, in which case the reasons for the exception should be articulated.[40]

Of the 130 prominent media people to whom Brill sent his questionnaire, 53 said they did not agree with the voluntary restrictions, 18 said they did agree, 3 offered mixed responses, and 56 refused to take any position on the restrictions.

Typical of those who rejected the restrictions was the response of Griffin Smith Jr., executive editor of the Arkansas *Democrat-Gazette*. "I can think of no good reason for a 'general rule' that purports to balance the newsworthiness of an activity occurring in a public place . . . against the desire of the participants in that activity to render conduct private," said Smith. CBS News president Andrew Hayward, one of the many respondents who refused to take a position on Brill's proposal, said, "We are not going to respond. I don't believe in industry guidelines at all. We handle these on a case-by-case basis." Howard Kurtz, media reporter for the *Washington Post*, was one of the few respondents to endorse the restrictions. "I'd be more than happy to have the *Washington Post* decline to publish pictures of grieving family members after a death," said Kurtz. "What the public despises about the media is the obnoxious intrusiveness with which we invade people's lives at times of tragedy, or buy telephoto-lens pictures from those who do."[41]

In an attempt to compare the broader public views on the privacy issue with those of media representatives, Brill retained the polling firm of Penn, Schoen & Berland to seek public reaction to the same proposed restrictions that the media had overwhelmingly rejected. The sample of 475 randomly selected registered voters overwhelmingly endorsed the proposed restrictions by an average margin of almost 80 percent.[42]

NOTES

1. "Diana Killed in a Car Accident in Paris," *New York Times* (August 31, 1997), A1.

2. Dan Ehrlich, "The Press under Fire," *Editor & Publisher* (September 13, 1997), p. 9.

3. Ibid.

4. Bill Thompson, "Paparazzi's Guilt Made Great Story, True or Not," September 6, 1997, texnews.com/opinion97/pap1090697.html.

5. "French Prosecutor Says Pursuers of Diana Did Not Cause Crash," *New York Times* (August 18, 1999), A6.

6. Ibid.

7. "French Magistrates Clear Photographers in Death of Diana," *New York Times* (September 4, 1999), A2.

8. Cited in Michael Gross, "The Princess and the Jackals," *New York* (September 15, 1997), p. 39.

9. Ibid.

10. Ibid.

11. Ibid.

12. Cited in Dan Ehrlich, "The Press under Fire," p. 10.

13. Cited in Tessa Mayes, ed., *Disclosure: Media Freedom and the Privacy Debate after Diana* (London: London International Research Exchange Media Group, 1998), p. 53.

14. Ibid., pp. 53–55.

15. "To Protect Their Baby," *Good Housekeeping*, (May 1986), p. 100.

16. "When Cameras Cross the Line," Fox TV, October 23, 2000, Ardent Productions, 2000.

17. "Photographers Sentenced in Schwarzenegger Case," *The News Media and the Law* (spring 1998), p. 18.

18. Cited in M. L. Stein, "Calif. Pols Want Press Limits," *Editor and Publisher* (September 13, 1997), p. 13.

19. Cited in Jenifer Joyce, "Lost Photo Opportunities," *ABA Journal* (November 1997), p. 36.

20. Ibid.

21. "When Cameras Cross the Line," October 23, 2000.

22. Congressional Universe, Congressional Information Service, Inc., 1999, http://web.lexis-nexis.com.

23. Cited in Joyce, "Lost Photo Opportunities," p. 37.

24. Ibid.

25. "Opening Statement, Chairman Henry J. Hyde, Legislative Hearing of H.R. 2448, the 'Protection from Personal Intrusion Act,' and H.R. 3224, the 'Privacy Protection Act of 1998,' " Committee on Judiciary, U.S. House of Representatives, May 21, 1998, www.house.gov/judiciary/10153.htm.

26. "Testimony by Michael J. Fox before the House Committee on Judiciary, U.S. House of Representatives," May 21, 1998, www.house.gov/judiciary/10142.htm.

27. "Testimony by Paul Reiser before the House Committee on Judiciary, U.S. House of Representatives," May 21, 1998, www.house.gov/judiciary/10143.htm.

28. "Testimony by Dick Guttman before the House Committee on Judiciary, U.S. House of Representatives," May 21, 1998, www.house.gov/judiciary/10150.htm.

29. "Testimony by Richard Masur, President, Screen Actors Guild, before the House Committee on Judiciary, U.S. House of Representatives," May 21, 1998, www.house.gov/judiciary/10147.htm.

30. "Testimony of Paul K. McMasters, H.R.3224, The Privacy Protection Act of 1998, the U.S. House of Representatives, Committee on the Judiciary," May 21, 1998, www.house.gov/judiciary/10145.htm.

31. "Testimony of David R. Lutman, on H.R.3224 and H.R.2448, U.S. House of Representatives, Committee on the Judiciary," May 21, 1998, www.house.gov/judiciary/10146.htm.

32. "Testimony of Paul C. Tash, *St. Petersburg Times* Executive Editor, on the Privacy Protection Act of 1998, U.S. House of Representatives, Committee on the Judiciary," May 21, 1998, www.house.gov/judiciary/10148.htm.

33. "Testimony of Barbara S. Cochran, President, Radio-Television News Directors Association, U.S. House of Representatives, Committee on the Judiciary," May 21, 1998, www.house.gov/judiciary/10149.htm.

34. "Testimony of Robert D. Richards, Associate Professor of Journalism and Law, Pennsylvania State University, U.S. House of Representatives, Committee on the Judiciary, Hearing on H.R.2448, Protection from Personal Intrusion Act, H.R.3224, Privacy Protection Act of 1998," May 21, 1998, www.house.gov/judiciary/10151.htm.

35. "Statement of Senator Dianne Feinstein upon Introduction of the Personal Privacy Protection Act, U.S. House of Representatives, Committee on the Judiciary," May 20, 1998, www.senate.gov/feinstein/speeches98/paparazzi2.html.

36. Cited in Todd S. Purdum, "Two Senators Propose Anti-Paparazzi Law," *New York Times* (February 18, 1998), A16.

37. "Statement of Senator Dianne Feinstein upon Introduction of the Personal Privacy Protection Act."

38. "Senator Dianne Feinstein Unveils Privacy Legislation Aimed at Paparazzi Abuses," February 18, 1998, www.senate.gov/feinstein/releases98/paparazzi.html.

39. Cited in Steven Brill, "Curiosity vs. Privacy," *Brill's Content* (October 1999), p. 98.

40. Ibid., p. 104.

41. Ibid., pp. 102–5.

42. Ibid.

From Plagiarism to Polemics

JOURNALISTIC PLAGIARISM

The 1980s and 1990s saw more highly publicized violations of journalistic ethics than longtime members of the press can recall in any previous generation. Countless allegations of plagiarism, phony sources, and unsupported reporting have stained the reputations of talented reporters and prominent publications. In some cases penitent reporters have confessed their wrongdoings. In others the alleged transgressions have been disputed, and in some the punishment meted out to reporters has served the purpose of censoring controversial stories. Nonetheless the sheer number of such scandals raises serious questions about the current generation of reporters and whether their values and professional ethics represent a profound change from those of the past.

Plagiarism is an ethical transgression, not a violation of law. The closest legal term would be "copyright infringement," which occurs if a person creates a work that is substantially similar to a copyrighted work to which he or she has had access. According to *Webster's Third New International Dictionary*, to commit plagiarism is "to steal or pass off as one's own" the ideas or words of another. How many borrowed words constitute plagiarism? How many paragraphs? The absence of a standard makes plagiarism an unlikely issue for the courts to decide, and although editors around the country consider plagiarism to be a cardinal sin, they are forced to deal with it on a case-by-case basis.

"This is something you never, never do," commented James Fallows,

Washington editor of the *Atlantic Monthly*. "If you're a soldier, you don't desert. If you're a writer, you don't steal anyone's prose. It should be the one automatic firing."[1]

Despite Fallows's dictum, such severe punishment of reporters is by no means automatic. Back in 1972 Nina Totenberg, today a prominent reporter and radio/television personality, was fired for plagiarism when she worked for the *National Observer*. Totenberg had used several paragraphs and verbatim quotes from a *Washington Post* report in her own story about House Speaker "Tip" O'Neill without attributing the source. "I was in a hurry," said Totenberg. "I used terrible judgment. The fact I used so many direct quotes obligated me morally to credit the *Post*. I should have been punished."[2]

Jonathan Broder is another successful journalist who seems to have transcended past incidents of plagiarism. In March 1988 Broder was fired from his job as Middle East correspondent for the *Chicago Tribune* after he plagiarized a story from the *Jerusalem Post*. *Tribune* editor James Squires said, "This was an aberration. There is an explanation for what happened, but there is no justification."[3]

Not all of Broder's colleagues were as understanding as Squires. Philip Terzian recently recalled Broder's *Tribune* incident and insisted that it was no aberration. Terzian described a 1981 story on Libyan leader Muammar Qaddafi by Broder that the *Tribune* transmitted over the wire. "I remember the occasion well," said Terzian. "I was associate editor of the *Lexington Herald* at the time, and as I read Broder's piece, it became quickly evident that he had lifted generous portions of a two-month-old *Newsweek* story on the Libyan dictator." As a courtesy, Terzian called the *Tribune*'s editor, Jack Fuller, and asked him to compare the two stories. He did, and shortly thereafter a "kill advisory" for the Broder piece appeared on the wire.

Broder is currently the Washington correspondent for the online magazine *Salon* and frequently appears on television. Such easy rehabilitation bothers Terzian. "There is no more despicable action by a writer than stealing someone else's words and, when caught, offering lame excuses for the deed," he said. "And yet plagiarists . . . seem to go from strength to strength, unbowed by anything like shame, honored and protected by their colleagues."[4]

Recent studies show that the severity of penalties for journalistic plagiarism has been mixed. The *Columbia Journalism Review (CJR)* looked at twenty cases of plagiarism that have occurred since 1988 and discovered that only eight of the offending reporters were fired, and two of those were rehired after arbitration; three of the twenty journalists were suspended for varying periods; one had his column briefly suspended; one had his column canceled but kept his job; one resigned but moved to another job in the same organization; one left the newspaper before his offense was discovered; and the remaining five received no punishment.[5] Following are some of the cases examined by *CJR*:

1. In 1989 Bob Hepburn, Washington bureau chief for the *Toronto Star*, used three paragraphs from a *Washington Monthly* story for his column. When the *Washington Monthly* complained publicly, the *Star* discontinued his column but maintained him as bureau chief.

2. Laura Parker was the *Washington Post*'s Miami bureau chief in 1991 when she was fired for using unattributed quotes from the *Miami Herald* and *Associated Press*. She moved on to the Washington bureau of the *Detroit News*, where she covered environmental issues.

3. In 1992 Michael Kramer, chief political correspondent for *Time* magazine, lifted a sentence from a *Los Angeles Times* column for use in his column. *Time* and Kramer apologized, but Kramer received no punishment.

4. Edwin Chen, Washington reporter for the *Los Angeles Times*, wrote a nonfiction book in 1992 that was based largely on a story in *Vanity Fair*. Chen's book included more than forty passages that closely resembled the *Vanity Fair* story. Chen continues to write for the *Times*.

5. Fox Butterfield, Boston bureau chief for the *New York Times*, actually plagiarized five paragraphs from a *Boston Globe* story about plagiarism. Butterfield was suspended for one week but remained bureau chief.

6. Bob Morris, a columnist for the *Orlando Sentinel*, wrote a column in October 1993 that was essentially the same as one written some years earlier in the *Columbus Citizen-Journal*. By the time the *Sentinel* discovered the plagiarism, Morris had moved on to another position. The *Sentinel* published an apology to its readers and made a cash settlement to the original author of the plagiarized material. Harris became a prominent journalist in Orlando, writing a syndicated column and functioning as editor at large for the magazine *Orlando*.

7. Gregory Freeman, a columnist for the *St. Louis Post-Dispatch*, used three sentences from a *Boston Globe* column in his own 1994 piece about Lani Guanier, Clinton's nominee to head the Civil Rights division of the Justice Department. The *Post-Dispatch* suspended Freeman's column for a month as Freeman took what the paper described as a "previously scheduled vacation." Freeman subsequently resigned his duties at the *Post-Dispatch*.

8. Ken Hamblin, *Denver Post* columnist and radio talk-show host, was suspended by the *Post* for two months during 1994 for plagiarizing five paragraphs from a story in the *Rocky Mountain News*. During his suspension, Hamblin's column and talk show were carried by numerous other media outlets.

9. Mark Hornung, editorial page editor for the *Chicago Sun-Times*, resigned in 1995 after the near-verbatim use of twelve paragraphs from a *Washington Post* editorial. He was reassigned to the circulation department.[6]

The variation of institutional response to plagiarism in the *CJR* study is in part a reflection of the absence of formal professional standards. Many newspapers and magazines have no written policy on plagiarism, and even the professional societies are imprecise or silent on the issue. The Code of Ethics of the Society of Professional Journalists simply says, "plagiarism is dishonest and unacceptable." Neither the American Society of Newspaper Editors nor the American Society of Magazine Editors mentions plagiarism in its statements on ethics.

Former *Washington Post* editor Ben Bradlee believes that anyone who plagiarizes should be fired. As described above, the *Post* fired Laura Parker for plagiarism, and Bradlee says the *Post* also refused to hire Elizabeth Wurtzel, a writer who had plagiarized some material for a story in the *Dallas Morning News*. Wurtzel was, however, later hired by the *New Yorker* and *New York* magazines.[7]

Not all newspaper editors are as consistent as Bradlee in meting out punishment. The *CJR* study showed that the *Denver Post* suspended Ken Hamblin, but several years earlier the paper had fired art critic Irene Rawlings for placing her byline over two articles from the *New Yorker*.

Some publications seem to wait for a second offense before firing a writer for plagiarism. In 1990 the *Toronto Globe and Mail* suspended Deirdre Kelly, its dance critic, for borrowing material from an article in *Music Magazine*, but just a few months later the paper fired Kelly for another incident. The paper then rehired Kelly after arbitration.[8]

The *Sacramento Bee* gave TV columnist Bob Wisehart a five-month suspension the first time he was caught plagiarizing but fired him the second time. "I don't believe one offense is worth destroying people's lives and careers," explained editor Gregory Favre. "The second time the institution of the newspaper was damaged."[9] Favre noted that Wisehart was an extremely talented writer whose original work was better than what he copied.

This seeming irony is, in fact, characteristic of most plagiarists, suggesting a compulsion comparable to kleptomania. Virtually all plagiarists become repeat offenders, and they don't really need the material they steal. They almost dare their institutions to catch them, and when caught they offer apologies and excuses. In his public statement Bob Hepburn said, "I simply forgot where I got the actual wording." Mark Hornung attributed his plagiarism to "deadline pressures" and "writer's block." Michael Kramer said the original wording "stuck in my mind."[10]

Ruth Shalit, a celebrated young journalist, may be the most prominent example of a plagiarist in denial. She burst on the scene at *The New Republic (TNR)* in 1993, and by the time she was 24 years old she was writing important political features for *GQ* magazine and the *New York Times Magazine*. In retrospect, colleagues at *TNR* say there was an alarming number of complaints by Shalit's sources claiming they had been misquoted, but at the time the editors chalked it up to the controversial nature of her stories. Her first real problem came in July 1994, when Daniel Klaidman, a reporter for the *Legal Times*, noticed the strong similarity of a Shalit story to one he had written a year earlier. Klaidman's editor complained to *TNR*, citing four examples of almost identical passages.

TNR issued a correction, saying that Shalit had mistakenly borrowed the material and "acknowledges her debt" to Klaidman. Shalit personally called Klaidman to explain that it was all a computer mistake, but the word was getting around that Shalit had a problem. When she heard that the *Columbia Journalism Review (CJR)* was planning to include her incident in an article on plagiarism, Shalit called Klaidman once more and said, "Now as I recall, you guys didn't formally accuse me of 'plagiarism.' " Klaidman recalled, "It flashed through my mind that she was looking for a quote to exonerate herself, and then I got a little mad. I said, 'Look, I'm not going to get into a semantic debate with you about plagiarism. You stole my writing and I didn't like it.'"[11]

Shalit then prevailed on an influential friend to intercede with *CJR* on her behalf, to explain that it had not really been plagiarism, just an electronic mistake. The *CJR* piece made only a brief mention of Shalit, referring to her "electronic fumble." But barely had *CJR* hit the newsstands when another of Shalit's borrowings was discovered. While reading a Shalit article on Steve Forbes, Paul Starobin, a reporter at the *National Journal*, noticed a number of similarities to his own recent article. Starobin, who was not aware of Shalit's earlier Klaidman incident, complained to *TNR*, which once more issued a correction under the heading, "Oops."

Both Starobin and Klaidman were astonished at Shalit's subsequent description of her plagiarism. In comments to the *Washington Post*, she said she would never do it again but noted that the material she had borrowed was "banal" and "boilerplate." Klaidman was outraged. "It's really hard to believe," he said. "In her apology, she managed to dis the writers she ripped off."[12]

In subsequent comments to the *American Journalism Review (AJR)*, Shalit tried to calm the waters. "I said there were banal sentences or boilerplate sentences," she explained. "That looks like I'm trying to minimize it. I don't. The fact is that someone else's words appeared in my story. Aside from lying, that's the most egregious offense in journalism. It doesn't matter that it happened inadvertently. That's an excuse." But after delivering her *mea culpas*, Shalit once more attributed her plagiarism to nothing more than sloppy computer habits. "In my case, the mistake came from having someone else's words on my screen," she explained. "From downloading Nexis searches as text files and then putting them on my screen and later conflating them with my own notes."[13]

Shalit's next bomb exploded when her article in the October 2, 1994, *New York Times Magazine* contained material from a *National Journal* article by Peter Stone. Amazingly, Shalit's editors continued to make excuses for her. *TNR*'s Andrew Sullivan explained that she was simply "overextended" and shouldn't be doing so much freelancing. Those from whom she had stolen were less understanding. Daniel Klaidman said, "What makes this so bizarre is that she flouted the everyday rules of the game that we all follow so stringently—and got rewarded for it."[14]

The most ironic example of Shalit's plagiarism occurred in her story on Bob Dole in the March 5, 1995, *New York Times Magazine*. Shalit wrote, "Like a British Tory rather than an American conservative, Dole distrusts visions and visionaries." *Mother Jones* discovered that the sentence was lifted without attribution from an April 5, 1993, article in *The New Republic* by Fred Barnes, the only difference being the use of the term "High Tory" instead of "Tory."[15] Fred Barnes was at that time Shalit's editor and mentor at *The New Republic*.

But Shalit was soon discovered to have borrowed material from a 1979 book by David Halberstam for her 1995 article about racial tension at the *Washington Post*. By now, Shalit's colleagues were responding to her transgressions with as much humor as horror. In noting some errors in Shalit's article, a *Post* reporter said, "One problem with stealing from the '70s is that your information might be out of date."[16]

Many publications that have been embarrassed by plagiarism are often reluctant to discuss the matter publicly. The *Rocky Mountain News* did not run an Editor's Note when it fired music critic Justin Mitchell for plagiarism. The *St. Louis Post-Dispatch* refused to discuss the punishment it gave to reporter Renee Stovsky for borrowing paragraphs from the *San Jose Mercury-News*. "I'm not going to tell you what specifically happened to her," said editor William Woo. "We take internal actions on a wide variety of matters that have to do with how well men and women do their jobs. They are between us and their personnel file."[17]

FROM PLAGIARISM TO FABRICATION

Journalistic fabrication, or passing off phony characters and stories as real, is a less common impropriety than plagiarism. The first big scandal involving fictionalized reporting occurred in 1981 when Janet Cooke, a young black reporter for the *Washington Post*, wrote a feature report entitled "Jimmy's Story," a sensational account of an 8-year-old heroin addict in Washington, D.C. The child's real name was withheld in the article, and indeed, Cooke's editor, Milton Coleman, did not ask Cooke for the name of the child, his mother, or their address, all in the name of confidentiality of sources.

Ironically, Bob Woodward of Watergate fame, whose confidential source "Deep Throat" was central to that historic story, was involved here as well, serving at the time as assistant managing editor for the metropolitan news (Metro) division. "In a way, both she and the story were almost too good to be true," he recalls. "This story was so well written and tied together so well that my alarm bells simply didn't go off. My skepticism left me. I was personally negligent."[18]

As soon as "Jimmy's Story" hit the streets, calls flooded the *Post* switchboard, most of them expressing outrage that nothing was being done to find and help the young addict. The D.C. police force responded with an intensive city-wide search, and the word on the street was that the police were prepared to offer up to $10,000 for the boy. When the search proved futile, Washington's black mayor and black police chief concluded that the child did not exist. D.C. mayor Marion Barry declared, "I've been told the story is part myth, part reality. We all have agreed that we don't believe that the mother or the pusher would allow a reporter to see them shoot up."

Some of the *Post's* black editors and reporters also doubted the authenticity of Cooke's story. Vivian Aplin-Brownlee, who was Cooke's first editor at the *Post*, said, "I never believed it, and I told Milton [Coleman] that." Courtland Milloy, a *Post* columnist, began doubting the story after spending seven hours driving Cooke through the area where she claimed to have met with the boy and his mother. After the unsuccessful attempt to locate the house, Milloy knew something was wrong. "It didn't take long to see that she didn't know the area," he said.[19]

Despite their growing doubts, the *Post's* editors continued to support Cooke's story and assert her First Amendment right to protect her sources. Indeed, *Post* editors wanted to submit the story for a variety of journalistic prizes. Coleman suggested that the story be nominated for the Sigma Delta Chi award, the Heywood Brown award, the Ellis Willis Scripps award, the Robert F. Kennedy award, and, of course, a Pulitzer Prize.

How could a story about which so many doubts had circulated be submitted for a Pulitzer? Woodward said, "I think that the decision to nominate the story for Pulitzer is of minimal consequence. . . . It is a brilliant story, fake and fraud that it is."[20]

Cooke actually won the Pulitzer, and the public announcement of the award was scheduled for April 13. But her deception soon began to unravel through a seemingly harmless series of events. Because of her celebrity status, newspapers across the country began preparing stories on Cooke. One paper, the *Toledo Blade*, noticed a discrepancy in Cooke's biography. The material provided by Cooke to the Pulitzer board said she had studied at the Sorbonne, had a master's degree from the University of Toledo and an undergraduate degree from Vassar, and spoke or read French, Spanish, Portuguese, and Italian. The *Blade* confirmed that Cooke had attended Vassar for only one year and had never attended the Sorbonne.

When the discrepancies were brought to Coleman's attention, he scheduled a meeting with Cooke and asked for an explanation. Cooke admitted that she had not graduated from Vassar but claimed that all the other information was correct. More important, she said that "Jimmy's Story" was true. Coleman didn't believe her. Executive editor Ben Bradlee and Bob Woodward were asked to join the meeting, and the questioning continued.

Cooke began to cry. Bradlee asked her to say something in Portuguese. She couldn't. He asked if she knew any Italian. She said no. She had similar difficulty with French. Soon, no one in the room believed either her resumé or her story. Bradlee made an accusation: "You're like Richard Nixon—you're trying to cover up."

Woodward told her, "I don't believe you on the 'Jimmy' story." It was the first time that Woodward had admitted it, even to himself.

David Maraniss, deputy Metro editor and a friend of Cooke's, joined the group, and the others left the two of them alone in the room. They talked for an hour. Finally, Maraniss said that if she would tell him the truth, he would explain it to the others. She would not have to humiliate herself before them.

"There is no Jimmy and no family," said Cooke. "It was a fabrication. I did so much work on it, but it's a composite. I want to give the prize back."

The others returned to the room. "I'm sorry I was such a son-of-a-bitch," Woodward said to Cooke.

"I deserved it," she responded.

The following day, she submitted her resignation and a written statement admitting the fabrication. The statement concluded: "I apologize to my newspaper, my profession, the Pulitzer board and all seekers of the truth."[21]

When the dust settled after the Janet Cooke scandal, it appeared that many major newspapers had learned their lesson. More demanding standards were imposed on reporters and editors with respect to anonymous sources. But the primary causes for Cooke's transgressions—personal ambition, competitive pressure, and editorial room indulgence—remained. It was only a matter of time before a similar scandal would surface. The most serious spate of journalistic fabrication occurred in 1998 when three media celebrities were disgraced for fictionalizing their reporting. Mike Barnicle and Patricia Smith of the *Boston Globe* and Stephen Glass of *The New Republic* met disaster within weeks of each other as the result their overactive imaginations.

Over a period of twenty-five years, Mike Barnicle's hard-boiled but sentimental coverage of the Boston working class earned him a reputa-

As an investigative reporter at the *Washington Post* during the 1972 Watergate scandal, Bob Woodward made heavy use of anonymous sources. A decade later, as an assistant managing editor at the *Post*, he had to fire reporter Janet Cooke for fabricating news stories under the cover of anonymous sources. Photo reproduced from the collections of the Library of Congress.

Admiral Thomas Moorer, chairman of the Joint Chiefs in 1970, found himself embroiled years later in the controversial Tailwind story concerning a secret military operation in Laos. Photo reproduced from the collections of the Library of Congress.

tion as the voice of the *Globe*. His outspoken style attracted controversy, but his political connections to the Kennedy family and California senator John Tunney insulated him from criticism. Through Tunney, Barnicle became friends with actor Robert Redford, adding further to the Barnicle mystique. Over time the mythology came to include claims that Barnicle wrote speeches for Bobby Kennedy and helped write the screenplay for *The Candidate*, Robert Redford's acclaimed 1972 film. Neither was true, but Barnicle did little to discourage such beliefs.

Barnicle's first major journalistic embarrassment occurred in 1973 when he wrote about the response of a Jewish gas station attendant, Edward Schrottman, to the racial changes in his neighborhood. Barnicle's column quoted Schrottman as saying that the neighborhood was "OK if you're a nigger."

Schrottman subsequently denied having said any such thing and took Barnicle to court. A judge ordered the *Globe* to pay Schrottman $40,000, noting that Barnicle had "interlineated" his notes, that is, scribbled Schrottman's name above the quote, apparently after the fact, in an effort to cover up the fact that it was manufactured.[22]

Accusations of plagiarism against Barnicle were also beginning to surface. *Globe* editor Matthew Storin said he received a complaint in the early 1980s about similarities between a column by Mike Royko and a Barnicle piece. Storin asked Barnicle if he got the material from Royko. Barnicle said no. "End of story," said Storin.[23]

Not quite. Barnicle's frequent appropriation of other writers' ideas and language was becoming a running joke. Royko, in particular, charged that at least three other Barnicle columns were either stolen or were strangely similar to his own. Barnicle also published a rewritten version of Jimmy Cannon's famous "Loser's Christmas" column and lifted quotes from an A. J. Liebling biography of Earl (Huey) Long. The *Globe*'s editors were willing to accommodate Barnicle's questionable practices because he was such a popular columnist, but by this time Barnicle had developed a disturbing new pattern. Instead of borrowing other reporters' stories and characters, he began making them up entirely.

Editors at the *Globe* discovered that most of the characters in Barnicle's columns were unverifiable. Still, they did nothing. "[A] good chunk of senior editors . . . gave him a lot more ethical running room than the rest of us," confided one newsroom source. "There were a lot of Barnicle enablers here."

In December 1993 Barnicle wrote a column about two unnamed off-duty policemen who caught two thieves breaking into a van, loaded them into the trunk of their car, drove them around for a couple of hours, threatened to kill them, and eventually let them walk away. The story caused a sensation. The *Globe*'s deputy managing editor wanted to assign a reporter to follow up and verify sources, but nothing more could be found about the tale. *Globe* editor Storin later warned Barnicle, "Mike, if you play with the truth, your whole career goes down." Storin says Barnicle responded with a shrug.[24]

At this point, a parallel tale of journalistic duplicity involving another *Globe* columnist was about to unfold. Patricia Smith, a bright, young black woman representing the *Globe*'s future, not its past, was hired in 1994 as part of a movement to make the paper reflect Boston's changing demographics. *Globe* editor Matthew Storin was fully aware that Smith, while previously working for the *Chicago Sun-Times*, had apparently written a review of a concert that she did not attend. Indeed, Storin was editor at the *Sun-Times* when Smith was reprimanded. "I called her in," recalled Storin, "put the fear of God in her, and that was the end of that."[25]

That episode was apparently only the beginning. By late 1995 the *Globe*'s assistant managing editor, Walter Robinson, began to suspect that some of Smith's columns were fictionalized. Feedback from the newsroom and a call from a reader led Robinson to review all ninety of Smith's 1995 columns. A column about Q-Silver, a supposed local gangbanger, stuck out like a sore thumb. Q-Silver's interview sound more like scripted dialogue than street talk. Another column featured the homespun musings of a character named Ernie Keane, who was hoping to meet with President Clinton. Robinson personally investigated the Keane column, checking voter registration rolls, motor vehicle registrations, and other databases. There was no Ernie Keane. Robinson called every Keane in the phone book, but no one knew an Ernie Keane. Similar checks on other characters in Smith's columns came up blank.

By the time he finished, Robinson had a list of forty characters that he couldn't find. He concluded that twenty-seven of Smith's columns were fiction and submitted them to Storin. Given the cloud of controversy already surrounding Mike Barnicle, Storin responded by imposing a requirement that Smith, Barnicle, and a third reporter submit information verifying the existence of all major figures appearing in future columns.

The consensus at the *Globe* was that Smith should have been fired, but Storin realized that if he fired Smith he would have to explain why he didn't fire Barnicle. Charges of racism would be inevitable. "To have fired her in January 1996—which everyone agrees would have been a better ending—would have meant dealing with the Barnicle problem then," said a *Globe* staff member.[26] So both remained.

In late 1997 the *Globe*'s editors met in Storin's office to select the best staff work to submit for the Pulitzer Prize, journalism's highest honor. They decided to enter Patricia Smith's work for the prize, despite the fact that at least three editors at that meeting knew of her pattern of journalistic fraud. In early 1998 Smith solidified her journalistic reputation by receiving the Distinguished Writing Award from the American

Society of Newspaper Editors. In April she was named as one of the three finalists for the Pulitzer.

By this time Smith's columns were no longer being checked for authenticity, and they had regained their old eloquence. In May 1998 Smith wrote about a woman named Claire who was dying of cancer. Like most of Smith's characters, Claire was extremely articulate and vaguely identified. Robinson was suspicious and decided once more to investigate Smith's recent columns. As he feared, they were replete with characters whose existence could not be verified. Smith had relapsed. In early June, Robinson and three other editors went to Storin with the bad news.

Storin was stunned, but he knew Smith had to go. On June 17, Smith was presented with a list of six of her characters and asked if they were real. After thinking for a few minutes, she admitted that four of them were fictitious, including Claire, the cancer victim. The next morning Storin asked for Smith's resignation.

Within hours of the announcement of Smith's resignation, Alan Dershowitz, a prominent attorney and syndicated columnist, faxed statements to the local media decrying the fact that a black woman had been fired for the same offenses that a white man, Mike Barnicle, had been committing for years. Faced with a journalistic crisis spreading beyond internal ethics, the *Globe* published a story on June 21 in which Storin admitted that he didn't fire Smith in 1995 because of lingering concerns about Barnicle.

Barnicle fought back in his own column, comparing himself to a martyred Irish revolutionary "shot to death by his own people." It appeared that Barnicle might survive through sheer determination, and in August he attempted to change the subject by writing a humorous column of one-liners. Just three days later, the *Boston Herald* reported that eight of Barnicle's jokes were lifted from George Carlin's best-selling book *Brain Droppings*. Storin immediately suspended Barnicle for a month.

At first, Barnicle insisted that he had never read Carlin's book. Then the local TV station ran a clip of Barnicle recommending it for summer reading. Believing that Barnicle had lied, Storin asked for his resignation. Barnicle turned to his numerous friends in the national media to defend him: Don Imus, Katie Couric, Larry King, Tim Russert, and others.

In early August, Barnicle met twice with *Globe* publisher Benjamin Taylor, who then released a statement saying that the decision on Barnicle "can not and will not be rushed. It involves the integrity and character of the *Globe* and the career of an employee who has served this paper well for 25 years."[27]

The next morning Storin was forced to announce that Barnicle would remain on the staff after serving a two-month suspension. The *Globe*'s minority reporters quickly organized a newsroom petition, signed by the white reporters as well, attacking Storin's reversal. The NAACP and local organizations also publicly criticized the decision to keep Barnicle.

Howell Raines, writing for the *Globe*'s parent paper, the *New York Times*, said, "Mr. Barnicle, like this writer, is a product of a male-dominated, mostly white tribal culture that takes care of its own. . . . Long after Mr. Barnicle settles back into his column, the historical bottom line of this event will be that a white guy with the right connections got pardoned for offenses that would have taken down a minority or female journalist."[28]

Meanwhile, journalists around the country were doing their own check on Barnicle's columns, and doing it better than the *Globe* had done. On August 18, Kenneth Tomlinson, former editor of *Reader's Digest*, wrote to the *Globe* saying that his editors had been unable to verify an earlier Barnicle column that the *Digest* had wanted to reprint. The column told of a black family and a white family, one rich and one poor, whose children became friends while fighting cancer. The *Digest*'s staff couldn't verify the existence of either family, said Tomlinson, and when Barnicle refused to help, "we concluded the column was fabricated."[29]

After *Globe* editors were unable to verify the column themselves, the paper asked once more for Barnicle's resignation, and this time Barnicle complied. His wide-ranging media connections began to crumble. He was given three-month leaves from his local TV show and from MSNBC, where he was a commentator. Public television's *NewsHour with Jim Lehrer* dismissed him. Although he would later make a remarkable comeback in television, he would never regain the full confidence of the public or of his journalistic colleagues.

Meanwhile, Patricia Smith, exiled from journalism, has embraced the poetry community, thanking it for standing by her in time of need. "When people in journalism who I thought were friends outside of our jobs just kind of freaked out and left skid marks running in the other direction, the poetry community rose up and went around me and just sheltered me," she said.[30]

Who could have predicted that even as Smith and Barnicle were beginning their downfall at the *Globe*, a third prominent journalist would be caught red-handed and dismissed in disgrace for fictionalizing his reporting? Stephen Glass was, in many ways, the most shameless of the three in spinning his fraudulent columns in *The New Republic (TNR)*. Glass had risen to associate editor at *TNR*, and his credits included contracts with *George* and *Rolling Stone*. But his house of cards began tumbling after a May 1998 column about a teenage computer hacker who was offered a lucrative position with the very company whose computer system he had penetrated.

Adam Penenberg, a technology reporter for the online publication

Forbes Digital Tool, initially thought he had been scooped. "It sounded amazing," he said. "I assumed it was true and that I missed it." Penenberg wanted to do a follow-up, but he could find nothing to substantiate the existence of the mysterious teenager or the company that supposedly recruited him. *Digital Tool* then did an in-depth search of every questionable entry in Glass's column, checking with the police, the Highway Patrol, the Justice Department, the FBI, the U.S. Customs Department, and any source that might have relevant information. They found nothing. Meanwhile, the enterprising Glass had gone to extraordinary lengths to cover his fraud, creating forged notes and interview transcripts and a Web page for the fictitious company, including a phone number that actually belonged to his brother's cell phone. Penenberg smelled a rat.

After Glass refused to return his calls, Penenberg reported his suspicions to *The New Republic*'s editor, Charles Lane, who began his own investigation. On May 8, Lane fired Glass after determining "to a moral certainty that the entire article is made up."[31] On June 1, 1998, *TNR* ran a penitent editorial, admitting that Glass's "hacker" article "was made up out of whole cloth" and that "a preliminary investigation of Glass's previous work suggests that there may be others." The editorial concluded, "[I]t is important to understand that our editing and fact-checking systems are designed to defend against the errors and mistakes that even good professionals sometimes make—not against the systematic and intentional deceptions of someone who has no business practicing journalism. We assumed that no person who calls himself a journalist . . . would attempt to work with us on any other basis. In Stephen Glass's case, this assumption was not warranted."[32]

Lane later declared, "Glass is a man without honor who operated out of hostility and contempt; he has no place in journalism. I've been wracking my brain to try to understand how this could have happened."[33] Within days of Glass's dismissal, the evidence against him had accumulated far beyond one phony story. Howard Kurtz, media writer for the *Washington Post*, found numerous unsubstantiated claims among Glass's articles. Eric Pooley of *Time* magazine concluded that Glass was "something rare in journalism: a genuine con man who made up not just quotations, but people, corporations, legislation."[34]

MODERN MUCKRAKING: IRRESPONSIBLE JOURNALISM OR CRUSADING REPORTERS?

The scandals involving plagiarism and fabrication in modern journalism were covered by the national media with nervous reluctance. For the most part, these stories were carried in the features sections of newspapers, if at all, and the media's obvious embarrassment at examining such issues gave the stories a short shelf life. The one kind of journalistic scandal that has demonstrated front page appeal and the ability to stay in the news derives from stories whose very content shocks and angers the political establishment, challenges the country's historical mythology, and arouses the hostility of the mainstream media itself.

Two such scandals erupted in the late 1990s, resulting in the same kinds of journalistic recrimination and soul-searching that followed the revelations of plagiarism and fabricated stories. As with the other scandals, the journalistic landscape was soon littered with fired journalists and editors, who, this time, were charged primarily with overreaching in their coverage of an incendiary issue. These were no mere newsroom squabbles over professional niceties. The stories challenged national morality and national security, a throwback to the muckrakers of the past.

In July 1995, Gary Webb, a respected investigative journalist working for the *San Jose Mercury-News*, received a message on his answering machine that would turn into the biggest story of his life—and his worst nightmare. The message was from a young woman whose boyfriend, Rafael Cornejo, was in prison awaiting trial on cocaine trafficking charges. When Webb called her back, she told him there was something about Cornejo's case that might interest him. "One of the government's witnesses is a guy who used to work with the CIA selling drugs," she told Webb. "Tons of it."[35]

For the next year and a half Webb researched the story of drug running by the CIA-backed rebel army in Nicaragua, the Contras. In a three-part series that appeared on August 18 through 20, 1998, in the *Mercury News*, Webb reported that CIA-backed supporters of the Contras had raised money by importing crack cocaine and selling it to Los Angeles street gangs. The articles did not state that the CIA itself was behind the drug dealing or was even aware of it, but many readers drew that conclusion. And thus began a national controversy of monumental proportions.

Some critics of the *Mercury News* series complained about the Web site for the story, which, in addition to supplying all source documents for the series, displayed a logo showing a man smoking a crack pipe superimposed over the CIA seal. This was meant to signify the clear CIA connection to the Contras, whose drug trafficking was well documented. The Web site itself, like the newspaper series, made no claims of direct CIA complicity and the logo never appeared in print, but it contributed to the frenzied public response, particularly in the black community.

Initially the *Mercury News* story was largely ignored by the major national media, but the growing public furor soon brought charges of a press coverup. Finally, on October 4, 1996, the *Washington Post* ran a front page story by Robert Suro and Walter Pincus under the headline, "The CIA and Crack: Evidence Is Lacking of Alleged Plot." The headline itself was misleading because the *Mercury News* series alleged no plot, but the content of the *Post* story dealt more directly with Webb's conclusions. Suro and Pincus declared that "available information does not support the conclusion that the CIA-backed contras—or Nicaraguans in general—played a major role in the emergence of crack as a narcotic in widespread use across the United States."[36]

The *Post* article affirmed what earlier congressional investigations had revealed: that some of the Contras and their supporters "were involved in drug smuggling in the region at a time when the CIA was deeply involved in contra operations there." In addition, Suro and Pincus said senior CIA officers and government officials admitted, "The CIA knew about some of these activities and did little or nothing to stop them." Where the *Post* article differed from Webb's account was in its conclusion that drug trafficking by the Contras and their supporters "accounted for only a small portion of the nation's cocaine trade."[37]

Not everyone found the *Post*'s article convincing. For one thing, Walter Pincus had himself been an undercover CIA agent as a young man, a fact that cast doubt on his credibility in defending the agency against Webb's charges. Even the *Post*'s own ombudsman, Geneva Overholser, was disappointed in the way Pincus addressed the question of the CIA's drug connection. "The *Post* . . . showed more passion for sniffing out the flaws in San Jose's answer than for sniffing out a better answer themselves," she wrote.[38]

But two other major newspapers, the *New York Times* and the *Los Angeles Times*, quickly followed with their own stories critical of Webb's series. Like the *Post* article, these stories did not challenge the fundamental information presented in the *Mercury News* series, but they denied a direct CIA connection with the domestic crack epidemic. Journalist Charles Bowden analyzed the articles in the *Post, New York Times*, and *Los Angeles Times*. "A common chord ran through the responses of all three papers: It never really happened, and if it did happen, it was on a small scale, and anyway it was old news. . . . What is missing from the press responses, despite their length, is a sense that anyone spent as much energy investigating Webb's case as attempting to refute it."[39]

Other critics suggested that the topic of the *Mercury News* series was too sensitive for normal journalistic standards to apply. Joann Byrd, editorial page editor of the *Seattle Post-Intelligencer*, complained, "The paper, in order to act responsibly, needed to recognize this story was going to have a huge impact, not just on the black community, but on everyone's faith in the government."[40] Even staff members at the *Mercury News* began to express similar concerns. "The relationship between the CIA, the drug-runners and black America is a sensitive topic," said Phil Yost, the paper's chief editorial writer. "We have not served well the cause of getting at the truth; we have served the cause of creating a sensation."[41]

As the media quibbled over the extent of CIA involvement in the American drug trade, anger grew among African Americans. CIA director John Deutch met with residents of South-Central Los Angeles to argue that the CIA had played no role in the city's crack cocaine epidemic. Few of those attending the meeting were convinced.

Meanwhile, even as the attacks on Webb were reaching a crescendo, he was honored with the Journalist of the Year award from the Northern California chapter of the Society of Professional Journalists (SPJ). Dave McElhatton, the well-known anchor for San Francisco's CBS affiliate, KPIX, presented the award to Webb, explaining, "Elements of the *Mercury News* series and presentation are open to dispute, as are criticisms of Webb's stories. A full airing is necessary and good for us all. But the [SPJ] chapter is convinced that the best journalism is that which is not afraid to venture into controversial areas of overwhelming national significance."[42]

McElhatton's comments summarized the crux of the controversy. Webb's severest critics did not dispute most of the factual detail in his series, and even his conclusions were accepted as at least arguable. The problem, said the critics, was that Webb had oversold the story, embarrassed the government, and cast doubt on its good faith.

Accompanying Webb at the award ceremony was his editor, Jerry Ceppos, who had himself received much criticism for the series. After accepting his award Webb turned to Ceppos and asked for his continuing support, drawing the parallel with a bomber pilot who receives most of the flak when he is over the target.

Ceppos was coming under increasing pressure to separate himself and the *Mercury News* from the controversial series. The newsroom tension eventually reached the point at which Ceppos and the other *Mercury News* editors told Webb to stop advancing the story and concentrate instead on a written response to the three major newspapers that had criticized it.

Webb argued, "The best way to shut them up is to put the rest of what we know in the paper and keep plowing ahead." Ceppos responded, "I don't want to get into a war with them,"[43] but he reluctantly agreed to let Webb make one more trip to Central America to pin down the CIA/Contra drug connection. Webb flew to Costa Rica and found an eyewitness, on the record, who had delivered drug money to the Contras and a top CIA official who admitted that the agency had received reports of the drug trafficking. But by the time Webb put the story together, Ceppos had decided to throw in the towel.

On March 25, 1997, Ceppos called Webb at his home and said the *Mercury News* was going to print a letter to its readers acknowledging mistakes in the series. Among the mistakes to be acknowledged was the failure to use the word "estimate" when describing the millions of drug dollars that went to the Contras. The editorial apology would also claim that the series had "oversimplified" the origins of the crack epidemic in the United States.

Webb was shocked. At a meeting with the *Mercury News* editors he asked, "How can we honestly say that we don't know that millions of dollars went to the Contras, or that the CIA didn't know about this, when we've got an eyewitness telling us that he personally gave drug money to a CIA agent?"

Ceppos responded, "You and I have very different views of the situation."

Webb warned, "You run this, and all we'll hear is 'The *Mercury News* has admitted it isn't true! The Contras weren't dealing cocaine! The CIA had nothing to do with it!' and you know as well as I do, that's not true."

Jonathan Krim, the editor who had most opposed the story, replied, "Well, you're the one who's always saying that we can't be held responsible for what other people read into things."

Webb would later recall, "There it is, I thought. The truth. They want the public to think there was nothing here. They want it all to go away. They're tired of fighting the current of mainstream opinion, tired of being journalistic outcasts."[44]

Webb was told there would be no more reporting on the story and was ordered to remove the Web site logo with the CIA seal. A few days later Webb was told to report to Ceppos to discuss his future with the *Mercury News*. At that meeting Ceppos announced that Webb would be reassigned to the West Bureau in Cupertino, California, the newspaper's "no-man's-land."

On November 19, 1997, under terms arbitrated by the Newspaper Guild, Gary Webb quit the news business after nineteen years as a reporter. Subsequently he has said, "Had I done what my editors wanted—kept my mouth shut and gone along with the charade—I would probably still be working at the newspaper. But I had no desire to hang around a place that was so easily cowed by the opinion of others. A reporter's job was to pursue the truth, I still believed, no matter how unpopular that pursuit became."[45]

Despite Webb's departure, the controversy persists. Many journalists believe that the mainstream media initially missed the story and then suppressed it. Bob Parry, the Associated Press reporter who first broke the Contra drug story in 1985, wrote a letter of condolence to Webb. "Like you, I grew up in the business thinking our job really was to tell the truth," wrote Parry. "By the 1990s, the media had become the monster. I wish it weren't so. All I ever wanted to do was report and write interesting stories—while getting paid for it. But that really isn't possible anymore and there's no use crying over it."[46]

Charles Bowden, writing for *Esquire*, took a similar view. "Gary Webb wrote a series of articles that said some bad things about the CIA and drug traffickers. The CIA denied the charges, and every major newspaper in the country took the agency's word for it. Gary Webb was ruined. Which is a shame, because he was right."[47]

But much of the media remained unconvinced. "In the end," wrote Alicia Shepard in the *American Journalism Review*, "many would argue that, by leading reasonable readers to believe that the CIA played a role in the origin of the crack explosion, the paper hurt its credibility, hurt journalism, caused irreparable damage in the black community and shed little light on the question of whether the CIA looked the other way while cocaine was smuggled into this country. Webb and his reporting have become as much the issue as the CIA and crack."[48]

The final official response to the controversy came on May 11, 2000, when the House Intelligence Committee issued a report saying it found no evidence of a CIA conspiracy to bring drugs into the United States. "Bottom line: the allegations were false," said committee chairman Porter J. Goss (R-Fla.).[49]

Shortly after Webb's controversial story on crack cocaine, a perhaps even more sensitive exposé hit the headlines. In June 1998 the media conglomerate Time/Warner, whose massive corporate holdings include *Time* magazine and the Cable News Network (CNN), introduced a project produced jointly by *Time* and CNN. Their televised report about Operation Tailwind, a secret 1970 U.S. military action in Laos, was the June 7 premiere show on CNN's *NewsStand: CNN & Time*. It was accompanied by a piece in *Time* entitled "Did the U.S. Drop Nerve Gas?" The *NewsStand* story, "Valley of Death," was the result of an eight-month investigation by CNN producers April Oliver and Jack Smith into allegations that sarin nerve gas was used by U.S. forces in Laos, possibly against U.S. military personnel suspected of defecting.

The *Time* story, which ran under the byline of CNN's April Oliver and Peter Arnett, began with a description of Operation Tailwind. A U.S. Special Forces unit had just wiped out a village base camp, said *Time*, "killing about 100 people that included not only women and children but also what some believed to be a group of American G.I.s who had defected to the enemy." After the American commandos came under heavy assault by a superior force of Vietnamese troops, Robert Van Buskirk, then a 26-year-old lieutenant in the unit, radioed for air support from two waiting A-1 Skyraiders that were to drop gas canisters containing what Van Buskirk called "the bad of the bad." The *Time* article described the results: "The G.I.s heard the canisters exploding and saw a wet fog envelop the Vietnamese soldiers as they dropped to the ground, vomiting and convulsing."[50]

Van Buskirk recalled, "All I see is bodies. They are not fighting anymore. They are just lying, some on their sides, some on their backs. They are no longer combatants."

Official military records say the Skyraiders dropped CBU-30—cluster bombs containing CS, a particularly virulent tear gas. But the *Time* article declared that military officials with knowledge of Operation Tailwind had told *NewsStand: CNN & Time* that "the gas dropped 25 years ago in Laos was nerve gas, specifically sarin."

Time quoted Admiral Thomas Moorer, chairman of the Joint Chiefs in 1970, confirming and justifying the use of sarin in Operation Tailwind. Other military officials told *Time* that sarin was also used the night before in order to prepare for the attack on the village. *Time* said, "[T]he targeted village was believed to be harboring a large group of American G.I.s who had defected to the enemy. The Special Forces unit's job was to kill them."[51]

Like the CNN broadcast, the *Time* article provided substantial detail on the American use of sarin, its effect on its victims (including some American commandos who were exposed to wind-blown gas), and the sighting of presumed American defectors among the enemy forces.

Needless to say, the story raised a firestorm of protest and criticism from the Pentagon and, as in the CIA/crack story, from the media itself. Immediately after the story was aired and published, CNN and *Time* were deluged with outraged calls. Initially the complaints came from Special Forces veterans, but soon former secretary of state Henry Kissinger and former chairman of the Joint Chiefs Colin Powell weighed in, followed by numerous Pentagon officials. CNN's own in-house military analyst, Major General Perry Smith (ret.) quit the network, claiming that CNN had failed to check the story with him. If it had, he said, he would have told them that there was no nerve gas in Vietnam and that the story had done serious damage to U.S. foreign policy.[52]

Oliver and Smith had submitted a 156-page briefing book on the story to all relevant superiors at CNN, all of whom signed off on it, but CNN and *Time* had not anticipated the violent official reaction. As the controversy continued to build, CNN/USA president Rick Kaplan put through a conference call to the story's producers, assuring the team that "this is not a journalism problem, it's a PR problem."[53]

When even the media began to criticize the story, *Time* was the first to blink. On June 29, *Time* published a statement distancing itself from CNN's reporting on the story. The statement recounted the strenuous denials from military experts, including CNN's own analyst, and concluded: "We believed that the original CNN report and article were based on substantial evidence. But we believe that the doubts raised deserve full exploration. So we plan to keep reporting this story. We also await the results of the Pentagon investigation, due out shortly. When we get more of these facts and, we hope, a clearer picture of what may have happened, we will report them to you, correct any mistakes and try to clarify any disputes that remain."[54]

Tom Johnson, CNN's chief executive, ordered April Oliver and Jack Smith, the producers of the CNN show, to assist the Pentagon in its investigation of the nerve gas charges. Meanwhile, retired military officers were threatening to pressure CNN's advertisers and local cable companies to sever their connections with CNN. Under such pressure, some of the story's sources were moved to hedge on their original statements. The atmosphere at CNN changed quickly from damage control to hysterical retreat. Johnson and Kaplan commissioned prominent media lawyer Floyd Abrams to work with David Kohler, senior vice president and general counsel of CNN, to examine the nerve gas story and prepare a report judging its accuracy.

In just over a week Abrams and Kohler compiled a 54-page report that concluded, "[A]lthough the broadcast was prepared after exhaustive research, was rooted in considerable supportive data, and reflected the deeply held beliefs of the CNN journalists who prepared it, the central thesis of the broadcast could not be sustained at the time of the broadcast and cannot be sustained now.... CNN's conclusion that United States troops used nerve gas during the Vietnamese conflict on a mission in Laos designed to kill American defectors is insupportable." The Abrams report acknowledged that Oliver and Smith committed no "falsification of an intentional nature" but said "CNN should retract the broadcast and apologize to the public."[55]

On July 2, CNN acknowledged serious faults in the Tailwind story and retracted it. Tom Johnson delivered the announcement: "We apologize to our viewers and to our colleagues at *Time* for this mistake."[56]

Oliver and Smith were promptly fired, and Peter Arnett was reprimanded and later fired. Johnson himself twice submitted his resignation but was retained at the insistence of Ted Turner, vice-chairman of Time Warner.

On July 13, *Time* published its retraction under the headline, "Tailwind: An Apology." *Time* said its findings "matched those reached by Abrams for CNN. The allegations about the use of nerve gas and the killing of defectors are not supported by the evidence." The *Time* statement concluded, "Like CNN, we retract the story and apologize. Our credibility is our most important asset. When we make mistakes, it's important to be open and honest about them, get all the facts out as quickly as possible and try to set the record straight. And to say we're sorry. We are."[57]

Norman Pearlstine, editor in chief of *Time* magazine, said the Tailwind fiasco was a classic breakdown in the relationship between reporters and editors. "If I fault myself at all, it's that, when the story came in to *Time*, I didn't fully appreciate that it was a controversial piece," he said. "I was saying, it's a twenty-eight-year-old story that's kind of interesting, but more of a footnote than something that's going to generate a lot of heat. So I probably should have been smarter about that."[58]

Richard Kaplan, head of CNN/USA, said the big problem was that Oliver and Smith had "fallen in love with their story . . . one of the biggest problems that any journalist can have."[59]

Jack Smith had quite a different view. "The only love affair going on was Rick Kaplan's love affair with his big-time job running a network," he said. "He didn't stand behind this story because he likes the power, he likes the money, he likes being boss just a little too much."[60]

Oliver and Smith were outraged by the Abrams/Kohler report, and they prepared a 77-page report of their own, rebutting all the charges in the Abrams/Kohler report. When their published rebuttal was largely ignored by the media, they attempted to speak directly to the public. "We got a star chamber proceeding," [a show trial with preordained outcome] said Smith. "It's a sham report, a fake that allowed the company to lynch us and get this behind them." Smith expressed disappointment at CNN's weakness in the face of political pressure and continued to defend the Tailwind story. "Tom Johnson caved in to the commercial pressure being brought on him," he said. "Kaplan caved. Johnson caved."[61]

In an op-ed piece for the *Washington Post*, Oliver was even more outspoken. "The Abrams/Kohler report was delivered to support a corporate whitewash, driven by executive fear, to avoid further controversy in the press, with the Pentagon and on Capitol Hill," she wrote. "One of the primary reasons CNN sacrificed this story was to protect its relationship with the Pentagon. Tragically, the CNN retraction, driven by enormous pressure and a hasty star chamber investigation, will paralyze further reporting of these serious matters and of other past and, more important, future black operations by America's secret army."[62]

The major sources for the story, particularly Admiral Moorer, former head of the Joint Chiefs, never retracted their original comments, although a number of other sources recanted. Oliver has said, "Remember, every individual on Tailwind was trained in plausible deniability."[63]

The mainstream media has not been supportive of Oliver and Smith. "The thing that's been most shocking to me," says Oliver, "is how passive the press corps has been, particularly the defense reporters who just seem to sit there and lap the briefings up instead of playing the skeptical role they're supposed to play." Oliver and Smith say they are being held to a previously unheard-of standard for investigative reporting: "proof beyond a reasonable doubt." Oliver observes, "By this standard, there would have been no Watergate."[64]

The substance of the Tailwind story soon receded from public view as the media focused exclusively on the controversy surrounding the reporters. "[I]t took less brainpower, less skill, and less resources to write the titillating media story . . . ," explains Oliver. "This is just more 'Entertainment Tonight'."[65]

Perhaps the clearest indication of the transformation of the Tailwind story into "infotainment" came in November 1998, when the popular TV military series *JAG* depicted a former ace pilot turned lawyer investigating a press report on the U.S. use of nerve gas to kill fellow Americans during the Persian Gulf War. The *JAG* episode, based on the real-life Tailwind story, cleared the U.S. military of any wrongdoing. More important, the episode drew its largest audience ever—about 17.1 million viewers, compared to only about 722,000 viewers for the original CNN telecast of the Tailwind story.[66]

There may be more serious journalistic fallout from the Tailwind controversy. On September 29, 1999, the Associated Press (AP) ran a powerful investigative story recounting a 1950 massacre of South Korean refugees by American troops.[67] The story had actually been completed in late July 1998, almost simultaneous with the Tailwind controversy, but AP president Louis Boccardi held the story for fourteen months. "There's absolutely no question that he wanted to shut down the effort and drop the story," said Robert Port, who subsequently resigned as AP's special assignment editor. Boccardi told Port that even if he could prove every detail of the story, "we don't have to be the ones to tell it. This isn't what we do."

Port acknowledged, "In the end, the AP did the right thing. They just had to be dragged kicking and screaming." Still, Boccardi insisted that words such as "massacre" and "war crimes" be deleted. "Every quotation from soldiers saying 'I committed a massacre' was expunged and censored from the story," said Port.

But what occurred after the story ran was an eerie echo of the Tailwind hysteria. Veterans groups began to criticize the story, and a few magazines, including *U.S. News and World Report*, joined in. Unlike the Tailwind fiasco, most of the media supported the story, but the public recriminations were ugly. "It looks like there are some veterans who don't like the message and are trying to kill the loudest messenger," concluded Port.[68]

Perhaps the most shocking example of this approach came in April 2000, when retired General Barry McCaffrey, the subject of a planned *New Yorker* magazine article about the Persian Gulf War, conducted a preemptive strike on the article's author, Pulitzer prize-winner Seymour Hersh. Hersh had won the Pulitzer in 1978 for exposing the My Lai massacre in Vietnam.

Having heard that the article in progress would document charges that the 24th Infantry Division, under McCaffrey's leadership during the Gulf War, had conducted a massacre of Iraqi noncombatants and prisoners of war, McCaffrey exploited his position as White House "Drug Czar" in an attempt to squelch the story. As director of the White House Office of National Drug Control Policy in the Clinton administration, McCaffrey used White House stationery and taxpayer funded services to send private correspondence and photocopied articles critical of Hersh to news organizations around the country.[69]

Howard Kurtz, the *Washington Post*'s media critic, commented that in making the material available to the *Post*, "McCaffrey is adopting the increasingly popular tactic of a news subject trying to make the journalist the issue before he delivers his findings."[70]

White House spokesman Joe Lockhart said the Hersh article was "another in a series of articles by a journalist who thinks if you throw enough stuff up against the wall, maybe something will stick. It's an attempt to gratuitously go after public officials and an attempt to try to revive a journalist's career."

The day before the *New Yorker* published Hersh's article, a White House aide to McCaffrey sent faxes to half-a-dozen human rights organizations saying, "Would ask for your help to discredit the Hersh article from your personal perspective."[71]

The big names in the military were quickly summoned to deny Hersh's charges. Retired General Norman Schwarzkopf, former Gulf War commander, expressed "100 percent support" for McCaffrey, and General Colin Powell, former chairman of the Joint Chiefs, was quick to follow.[72] However, a number of less-prominent military men were willing to step forward and verify Hersh's account. "[T]here was no need to be shooting anybody," said Lt. General James H. Johnson Jr. "They [the Iraqis] couldn't surrender fast enough. The war was over."[73]

Conservative syndicated columnist Robert Novak noted that the White House, Congress, the Pentagon, and leaders of both political parties had turned a blind eye on Hersh's charges. "The governmental establishment's attitude is that the horrifying events Hersh alleges in the *New Yorker* magazine never happened, but we don't want to know about it if they did. Since Hersh's Gulf War exposé was published two weeks ago, military and political leaders have joined to kill the messenger." Novak said that McCaffrey's "turkey shoot" had been whispered about for years inside the military. One retired army officer told him, "Hersh has it about 85 percent right. Everybody knows that. The old boys' network has just circled the wagons."[74]

NOTES

1. Cited in Trudy Lieberman, "Plagiarize, Plagiarize, Plagiarize . . . Only Be Sure to Call It Research," *Columbia Journalism Review* (July/August 1995), pp. 1–2. www.cir.org/year/95/4/plagiarize.

2. Philip Terzian, "The Plagiarist's Salon," *The Weekly Standard* (May 11, 1998), p. 2, www.freerepublic.com/forum.

3. Ibid.

4. Ibid.

5. Lieberman, "Plagiarize, Plagiarize, Plagiarize," p. 2.

6. Ibid., pp. 2–4.

7. Ibid.

8. Ibid.

9. Ibid., pp. 5–6.

10. Ibid.

11. Cited in Lisa DePaulo, "The Truth about Ruth," *George* (February 1, 1996), p. 153.

12. Ibid., p. 154.

13. Cited in "Too Much Too Soon?" *American Journalism Review* (December 1995), p. 36.

14. DePaulo, "The Truth about Ruth," p. 154.

15. "Repeat Offender," *MOJO Wire* (January/February 1996), p. 1. bsd.motherjones.com/mother__jones/JF96/outfront.

16. DePaulo, "The Truth about Ruth," p. 154.

17. Cited in Lieberman, "Plagiarize, Plagiarize, Plagiarize," p. 6.

18. Cited in Bill Green, "Janet's World," *Washington Post* (April 19, 1981), A12.

19. Ibid., A13.

20. Ibid., A14.

21. Ibid.

22. Cited in Sean Flynn, "Scandal Racks Hub Daily," *Boston Magazine* (October 5, 1999), p. 13, www.bostonmagazine.com/highlights/.

23. Ibid.

24. Ibid., pp. 14–15.

25. Ibid., p. 5.

26. Ibid. p. 16.

27. Ibid.

28. Howell Raines, "The High Price of Reprieving Mike Barnicle," *New York Times* (August 13, 1998), A22.

29. "You Can Quote Her," *Washington Post* (May 6, 1999), C3.

30. Ibid.

31. Cited in "Shattered Glass at the New Republic," *American Journalism Review: AJR Newslink* (November 2–8, 1999), p. 2, ajr.newslink.org.

32. "To Our Readers," *The New Republic* (June 1, 1998), pp. 8–9.

33. Eric Pooley, "Too Good to Be True," *Time* (May 25, 1998), p. 62.

34. Ibid.

35. Gary Webb, *Dark Alliance: The CIA, the Contras, and the Crack Cocaine Explosion* (New York: Seven Stories Press, 1998), p. 3.

36. Robert Suro and Walter Pincus, "The CIA and Crack: Evidence Is Lacking of Alleged Plot," *Washington Post* (October 4, 1996), A1, A19.

37. Ibid.

38. Charles Bowden, "The Pariah," *Esquire* (September 1998), p. 159.

39. Ibid.

40. Cited in Alicia C. Shepard, "The Web That Gary Spun," *American Journalism Review* (January/February 1997), p. 36.

41. Ibid., p. 37.

42. Ibid., p. 36.

43. Cited in Webb, *Dark Alliance*, p. 470.

44. Ibid., pp. 474–76.

45. Ibid., p. 477.

46. Ibid., p. 480.

47. Bowden, "The Pariah," p. 150.

48. Shepard, "The Web That Gary Spun," p. 45.

49. "House Probe Exonerates CIA on Crack Cocaine Allegations," *Washington Post* (May 12, 2000), A26.

50. April Oliver and Peter Arnett, "Did the U.S. Drop Nerve Gas?" *Time* (June 15, 1998), p. 37.

51. Ibid.

52. Cited in April Oliver, "I Produced That Program—and Was Fired," *Washington Post* (July 12, 1998), C7.

53. Ibid.

54. "To Our Readers: The Nerve Gas Story," *Time* (June 29, 1998), p. 4.

55. Floyd Abrams and David Kohler, "Report on CNN Broadcast 'Valley of Death,'" (July 2, 1998), pp. 1–2, www.freedomforum.org/fpfp/specialprogram/tailwind.contents.

56. Cited in Neil Hickey, "Ten Mistakes That Led to the Great CNN/Time Fiasco," *Columbia Journalism Review* (September/October 1998), p. 28.

57. "Tailwind: An Apology," *Time* (July 13, 1998), p. 6.

58. Norman Pearlstine, "The Trouble with Ground Rules," *Columbia Journalism Review* (October 1998), p. 29.

59. Cited in Hickey, "Ten Mistakes," p. 31.

60. Ibid.

61. Cited in Howard Kurtz, "CNN Staffers Wait for the Other Shoe to Drop," *Washington Post* (July 7, 1998), C7.

62. Oliver, "I Produced That Program—and Was Fired," C7.

63. Cited in Arthur Allen, "April's War: How a Single-Minded Journalist Tripped Over the Ghosts of Vietnam," *Washington Post Magazine* (November 29, 1998), p. 30.

64. Cited in Victoria Calkins, "CNN Reporters Casualty of Corporate and Military Fire," *Censored Alert: The Newsletter of Project Censored* (Summer 1998), p. 3.

65. Ibid.

66. Lisa de Moraes, "'JAG' Tears into CNN Nerve Gas Story with a Vengeance," *Washington Post* (November 12, 1998), C7.

67. Associated Press, "GI's Tell of a U.S. Massacre in Korean War" *Washington Post* (September 30, 1999), A1.

68. Cited in Howard Kurtz, "AP Reporters Facing Fire on 2 Fronts," *Washington Post* (May 16, 2000), C8.

69. Howard Kurtz, "McCaffrey's Preemptive Strike," *Washington Post* (April 18, 2000), C7.

70. Ibid.

71. Howard Kurtz, "Media Notes," *Washington Post* (May 22, 2000), C7.

72. Kurtz, "McCaffrey's Preemptive Strike," C8.

73. Associated Press, "McCaffrey Defends Gulf War Actions in Face of Officers' Quotes," *Washington Post* (May 16, 2000), A22.

74. Robert D. Novak, "An Exposé that Went Thud," *Washington Post* (May 29, 2000), A23.

CHAPTER 8

Anonymous Sources and the Reporter's Privilege

THE REPORTER'S PRIVILEGE

Most journalists agree that there are some stories, often very important stories, that could never be brought to the public unless the sources were promised confidentiality. This is necessary when the information comes from "whistleblowers," that is, individuals who call attention to negligence, abuses, or dangers that threaten the public interest, often from within the very organization in which they work. These people would risk their livelihood, even their personal safety, by speaking on the record to reporters. Such confidential sources played an indispensable role in revealing the Pentagon Papers, the Watergate scandal, and the more recent tobacco industry scandals.

Frequently the government subpoenas reporters in an effort to force them to reveal their sources, but it is a longstanding principle within the journalism profession that such subpoenas are resisted. To do otherwise, journalists say, would dry up their sources and chill the free flow of information to the public.

Such principled journalistic resistance to forced testimony on confidential sources predates the American Revolution. In 1722 Benjamin Franklin's older half-brother, James, was summoned before the Massachusetts Assembly, which demanded that he identify the author of an article in his newspaper, *The New England Courant*. When Franklin refused, he was imprisoned for a month and was prohibited from serving as publisher of the *Courant*. James solved this problem by placing the paper under his brother Ben's name.

Ben himself, who at the time served as an apprentice at the newspaper, was then summoned before the assembly, and he later described the episode: "He [James] was taken up, censur'd, and imprison'd for a month, by the speaker's warrant. . . . I too was taken up and examined before the council; but tho I did not give them any satisfaction, they contented themselves with admonishing me, and dismissed me, considering me, perhaps, as an apprentice, who was bound to keep his master's secrets."[1]

The most widely reported nineteenth-century case in which a reporter was punished for withholding the identity of a source occurred in 1848 while the U.S. Senate debated the treaty to end the Mexican-American War. When John Nugent, a reporter for the *New York Herald*, acquired a confidential draft of the treaty and other secret documents, he was subpoenaed before the Senate and ordered to reveal his source. Nugent refused and was jailed for contempt of Congress.[2]

Throughout the first half of the twentieth century, reporters continued to invoke journalistic principle in protecting the identity of their sources, despite the absence of any legal authority to do so. For example, in *Clein v. State* (1950) the Florida Supreme Court rejected a reporter's appeal of a contempt sentence, arguing that a journalist's professional interest in protecting a source must yield to the public interest in the administration of justice.

The notion of a "reporter's privilege," a legal right to withhold information such as the identities of confidential sources from courts and executive bodies, is a relatively recent phenomenon in American history. Journalists did not even raise First Amendment issues in resisting official demands for the revelation of sources until the 1950s. In 1958 columnist Marie Torre became the first journalist to claim a reporter's privilege under the First Amendment before an appellate court. In *Garland v. Torre* she refused to reveal her source for an allegedly libelous comment about motion picture star Judy Garland, claiming that such forced revelation of a source would violate the First Amendment's free press guarantee by chilling the flow of news to reporters and to the public.

Appeals court judge Potter Stewart, who was named to the U.S. Supreme Court later that same year, wrote the opinion for a unanimous appeals panel that rejected Torre's claim. Stewart said there was no precedent for a First Amendment–based privilege for journalists and that Torre should reveal the identity of her source because it "went to the heart" of Garland's libel claim.[3]

In this climate of judicial indifference to the need for confidentiality of journalists' sources, reporters became the favorite target of government subpoenas. "Prosecutors, criminal defense attorneys and other litigants

In the famous print "Franklin the Printer" by Charles Mills, young Ben Franklin is shown working as an apprentice for *The New England Courant*, a paper owned by his half-brother, James. Ben and James were summoned before the Massachusetts Assembly, which demanded that they identify the author of an article in the paper. Photo reproduced from the collections of the Library of Congress.

The most famous use of anonymous sources by a reporter occurred during Woodward and Bernstein's coverage of President Richard Nixon's cover-up of the 1972 break-in at Democratic Party national headquarters in the Watergate complex. The sensational story eventually led to Nixon's resignation. Photo reproduced from the collections of the Library of Congress.

treated newspapers and television stations like the reference room at the public library," said First Amendment attorney Bruce Sanford. If prosecutors needed a videotape of an automobile accident, they simply subpoenaed the footage from the local station. If a reporter had interviewed an accused person about a crime, the reporter's notes—published and unpublished—were subpoenaed. "This appetite for news material and testimony from reporters began to make the press look like the research arm of law enforcement," stated Sanford. "Besides the disruption to ongoing operations, (reporters couldn't be covering the news if they were sitting around the courthouse waiting to testify), this over-reliance on the media to do the legwork and the homework that could be done by others also endangered the media's appearance of neutrality or impartiality. It didn't take long for reporters to hear from people with stories to tell: 'I'm not talking to you. You'll just tell the cops.' "[4]

For twelve years after *Garland v. Torre* journalists continued to press First Amendment claims for the protection of their sources, but with little success. Finally, in *Caldwell v. United States* (1970), the Ninth Circuit Court of Appeals became the first federal appellate court to recognize such claims. Here, Earl Caldwell, a *New York Times* reporter covering the Black Panthers in California, argued that his appearance before a federal grand jury would jeopardize his working relationship with the Panthers. The appeals court agreed, saying that the government had failed to show a "compelling need" for Caldwell's testimony about possible illegal acts by the Panthers.[5]

The government sought review of the case by the U.S. Supreme Court, which agreed to consider *Caldwell* as part of a trio of cases, including two in which a reporter's privilege had been rejected by lower courts. In one of those cases, *Branzburg v. Hayes* (1971), the Kentucky Court of Appeals had held that Kentucky's law granting a reporter's privilege to withhold confidential sources did not apply to journalists who had witnessed criminal activity. The third case that was consolidated with *Caldwell* and *Branzburg* was *In re Pappas* (1971), in which Paul Pappas, a Massachusetts reporter, was subpoenaed to testify before a grand jury about his confidential dealings with local Black Panther leaders. The Supreme Judicial Court of Massachusetts had held that there was no constitutional privilege allowing a journalist to refuse to appear before a grand jury.

In considering the trio of cases under the case name *Branzburg v. Hayes* (1972), the U.S. Supreme Court conceded that news gathering deserved some First Amendment protection but ruled that the First Amendment did not prohibit any "incidental burdening" of the press caused by enforcement of laws applying to all citizens. In particular, Justice Byron White's majority opinion rejected the claims made by reporters in the trio of cases that revealing their sources would deter the free flow of

While serving as an appeals court judge in 1958, Potter Stewart wrote the opinion that rejected the first claim of a reporter's privilege before an appellate court. Ironically, he later wrote a Supreme Court opinion which devised a three-pronged test that would form the basis for many states' "shield laws." Photo reproduced from the collections of the Library of Congress.

Justice Byron White's majority opinion in *Branzburg v. Hayes* (1972) represented the Supreme Court's first recognition that the use of confidential sources for news gathering deserved some degree of First Amendment protection. White, however, was unwilling to support the notion of a reporter's privilege. Photo reproduced from the collections of the Library of Congress.

information. White said the Court could not "seriously entertain" the idea that journalists had a right to conceal the criminal conduct of their sources "on the theory that it is better to write about crime than to do something about it." He concluded that there was no compelling evidence that forcing reporters to reveal their sources would chill the news-gathering process. White was unwilling to accept even a qualified reporter's privilege, claiming that it would embroil courts in proceedings to determine whether the government had a compelling need for the reporter's information or even to determine who qualifies as a journalist.[6]

Justice Lewis Powell wrote a concurring opinion, but he noted the "limited nature" of the Court's holding. Indeed, many believe that he summarized the essence of a reporter's privilege when he wrote, "[I]f the newsman is called upon to give information bearing only a remote and tenuous relationship to the subject of the investigation, or if he has some other reason to believe that his testimony implicates confidential source relationships without a legitimate need of law enforcement, he will have access to the court on a motion to quash [the subpoena]."

Justice Potter Stewart, joined by Justices William Brennan and Thurgood Marshall, wrote a dissenting opinion, warning that the majority decision would lead state and federal authorities to "annex the journalistic profession as an investigative arm of the government." Stewart said the right of journalists to protect confidential sources was necessary for "a full and free flow of information to the public."[7]

Stewart said courts should weigh First Amendment interests against the need for a reporter's testimony on a case-by-case basis, and he proposed a standard for making such determinations. Before a journalist should be required to reveal confidences, said Stewart, the government would have to show: "(1) . . . that there is probable cause to believe that the newsman has information that is clearly relevant to a specific probable violation of the law; (2) . . . that the information sought cannot be obtained by alternative means less destructive of First Amendment rights; and (3) . . . a compelling and overriding interest in the information."[8] Stewart derived his three-pronged qualified privilege from two First Amendment values: the need to ensure the free flow of information to the public, and the need to avoid unwarranted government interference with the autonomy of the press.

Justice William O. Douglas wrote a separate dissent arguing that the journalist's privilege should be absolute. Douglas rejected the idea of a balancing test, declaring that "all of the 'balancing' was done by those who wrote the Bill of Rights" when they expressed the First Amendment in "absolute terms."[9]

In the wake of the fractured *Branzburg* opinion, lower federal courts, state courts, and state legislatures responded in a variety of ways. Within a year three federal appeals courts recognized a qualified reporter's privilege similar to Justice Stewart's three-pronged standard. Indeed, in 1975 a federal district court in Florida became the first to apply the reporter's privilege to nonconfidential information. In a civil suit the court rejected a motion to compel a newspaper reporter to answer questions regarding a published interview that was "on the record" and involved no confidential sources. The judge said that the distinction between confidential and nonconfidential material was "utterly irrelevant" to the "chilling effect" on the flow of information to the public that would result from enforcing the subpoena. "The compelled production of a reporter's resource materials," said the court, "is equally as invidious as the compelled disclosure of his confidential informants."[10]

According to Bruce Sanford, "Steadily, throughout the nation, federal and state courts built up substantial protection not just for reporters' confidential sources but also for the central notion that the news media ought to be independent from government's law enforcement activities."[11]

Clearly, the mixed *Branzburg* decision increased judicial sympathy for a qualified reporter's privilege. In addition, although Justice Byron White's majority opinion did not exempt reporters from grand jury subpoenas, it did suggest that state legislatures could "fashion their own standards in light of the conditions and problems with respect to the relations between law enforcement officials and press in their own areas."[12] In the years following *Branzburg*, fourteen states and the District of Columbia have passed "shield laws" doing just that.

SHIELD LAWS: CODIFYING A REPORTER'S PRIVILEGE

Although *Branzburg* energized many state legislatures to provide a statutory basis for the reporter's privilege, such laws already existed in seventeen states. The nation's first "shield law" was enacted in Maryland in 1896 after John Morris, a *Baltimore Sun* police reporter, was jailed for his refusal to identify to a grand jury his confidential source for a story about voting bribery. The Maryland law was designed "to protect reporters and other newspaper men from being compelled to disclose the source of any news or other information procured for publication in any legal or legislative proceeding."[13]

Thirty-seven years passed before another state enacted a shield law, but a spate of highly publicized jailings of journalists resulted in ten such laws being passed between 1933 and 1941. By the time of the 1972 *Branzburg* decision, seventeen states had enacted shield laws, and today thirty-one states and the District of Columbia have them. These state laws vary significantly in scope. All of them apply to court proceedings generally, and some apply to legislative hearings as well. All shield laws give protection to reporters' confidential sources, and most of them protect news products such as notes, documents, or tapes. Employees of newspapers, magazines, and broadcast media are explicitly protected in virtually all shield laws, and book authors, cable TV operators, and motion picture photographers are included in some.

Shield laws can be divided into two categories: absolute and qualified. Absolute protection for reporters is usually accomplished by absolving them of any obligation to reveal their sources. However, three states—California, Montana, and New York—provide unqualified protection by removing the courts' contempt powers in such cases, an approach that some legal scholars believe violates the constitutional separation of powers.

The majority of state shield laws are qualified (or divestitory), meaning that the court has the authority to divest the reporter of the privilege under certain circumstances. In such cases the court must weigh the need for a reporter's evidence against the chilling effect of compulsory disclosure on the free flow of information. Several tests have been applied in shield laws to resolve these competing issues. Among them are the requirements that the reporter's information be relevant to the judicial inquiry or crucial to the development of the case. Some shield laws use a test approximating Justice Stewart's three-part standard in *Branzburg*: (1) relevance of the information sought, (2) a compelling interest in the information, and (3) the lack of alternative means to acquire the information.

Two recent cases, one in South Carolina and one in California, demonstrated the uncertain judgments likely to be rendered in states with either qualified or absolute shield laws. The 1995 case in Union, South Carolina, tested that state's qualified shield law, whose privilege can be overcome by a "clear and convincing" showing that the material is relevant to the proceeding, cannot be obtained by alternative sources, and is necessary to the proper preparation or presentation of the case.[14] In *South Carolina v. Smith* (1995) Susan Smith, on trial for drowning her two young sons, was examined by a psychiatrist to determine her competency to stand trial. Judge William Howard had the State Mental Health Department's report sealed, but Twila Decker, a reporter for the *Columbia State*, obtained a copy and reported its conclusion that Smith was competent to stand trial. Judge Howard asked Decker to reveal the source of her news report, but Decker refused, saying she had "a contract with the source not to reveal their identity."

Smith's attorney asserted Decker's right against compelled disclosure of confidential information under South Carolina's 1993 shield law, but Judge Howard found Decker in contempt of court, declaring that a reporter's privilege under the law was not absolute. The trial court held that the shield law was inapplicable because the court itself, which was not a party to the action, was the entity seeking disclosure. The ruling also specified that court-compelled disclosure does not interfere with the statute's aim of protecting "a free flow of information to the public." The South Carolina Supreme Court affirmed the lower court's judgment, holding that the shield law applies only where a "party" to a case seeks disclosure.[15]

"The ruling by the South Carolina Supreme Court saying that Twila Decker must reveal her sources is a direct violation of the First Amendment," said Paul McMasters, executive director of the Freedom Forum First Amendment Center. "They are telling the reporter that she must violate the contract she had with the person from whom she got her information. The reporter is facing jail time if she refuses to name her sources, as I expect she will. If the ruling is upheld then much good investigative reporting from around the country will go down the tubes. That's a real loss for the American public."[16] Decker eventually avoided jail time by swearing that her source was not subject to the court's gag order, leading the trial judge to rescind the contempt order.

Just weeks after *South Carolina v. Smith*, the spectacular O. J. Simpson murder trial in California[17] produced a different judgment based on California's supposedly "absolute" shield law. In that trial Judge Lance Ito upheld the rights of two journalists under the state's shield law to refuse to reveal their confidential sources. The California law, embodied in the state's constitution and evidence code, protects publishers, editors, reporters, or other persons connected with a newspaper, magazine, radio or television station, or press association from revealing information obtained "for communication to the public."[18] Although the law as written appears to provide absolute protection, those protections have been narrowed by court interpretation.

The courts have interpreted California's shield law as covering both confidential and nonconfidential information, but recent cases have ruled that a criminal defendant may overcome the statutory and state and federal constitutional privilege by showing "a reasonable possibility the information will materially assist the defense."[19] The court must then balance the media's interest in confidentiality against the defendant's interest in the information by considering the importance of the information to the defendant, whether the information is confidential, whether free press interests are at stake, and whether there are alternative sources for the information. In addition, the California Supreme Court has held that the state's shield law does not require courts to quash subpoenas, but instead immunizes journalists from being held in contempt for refusing to testify.

In the O. J. Simpson trial Tracie Savage, a reporter for KNBC in Los Angeles, used unnamed sources in reporting that DNA tests suggested that Nicole Brown Simpson's blood was found on O. J.'s sock. In addition, freelance writer Joseph Bosco published a report in *Penthouse* magazine claiming that a police officer, who was not named, had offered the preliminary DNA report to reporters around town until he found someone willing to use it in a story. Both Savage and Bosco asserted their rights under California's shield law to protect the identity of confidential sources. Simpson's attorneys, on the other hand, insisted that the identities of the confidential sources were necessary to conduct their defense.

Judge Ito ruled that the circumstances in this case did not demonstrate that the disclosure of the identities of the confidential sources would materially assist the defendant.

THE RECENT EROSION OF THE REPORTER'S PRIVILEGE

Today, forty-three states have either passed shield laws or recognized a state or common law privilege to protect the press. Yet serious erosion in the application of the privilege occurred during the 1990s. "The results," according to First Amendment lawyer Bruce Sanford, "put some reporters exactly where a lot of people would like to see them—behind bars."[20]

For example, in 1990 Libby Averyt, a Texas reporter, was jailed over a weekend after she refused to reveal the source of a jailhouse interview. Also in 1990 Brian Karem, another Texas television reporter, was jailed for 13 days for withholding the names of individuals who arranged a jailhouse interview. Tim Roche, a Florida reporter, was subpoenaed in 1990 and sentenced to 30 days in jail for criminal contempt after refusing to reveal his source for a leaked court order. Roche eventually served 18 days in 1993. Lisa Abraham, an Ohio newspaper reporter, was jailed from January 19 to February 10, 1994, because she would not testify about a jailhouse interview. In 1996 Bruce Anderson, a California newspaper editor, was jailed for 13 days for refusing to provide the court with a letter to the editor from a prisoner.[21]

A dramatic example of the courts' harsh treatment of reporters occurred in 1996 when David Kidwell, a *Miami Herald* reporter, was jailed for refusing to testify about his jailhouse interview with accused murderer John Zile. Zile had already confessed to the murder, and he talked with Kidwell about the crime. Prosecutors called Kidwell to testify, but he refused, saying he could not serve as both an arm of the prosecution and an effective reporter. Judge Roger Cotton sentenced Kidwell to seventy days in jail for criminal contempt.

Kidwell told the court, "I want you to know I've struggled with this decision for months. I've spoken with friends and colleagues and ethics experts across the country, searching for a way out, looking for a cohesive argument as to how I can maintain my professional convictions and stay within the law. I haven't found one. I have spoken with other reporters who won't interview criminal defendants anymore for fear of subpoenas. I have spoken with media lawyers who say the law has abandoned us.

"All of this only helped firm my resolve. I don't want to go to jail. I'd rather go back to work this afternoon. But either way, when I do go back to work, I have to know I'm free to pursue all sides of a story without interference from the government, that I can represent myself as fair and impartial and know it's true. I know the law is against me. The courts have retreated from the idea that these principles are worth protecting. I'm convinced I cannot allow my ethics to retreat with them."[22]

As courts handed out more severe punishment to reporters, they were particularly unsympathetic to claims of a reporter's privilege when it involved nonconfidential information. This was a disturbing trend, because the overwhelming majority of subpoenas issued to reporters concern information provided without an explicit promise of confidentiality. Surveys by the Reporters Committee for Freedom of the Press had documented that in 1989 only 5.1 percent of subpoenas received by news organizations were for confidential sources or information, and in 1991 and 1993 that percentage dropped to just 3.4 and 3.8, respectively.

A decision by the influential Second Circuit Court of Appeals in 1993 signaled the new direction of the judiciary. In a New York case involving Bruce Cutler, the lawyer for alleged Mafia boss John Gotti, Cutler was charged with violating a gag order by making statements to the press during Gotti's criminal trial. As part of his defense, Cutler subpoenaed notes from the reporters with whom he had spoken as well as the outtakes from television stations. The news organizations involved attempted to quash the subpoena, but the Second Circuit ignored its own precedent and brushed aside all First Amendment arguments.[23]

A very recent, highly publicized case involving CBS produced a similar judgment. In late 1999 Texas prosecutors demanded that CBS-TV turn over the entire text of an interview that Dan Rather had conducted with Shawn Allen Berry, a defendant in the death of James Bird Jr. Texas is one of nineteen states that does not have a shield law protecting journalists' sources and news products. The prosecutors argued that they needed to examine the entire transcript because the edited interview broadcast on *60 Minutes II* contradicted details Berry had given the police. After CBS refused to comply, Texas prosecutors subpoenaed the transcript, threatening Dallas-based CBS producer Mary Mapes with jail time if she didn't turn over the material. Meanwhile, in New York, Dan Rather was subpoenaed to turn over the interview tapes and to testify in Berry's trial.

In court Rather declared, "I believe in the rule of law deeply and completely. And that's the reason we're here today, because an important principle is involved, and it's the principle of the public's right—not the press—but the public's right to have a free and independent press."[24]

First Amendment lawyer Floyd Abrams, who represented Rather and CBS in New York, said, "CBS fought very hard on this because it believed and believes that there's a principle at stake here. The principle is that Dan Rather doesn't work for the police, and that people that speak to Dan Rather understand that he's a journalist and not a police agent. ... If the word gets out, if the perception exists that by speaking to a CBS journalist you are, therefore, inevitably, immediately speaking to the police, I don't think there's any doubt that people won't talk. And, therefore, the public won't learn."[25]

Guy James Gray, the criminal district attorney in Texas, made it clear that in the absence of a Texas shield law the principle being argued by CBS was overridden by state law. "There would certainly be some merit if you're talking about a confidential source," said Gray. "There would be some merit if you're talking about a reporter's private notes. But the law in Texas is clear. If you interview a defendant, what that defendant says is admissible in the courtroom."[26] In November 1999, CBS made the interview transcript available to the prosecutor, who then dropped the subpoena against Rather for the video outtakes.

Abrams explained, "The question at the end of the day was, the courts having found there was no defense ... , should CBS in effect tell the producer to go to jail even though there is no law at all that we can use to get you out of jail? ... Were this not [Texas] ... where there were no protections at all and where the law was clear on that, I think CBS and Mary Mapes and Dan Rather and all of us had a very good chance of winning. So this is an ongoing battle about an issue of principle."[27]

THE GRADUAL ABUSE OF ANONYMOUS SOURCES

All confidential sources are anonymous, but not all anonymous sources are confidential. If a reporter extends a promise of confidentiality to a source in order to protect that individual from official reprisal, such anonymity can serve the interest of the press and public alike. If, on the other hand, anonymity is simply a cloak behind which government officials can circulate propaganda or disinformation with impunity, it serves no public or journalistic interest. Indeed, it undercuts the watchdog function of the press and the public's right to know.

Throughout the twentieth century most American journalists applied a common set of rules to the use of information provided by their sources. Even the general public is familiar with the notion of information being on or off the record. If a source indicates that his or her comments are "on the record," then any information provided may be printed and attributed. If the comments are "off the record," the information should not be printed unless confirmed elsewhere and proved to the original source.

There are other less publicized journalistic rules that contribute to the increasing use of anonymous sources. If a source provides information that is "not for attribution," then it cannot be attributed by name to the source. For example, the reporter could attribute the information to "a Defense Department official," but not to Defense Secretary Bill Cohen. A roughly equivalent phrase is "on background." The most murky of these journalistic rules is called "deep background," which requires the reporter to print the information as if he or she knows it to be true. It cannot even be attributed to an anonymous source. This has come to be known as the "Lindley Rule," devised by former *Newsweek* reporter Ernest K. Lindley. A common example of such use is, "The president is known to believe . . ."

Mike Hoyt, senior editor of the *Columbia Journalism Review*, has warned that using anonymous sources places one on a slippery slope. "That slope increases its pitch this way. Anonymous but well identified. Anonymous and weakly identified. Anonymous and no I.D. Anonymous but deceptively identified. Anonymous and protected with a false no-comment. I can imagine a rational for each of these steps down the slope. But at the same time, each step exponentially gambles our store of credibility."[28]

Veteran reporter Dan Thomasson recently wrote, "Anonymous sources always have been a part of modern investigative reporting. But in the 35 years I have been in Washington, the reliance on these sources has grown dramatically, beginning with the 1972 break-in at the Democratic National Headquarters in the Watergate."[29]

The Watergate story may have been media's highpoint in the twentieth century. Reporters like Bob Woodward and Carl Bernstein became celebrities. In the popular motion picture *All the President's Men*, Robert Redford played Woodward and Dustin Hoffman portrayed Bernstein as heroes challenging the seemingly invincible centers of corrupt power—and winning. Their dogged pursuit of the truth behind President Nixon's Watergate cover-up relied heavily on an anonymous source, referred to only as "Deep Throat." In their best-selling Watergate books, Woodward and Bernstein emphasized that every detail of their story had to be doubly verified by Deep Throat.

The identity of Deep Throat may be the best-kept secret in American politics and journalism. Only four people knew the source's name: Woodward, Bernstein, Ben Bradlee (former executive editor of the *Post*), and Deep Throat himself. Woodward has kept his 1972 promise to protect his source's identity, but some information has been disclosed over the years. It is now known that Deep Throat is a real person, not a composite. Woodward says he is a smoker who drinks Scotch, "an incurable gossip, careful to label rumor for what it was, but fascinated by it."[30]

Deep Throat's continuing anonymity has not discouraged speculation about his identity. The most common suspects are Nixon administration members Henry Kissinger and Alexander Haig; CIA officials Cord Meyer and William Colby; and FBI officials L. Patrick Gray, W. Mark Felt, Charles W. Bates, and Robert Kunkel. In August 2000, Leonard Garment, former law partner and White House confidant to Richard Nixon, claimed to have unmasked the shadowy Watergate leaker. In his book, *In Search of Deep Throat*, Garment pointed the finger toward John Sears, former Nixon campaign operative and White House aide.

"This is a very strong, well-researched belief, but it's not a slam dunk," admitted Garment. "I think I've come as close to making an identification as can be made." Sears quickly rejected Garment's claim. "I categorically deny this," he said. "I offered to take a lie detector test to prove my innocence of this charge. Neither the author nor his publisher were willing to accept this offer."[31]

The media coverage of the Watergate scandal not only legitimized the use of anonymous sources, but made it difficult to distinguish them from "leaks," the self-serving information planted in the press by government officials. "Watergate was from beginning to end primarily a leak story," said Thomasson, "with the leaks coming from official Washington, frequently those agencies charged with uncovering the cover-up—the FBI, the Justice Department, and, of course, the CIA."[32]

The ease with which post-Watergate journalists rely on anonymous sources is an unanticipated negative consequence of Woodward and Bernstein's crusading reporting. "Before Watergate, if you wrote a story that raised questions about someone's conduct or integrity, you had to have something more than anonymous sources," claimed Jack Nelson, former Washington bureau chief for the *Los Angeles Times*. "After Watergate, some people decided they could just go with anonymous sources."[33]

The American public began to notice that an increasing number of the "authoritative" sources being quoted in news stories were unidentified. Whether described as "a reliable White House source" or "a high-ranking Pentagon spokesman," these voices spoke with authority, but their anonymity made them unaccountable and the news story itself unverifiable. Government officials have always manipulated leaks to serve their own purposes, but the extent and effectiveness of such practices had been limited by the press's reluctance to tolerate it. Now it was common practice.

"For years, everybody believed that if you could name your source you had a harder and more reliable story," said Associated Press reporter Michael Sniffin. "But there are some reporters who stand that principle on its head. They think they have a better story if it comes from an unnamed source."[34]

As more and more news stories featured unidentified and unverifiable sources, it was inevitable that some reporters would begin manufacturing false sources. The most spectacular example of this occurred in 1981 when Janet Cooke, a young black reporter for the *Washington Post*, received a Pulitzer Prize for "Jimmy's Story," the compelling account of an 8-year-old cocaine addict. Cooke said young Jimmy and his mother were confidential sources whose identity had to be withheld to protect their safety, as well as her own. It turned out there was no Jimmy. Cooke had made up the entire story (see Chapter 7). The irony was that Cooke's boss at the *Post* was none other than Bob Woodward, formerly of Watergate fame. Woodward and the other *Post* editors accepted Cooke's claims of confidentiality and never checked on the existence of her sources.

Eventually Cooke's manufactured story crumbled. Forced to return her Pulitzer, she left the *Post* in disgrace, and newspaper editors around the country began to question the excessive use of unverified sources. The *Post* published an 18,000-word confession and apology in which Woodward admitted, "We went into our Watergate mode. Protect the source and back the reporter."[35] The public was unforgiving. Having learned that Cooke's anonymous "Jimmy" was a hoax, they began to question the legitimacy of the Watergate story. One letter to the *Post* asked, "Is it possible that little 'Jimmy' does, in fact, exist and is living on the very street with 'Deep Throat'?"[36]

TABLOID SOURCES

Concern with excessive use of anonymous sources continued into the 1990s, when two sensational stories once more brought the issue before the public. In the course of the O. J. Simpson murder trial in 1994, numerous press stories appeared based on false information attributed to unnamed sources. Among them were reports that:

- A bloody ski mask was found at the murder scene. ("There is no ski mask," prosecutor Marcia Clark would later tell the court.)
- The murder weapon was a military digging tool. (A deputy medical examiner would testify that the murders were carried out with a knife.)
- Simpson behaved strangely during his airplane flight to Chicago after the murders, keeping his hand in a bag throughout the flight. (Several passengers on the plane said Simpson behaved normally on the flight and did not hide his hand in any way.)
- Simpson had cuts on his body at the time of his arrest that were consistent with injuries from a fight. (Police witnesses said Simpson had only a small scratch on one finger.)
- DNA testing showed that blood on a sock found in Simpson's bedroom

matched Nicole Brown Simpson's blood. (This story, reported by KNBC-TV in Los Angeles, was refuted by the prosecution, the defense, and Judge Lance Ito.)

After the phony DNA story, Judge Lance Ito threatened to close Simpson's trial to TV cameras, calling the KNBC report "outrageous" and "irresponsible." KNBC reporter Tracie Savage had reported the information from an unnamed source. Initially KNBC said it had "reported accurately the information our sources have told us," but several days later the station admitted that parts of its report were "in some respect, factually incorrect."[37]

Once more, the public and many in the media responded negatively to the apparent misuse of anonymous sources. "My hope is that the O. J. story will be to anonymous sources what the 'Jimmy's World' story [by Janet Cooke] . . . was to deception, fictional and composite characters," said Tom Brislin, professor of journalism at the University of Hawaii. Brislin expressed hope that in ten years "we'll look back on O. J.'s world and anonymous sources as those bad old days in our ethical evolution."[38]

Perhaps, but first the public would have to endure the Clinton/Lewinsky scandal and its profusion of anonymous sources, which made their use in Watergate pale in comparison. Both the print and broadcast media were equally guilty, but the only reliable statistical study available examined television news coverage. That study, published in September 1999 by Steven Esposito, currently a professor of communications and formerly a TV reporter, documented the use of anonymous sources in television coverage of "Monicagate" from January 21, 1998 (the day the story broke) to September 9, 1998 (the day the independent counsel's report was delivered to Congress). During this period not only were anonymous sources used frequently in covering the scandal, but the independent prosecutor, Kenneth Starr, was himself investigated by a federal judge for leaking grand jury testimony to the press.

The statistical results of the study were astounding. Fully 72 percent of the 1,107 stories carried on NBC, ABC, CBS, and CNN contained at least one anonymous source. Nearly half (45.1 percent) of the 4,833 sources cited were anonymous. In all, 2,179 anonymous sources were included in the 1,107, stories, averaging 1.03 anonymous attributions per minute. The number of unnamed sources originating from the White House was five times greater than the number of those leaked from Starr, but, of course, Starr's office was supposed to be prevented by law (Rule 6(e)) from disclosing matters before the grand jury.[39]

Steven Esposito, the author of the study, explained the alarmingly high incidence of anonymous sources. "First, the Clinton-Lewinsky story originated from Washington D.C. (the anonymous-source capitol of the world), where few sources appear to say anything of substance on record and where background and deep background are a way of life," said

Esposito. "Secondly, what really matters is not whether a source is named or unnamed, but whether the information gathered is factual." Esposito concluded, "The findings of this study, however, indicate that the networks may be over-using, perhaps even abusing, the use of anonymous sources as a news-gathering device."[40]

In July 1998 U.S. District Judge Norma Holloway Johnson began investigating Starr for illegal leaks, and that story was reported on all four TV networks—using unnamed sources, of course. In response to Judge Johnson's decision to investigate alleged violations of Rule 6(e), one "White House source" told NBC that the judge was "intent on taking Starr to the woodshed." One of Clinton's "top aides" referred to Starr and his staff as "Keystone Cop Central." Unnamed "White House officials" admitted the strategy of having aides criticize Starr "behind the scenes" but "not do so publicly."[41]

In June 1998 journalist Steven Brill caused an uproar when he published an interview with Starr in his magazine *Brill's Content*. In that interview Starr admitted that people in his office, including his deputy, Jackie Bennett, had supplied information to reporters and had talked "extensively" with Susan Schmidt of the *Washington Post*, Michael Isikoff of *Newsweek*, and Jackie Judd of ABC. Those three journalists refused to discuss their sources, which is to say, they protected Starr's anonymity, despite the fact that Starr himself had admitted leaking information to them. The shoe was now on the other foot, and many in the media began to debate whether it was proper for a leaker to identify those to whom he leaks.

"It chills the relationship between source and journalist, and thereby inhibits a free flow of information to the public," said Marvin Kalb, director of a Harvard University center on the press. Kalb said it could create a perception that reporters were in "cahoots" with those who supply them with information.[42]

Howard Kurtz, media reporter for the *Washington Post*, said there was "a genuine sense of discomfort in media ranks" when Starr revealed those to whom his office had leaked information. Kurtz said that most reporters assume that "anyone who gives them information without their name attached is not going to blab to the world about the shadowy transaction."[43]

In addition to the federal courts, the House Judiciary Committee also wanted to hear from Starr. On the day of his testimony, Steven Brill issued a public challenge to Starr. "Mr. Starr, I want to give you a chance to clear your name on the serious accusation made against you by the judge presiding over your grand jury," said Brill's statement. "We all appreciate the need for reporters to keep their sources of information confidential if they have promised confidentiality. But news sources are free to release reporters from this obligation, and that is what I am asking you to do today. . . . If you've been unfairly accused, as you insist, sir, you should want these reporters to talk freely and honestly about what you and Mr. Bennett did or did not tell them."[44]

Brill repeated his challenge on public television's *NewsHour With Jim Lehrer*, but he also complained that the media had a conflict of interest that prevented them from properly covering Starr's leaks.

"Are you saying reporters are not covering this because they are the beneficiaries of the leaks?" asked the show's moderator.

"We have in Washington right now a supremely powerful, high federal officer [Starr], whom a judge has said probably committed what she considered to be crimes," answered Brill. "She's laid out the 24 instances, and yet, this is one investigation that has no leaks. . . . [O]ne of the great ironies now is that everything else about the Lewinsky grand jury is totally public, except the leaks investigation." *Newsweek*'s Evan Thomas had to agree that Brill was on to something, a conflict of interest within the press coverage. "[T]he conflict," said Thomas, "is we don't like to report on our sources."[45]

The bickering about leaks and anonymous sources in Ken Starr's office soon came to a bizarre conclusion when Charles Bakaly III, Starr's spokesman during the investigation of illegal leaks, was fired because he leaked information to *New York Times* reporter Don Van Natta Jr., whose story was sourced to unnamed associates of Starr's. Bakaly was subsequently charged with criminal contempt for having lied to federal investigators about the leaks.[46]

On October 6, 2000, Judge Johnson ruled that though Bakaly was a "direct" or "confirming" source for much of the information in the *Times* article, federal prosecutors had not proved that he had intentionally lied about his role. Judge Johnson made it clear that she held the *Times* as responsible as Bakaly for the entire matter. In noting that the *Times* had "misleadingly attributed to 'associates of Mr. Starr' " a twenty-four-year-old memo from Watergate prosecutors, Judge Holloway Johnson said, "The impression that this journalistic sleight of hand produced is quite troubling for what it shows about the reliability of anonymously attributed information."[47]

CONCLUSION: WHEN ARE ANONYMOUS SOURCES NECESSARY AND APPROPRIATE?

The debate over anonymous sources becomes more intense after scandals like the Janet Cooke affair, the O. J. Simpson trial, or Monicagate, but even then, few journalists suggest that anonymous sourcing be ended. One of the few who has made such a proposal is Allen Neuharth, founder of *USA Today*, who instituted a ban on blind sources when he began the paper. "There's not a place for anonymous sources," said Neu-harth. "I think there are few major historical developments that hap-pened in journalism—the Pentagon Papers, maybe Watergate—where anonymous sources had a more positive influence than a negative im-pact. But on balance, the negative impact is so great that we can't over-come the lack of trust until or unless we ban them."[48]

It is significant that *USA Today*'s subsequent editor, Peter Prichard, admitted, "We don't exactly have a no anonymous source policy. A bet-ter way to put it is we try not to abuse or overuse them."[49]

Because the use of anonymous sources appears to be a permanent part of the journalistic landscape, the only meaningful debate within the pro-fession centers on appropriate guidelines for their use. During the 1990s a number of media scholars and newspeople have made formal propos-als in this regard. In 1990 David E. Boeyink wrote of the journalist's ethical obligations of "truth telling, doing no harm and seeking justice," and he concluded that the use of anonymous sources may at times be necessary to meet these ethical goals. Boeyink offered seven guidelines by which journalists could decide whether to use anonymous sources:

Promises of anonymity must be authorized by the editor;

Anonymous sources should be used only for a just cause;

Anonymous sources should be used only as a last resort;

Sources should be as fully identified as possible, with reasons for anonymity explained in the story;

Editors should balance the potential harms and benefits in any use of anonymous sources;

Anonymous sources can only be used with just intentions by the reporter, the media, and the source; and

Use of anonymous sources requires independent verification by a second source. [50]

Felix Winternitz, a veteran magazine and newspaper editor, offered the following additions to the list:

Warn the source that the agreement of confidentiality is off if you later discover that the source lied; and

Forbid personal attacks by unnamed sources.[51]

A 1997 study of newspaper ombudsmen gave another view of news-paper policies toward anonymous sources. Nine ombudsmen were in-terviewed at length and thirty-seven others responded to a mail survey. In the mail survey, 83 percent of the respondents said their papers relied on anonymous sources in "about the right amount," whereas only 13 percent thought their papers used them "too much or far too much." In their separate responses, the ombudsmen suggested possible standards for the use of anonymous sources, some of which are paraphrased here:

Grant confidentiality as a last resort;

Reveal the identity of the source to the ranking editor and have him approve confidentiality in advance;

Use confidential sources only when there is no other way to obtain important information;

Public interest must be served.

The ombudsmen also described some particular circumstances under which confidentiality should be granted:

For major stories on which no public records or information are available;

For major investigations in which a source's safety or job would be in jeopardy;

For stories involving national security;

For major stories on public policy, including corruption in government or information on ethical issues;

For any newsworthy story.

Fifty-seven percent of the ombudsmen felt that when confidentiality is granted the story should clearly explain why, and about half of the respondents agreed that information from an anonymous source should be verified with an independent source. It is surprising that 39 percent said that some circumstances justified revealing the identity of a confidential source, traditionally a taboo among journalists. Among those circumstances mentioned were cases when the source is lying or manipulating confidentiality to take advantage of the reader or has been granted confidentiality without authorization.[52]

Many news organizations have adopted policies on the use of anonymous sources that draw on the basic standards listed here. A study of newspapers and TV stations during the 1980s found that 32 percent of the papers and 16 percent of the stations surveyed had formal written policies on the use of anonymous sources, and 69 percent of the papers and 72 percent of the stations had informal policies. A 1996 survey of sixty-four large-circulation newspapers found that 40 percent had written policies and 92 percent had either a written or nonwritten policy on anonymous sources.[53]

For example, the *Cincinnati Enquirer* has one of the most elaborate and restrictive policies with respect to the use of anonymous sources. As summarized, the policy states:

The identities of all sources must be verified and confidentiality disclosed to the editor and, if requested, to the newspaper's attorney;

Misleading information about the true identity of a source may not be used in a story;

Information supplied by an unnamed source should be verified independently or confirmed by at least one other source. An exception may be made for individuals who are the sole possessors of the information or whose integrity is unassailable;

The motive of the anonymous source should be fully examined to prevent the reader from being used unwittingly;

The use of anonymous sources on information that calls someone's judgment into question or on statements that are a matter of opinion should be avoided;

Information attributed to an anonymous source must be factual and important to the story;

Reporters and editors should satisfy themselves that the source is appropriate to provide the information sought and that he or she is in a position to know;

When an unnamed source must be used, the story should explain why his or her identity is being withheld, and enough information should be given to establish his or her authority to speak on the subject;

Stories containing unnamed sources may not be published without the approval of the editor;

Reporters should not quote people whose identities they do not know or cannot verify.[54]

The *Washington Post*, a newspaper frequently criticized for its reliance on unnamed sources, has a brief policy statement on sourcing in its stylebook: "Before any information is accepted without full attribution, reporters must make every reasonable effort to get it on the record. If that is not possible, reporters should consider seeking the information elsewhere. If that in turn is not possible, reporters should request an on-the-record reason for concealing the source's identity and should include the reason in the story."[55]

Recently an embarrassing public debate arose between the *Post*'s editors and its ombudsman over whether the paper was adhering to its stated policies regarding anonymous sources. Geneva Overholser, the paper's ombudsman, used her column to strongly criticize the *Post*'s legendary Bob Woodward for excessive use of unnamed sources, charging in particular that he had violated the *Post*'s stylebook in a story on Vice President Al Gore. As if that were not embarrassing enough, Managing Editor Robert G. Kaiser raised the level of the debate with an op-ed column refuting Overholser and defending Woodward. "People have jobs, relationships and other interests that they may be unwilling to put at risk, even when they are willing—anonymously—to give us valuable information," wrote Kaiser. He concluded that "readers can decide for themselves" if anonymity is appropriate. In other public statements, Kaiser questioned Overholser's criticism of Woodward's work. "She devoted no space in her column to issues of the import or accuracy of the [Woodward] story," he said. "She totally focused on the sourcing, and I thought that was an imbalance." Woodward insists that he followed the *Post*'s stylebook to the letter, but in any case he thinks the dispute with Overholser may have created "a new awareness that the goal is to get things on the record if you can. It doesn't hurt to be reminded of that."[56]

Nevertheless Woodward makes no apologies for his use of unnamed sources. "Look at all the stuff that's been from anonymous sources over the years and very little of it has been wrong," he has told fellow journalists. "In fact, I would argue it's often more correct because the reporter knows his or her rear end is on the line. . . . The standard has to be: What's the quality of the information?"[57]

The debate continues. Lawrence Latto, a Washington attorney and media critic, responded to Kaiser's defense of the *Post*'s policies by suggesting a law that would hold accountable those who use anonymous sources. "It would confirm that a newspaper can never be held civilly liable for a story that is attributed to another person and accurately reports what that person has said—regardless of whether the subject of the report is newsworthy or unknown and without regard for whether the motivation for publishing was malicious," said Latto. "The publisher of a story based on undisclosed sources, on the other hand, would be liable for any damage caused by any inaccuracy in the story. . . . Why am I dubious that journalists would be willing to support the adoption of such a law?"[58]

NOTES

1. Louis A. Day, "Shield Laws and the Separation of Powers Doctrine," in *Censorship, Secrecy, Access, and Obscenity*, ed. Theodore R. Kupferman (Westport, Conn.: Meckler, 1990), p. 135.

2. Ibid.

3. *Garland v. Torre*, 259 F. 2d 545 (2d Cir. 1958) at 549–50.

4. Bruce W. Sanford, *Don't Shoot the Messenger: How Our Growing Hatred of the Media Threatens Free Speech for All of Us* (New York: The Free Press, 1999), pp. 166–67.

5. *Caldwell v. United States*, 434 F. 2d 1081 (9th Cir. 1970) at 1089.

6. *Branzburg v. Hayes*, 408 U.S. 665 (1972) at 692–94, 702–5.

7. Ibid., at 709–10, 725–27.

8. Ibid., at 743.

9. Ibid., at 711–13.

10. *Loadholtz v. Fields*, 389 F. Supp 1299 (M.D. Fla. 1975) at 1303.

11. Sanford, *Don't Shoot the Messenger*, p. 166.

12. *Branzburg v. Hayes*, 408 U.S. 665 (1972) at 706.

13. Laurence B. Alexander and Leah G. Cooper, "Words That Shield: A Textual

Analysis of the Journalist's Privilege," *Newspaper Research Journal*, vol. 18, no. 1–2 (winter/spring 1997), p. 53.

14. South Carolina Code, Annotated sec. 19–11–100.

15. *South Carolina v. Smith*, 471 S.E.2d 462 (S.C. 1995).

16. "McMasters Blasts Decision by South Carolina Supreme Court," First Amendment Center Homepage (July 10, 1995), www.fac.org/releases/decker.

17. On October 3, 1995, O. J. Simpson was acquitted of the brutal stabbing murders of his ex-wife Nicole Brown Simpson and her friend, Ronald Goldman.

18. California Constitution, art. 1, sec. 2; California Evidence Code, sec. 1070.

19. *Delaney v. Superior Court*, 50 Cal.3d 785, 268 Cal. Rptr 753, 789 P.2d 934 (1990).

20. Sanford, *Don't Shoot the Messenger*, p. 167.

21. Cited in Noreen Marcus, "Squeezing the Press," *Broward Daily Business Review* (October 8, 1996), A1–A3.

22. Ibid.

23. *United States v. Cutler*, 6 F. 3d 67 (2d Cir. 1993).

24. "Free Press vs. Fair Trial," Online NewsHour, (November 12, 1999), p. 2, www.pbs.org/newshour/bb/media.

25. Ibid.

26. Ibid.

27. Ibid., pp. 4–5.

28. Mike Hoyt, "Anonymous Sources, Slippery Slopes," *Columbia Journalism Review* (May/June 1999), p. 70.

29. Dan Thomasson, "Anonymous Whispers Growing into Roars," *The American Editor* (November 1998), p. 14.

30. Cited in Lisa Todorovitch, "Deep Throat Suspects" (June 13, 1997), p. 1, washingtonpost.com.

31. Deb Riechmann, "Nixon Confidant Says He Knows Identity of 'Deep Throat,'" Starnet, c2000, p. 1, www.azstarnet.com/breaking.

32. Thomasson, "Anonymous Whispers Growing into Roars," p. 14.

33. "A Searching of Conscience," *Newsweek* (May 4, 1981), p. 53.

34. Ibid.

35. Cited in Thomas Griffith, "The Pulitzer Hoax—Who Can Be Believed?" *Time* (May 4, 1981), p. 50.

36. Ibid.

37. Jacqueline Sharkey, "Offside on O. J.," *American Journalism Review* (December 1994), p. 21.

38. Cited in Alicia C. Shepard, "Anonymous Sources," *American Journalism Review* (December 1994), p. 20.

39. Steven A. Esposito, "Anonymous White House Sources: How They Helped Shape Television News Coverage of the Bill Clinton–Monica Lewinsky Investigation," *Communication and the Law* (September 1999), pp. 7–8.

40. Ibid, p. 16.

41. Ibid. p. 14.

42. "When Anonymous Sources Identify Themselves, Reporters Cringe," Associated Press (June 16, 1998), www.freedomforum.org/professional/1998.

43. Ibid.

44. Steven Brill, "A Question for Ken Starr" (November 17, 1998), www.housecenter.com/clinton.

45. "Leaking the Story?" Online Newshour (November 18, 1998), pp. 3–4, www.pbs.org/newshour.

46. David Vise, "Ex-Starr Aide Acquitted of Lying about Leaks," *Washington Post* (October 7, 2000), A10.

47. Howard Kurtz, "Making Their Heads Spin," *Washington Post* (October 9, 2000), C7.

48. Cited in Shepard, "Anonymous Sources," p. 20.

49. Ibid, p. 24.

50. Sherrie L. Wilson, William A. Babcock, and John Pribek, "Newspaper Ombudsmen's Reactions to Use of Anonymous Sources," *Newspaper Research Journal* (summer/fall 1997), p. 145

51. Felix Winternitz, "When Unnamed Sources Are Banned, Reporters' Hands Are Tied," *Quill* (October 1989), p. 40.

52. Wilson et al. "Newspaper Ombudsmen's Reactions to Use of Anonymous Sources," pp. 147–49.

53. Ibid., p. 142.

54. Shepard, "Anonymous Sources," p. 25.

55. Lori Robertson, "A Public Debate over Unnamed Sources," *American Journalism Review* (May 1997), p. 11.

56. Ibid.

57. Shepard, "Anonymous Sources," p. 24.

58. Lawrence J. Latto, "Vouching for Sources Isn't Enough," *Washington Post* (April 6, 1998), A25.

C H A P T E R

Pacifying the Internet's Electronic Frontier

THE LOST PROMISE OF A CENSOR-PROOF MEDIUM

When the worldwide system of linked computer networks called the Internet burst on the scene, it offered the promise of a truly democratic form of information exchange, combining the power and intimacy of the telephone, television, postal service, and community bulletin board. Although the Internet had been established in the early 1970s by the U.S. Department of Defense, it soon became a public fixture.

The giddy optimism of the new Internet advocates was typified by their belief that the unique new medium was censor-proof. After all, potential government or corporate censors would have no more authority or ability to control the content of the Internet than they have to censor phone conversations. Or would they?

At the heart of the Internet are the linked central computers and their system operators (sysops). It now appears that these sysops and the commercial Internet providers are vulnerable to the same kinds of pressures to censor content that publishers and broadcast networks face. The constitutional protections and obligations of Internet providers such as America Online, Prodigy, and CompuServe are unsettled by the courts. The law has not clearly established whether these providers are comparable to (1) a newspaper publisher or editor, (2) a secondary publisher, such as a library or bookstore, (3) the broadcast media, (4) a common carrier, such as the telephone, or (5) a private real property owner.

This legal ambiguity has encouraged a growing mentality of self-censorship among Internet providers, who are fearful of liability for the expression of their users. If a provider assumes responsibility, hence liability, for the messages of its users, it is inclined to assert control over them. A good example of this is seen in the behavior of Prodigy, one of the earliest commercial Internet providers. Prodigy claims to be responsible for its users' messages and therefore claims the right of a print publisher to selectively disseminate or suppress those messages. Under this assumption, Prodigy has prescreened all messages to ensure that they are suitable for readers of all ages.

In 1990 Prodigy aroused particular concern among Internet advocates when it imposed formal content restrictions on the messages that could be posted on its electronic bulletin boards. Prodigy claimed that it was only screening out public postings about subjects such as suicide, crime, sex, or pregnancy, but it was soon discovered that controls were also being imposed on messages that were considered contrary to Prodigy's corporate interests. For example, when some Prodigy customers posted messages complaining about a proposed rate increase, Prodigy announced that public postings about the company's fee policies would no longer be allowed. When Prodigy customers turned to private e-mail messages to voice their complaints, the company canceled the protesters' accounts and imposed a general ban on e-mail communications with merchants.

Prodigy defended its policy by claiming that it was not a common carrier that is required to carry all messages, and the Internet community feared that all commercial providers would subsequently renounce any obligation to free speech. Jerry Berman of the American Civil Liberties Union (ACLU) and Marc Rotenberg of Computer Professionals for Social Responsibility concluded, "Prodigy's dispute with its subscribers shows why, to protect First Amendment rights in the electronic age, we need to press Congress to establish the infrastructure for an accessible public forum and electronic mail service operating under common carrier principles."[1]

In 1995 an international Internet scandal brought into question the legendary borderless character of cyberspace, something always assumed to be one of its strengths. CompuServe, one of the most popular Internet providers, announced that it was blocking access to 200 online newsgroups in response to complaints from German authorities who said the newsgroups contained indecent material. CompuServe responded by banning the newsgroups from *all* of its subscribers, including those in the United States. Thus a complaint originating in Germany, unaccompanied by formal charges or a court judgment, resulted in worldwide Internet censorship. Among the subjects blocked from the public at large were discussions about an Internet censorship bill introduced in the U.S. Congress.[2]

LEGISLATING DECENCY ON THE INTERNET

It was, of course, naive for Internet advocates to expect Congress to protect them from the censors. Capitol Hill's attitude toward free expression has not changed significantly since 1873 when Congress passed the Comstock Act, which criminalized the use of the mails for any "obscene, lewd, lascivious, filthy book, pamphlet, print or other publication of a vulgar or indecent character."[3] Politicians in the 1990s were outraged to discover that despite over a century of legislative attempts to muzzle the media, sex was alive and well in cyberspace.

Studies were commissioned to document the extent of cyberporn, and one unusual report by Marty Rimm, a twenty-nine-year-old undergraduate at Carnegie Mellon University (CMU), became the basis for punitive legislation against the Internet. In late 1994 Rimm presented a study to the CMU faculty in which he made such extravagant estimates of the amount of explicit sexual material on the Internet that the university's administration felt obliged to censor a wide range of material from CMU's computer systems. CMU officials acknowledged that every university in the nation provides access to the same Internet content, but they claimed that once Rimm had notified them of specific examples of alleged cyberporn, CMU became vulnerable to a state law that made it illegal to *knowingly* distribute sexually explicit material to anyone under age eighteen, as many college freshmen are. "It didn't take a lawyer to read those pornography and obscenity laws to know we were really vulnerable," said Erwin Steinberg, CMU's vice provost for education.

CMU's decision to restrict student access to the Internet infuriated the university's students, but it was celebrated in national publications and on network news shows. Rimm himself became an overnight celebrity, appearing on the front pages of 136 of America's largest newspapers. The most spectacular spinoff from Rimm's study was *Time* magazine's July 1995 cover story, headlined "CYBERPORN: A New Study Shows How Pervasive and Wild It Really Is." The *Time* article began, "If you think things are crazy now . . . wait until politicians get hold of a report coming out this week. A research team at Carnegie Mellon University . . . has conducted an exhaustive study of online porn . . . and the findings are sure to pour fuel on an already explosive debate."[4]

The "research team" mentioned by *Time* was Marty Rimm. Senator Charles Grassley (R-Iowa) was so impressed by the Rimm report that he had the full text entered into the *Congressional Record*. After praising the Rimm report on the Senate floor as "a remarkable study conducted by researchers at Carnegie Mellon University," Grassley introduced S.892, the Protection of Children from Computer Pornography Act of 1995. Grassley concluded, "I urge my colleagues to give this study by Carnegie

Mellon University serious consideration, and I urge my colleagues to support S.892."[5]

Some of Grassley's colleagues supported his bill, and others introduced their own cyberporn legislation. Senator James Exon (R-Nebr.) made the Rimm study the cornerstone of his Communications Decency Act, submitted as an amendment to a broader telecommunications bill. To gain support for his amendment Exon downloaded sexually explicit images from the Internet, bound them in a three-ring binder, and hand-carried them from desk to desk in the Senate chamber. The Senate promptly passed Exon's Communications Decency Act by a vote of 84 to 16.

The Senate then scheduled hearings on cyberporn, an unusual move because hearings on a topic are normally held prior to the passage of an associated bill. Marty Rimm was to be the star witness in the July 1995 hearings, but suddenly disturbing information about Rimm and his study began to surface. It turned out that Rimm had earlier written a scatological book, the unpublished, *The Pornographer's Handbook: How to Exploit Women, Dupe Men and Make Lots of Money.* His supposedly authoritative pornography study now came under scrutiny.

CMU faculty members whom Rimm had cited as advisers on his study denied playing any role in the report, and a three-member faculty committee was assembled to determine whether Rimm had violated CMU's ethical and academic guidelines. Social scientists around the country also criticized the Rimm study as poorly designed and said its conclusion—that the majority of images exchanged on computer bulletin board systems were pornographic—could not be supported. As for Rimm's much quoted claim that 83.5 percent of Internet content is pornographic, a new study showed that figure to be a mere 0.5 percent.[6]

With his study discredited and his anti-pornography credentials tarnished, Rimm was no longer Capitol Hill's Golden Boy. He was promptly removed from the witness list for the Judiciary Committee's hearings. But despite the loss of their star witness, the hearings continued.

On Monday, July 24, 1995, the Senate Judiciary Committee broke new ground by convening the first congressional hearing on Internet pornography. The principal focus of the hearing was Senator Grassley's bill (S.892), which had been cosponsored by prominent members such as Bob Dole (R-Kans.), Orrin Hatch (R-Utah), and Strom Thurmond (R-S.C.). Witnesses included Donnelle Gruff, a fifteen-year-old Florida girl described as a victim of an online stalker; Patricia Shao, a mother of two who worked for an anti-pornography group; Dr. Susan Elliot, a mother from McLean, Virginia; Bill Burrington, assistant general counsel for America Online; Barry Crimmins, a children's rights advocate; Stephen Balkam, executive director of the Recreational Software Advisory Council; Jerry Berman, executive director of the Center for Democracy and Technology (CDT); Michael S. Hart, executive director of Project Gutenberg; and Dee Jepson, a member of the anti-pornography group Enough Is Enough.

Elliot and Shao described how their children had used commercial online services to access files that they (the mothers) considered inappropriate. Gruff testified that she had been harassed by the systems operator of an online bulletin board she was using. During questioning, however, Gruff's stepfather told Senator Patrick Leahy (D-Vt.) that Florida police working on the case gave no indication that current law was inadequate to prosecute such cases.

Crimmins testified that he had found numerous images of child pornography on America Online (AOL), and he accused AOL of neglecting to police its network. Nonetheless, under questioning from Senator Leahy, Crimmins acknowledged that current law already prohibited such images from publication or display in any medium.

It soon became apparent to the committee that whereas some of the material described by witnesses could be considered obscene, and hence covered by existing law, some material, such as that described by Shao, was merely "indecent," a constitutionally protected category. Senator Russ Feingold (D-Wis.) urged the committee to carefully consider the distinction between "obscene" and "indecent" expression and to "exercise caution and restraint" in proposing legislation. Feingold asked Elliot, "Where should we draw the line? Should we prohibit *Playboy*? Swearing? *The Catcher in the Rye*? What about a discussion forum about how to avoid getting AIDS?"

Senator Grassley insisted that his legislation was narrowly crafted to preserve the First Amendment rights of adults while protecting children from inappropriate material. But CDT's Jerry Berman and AOL's Bill Burrington argued that the ambiguity of the statute could lead to a severe chilling effect on the free flow of legitimate information in cyberspace. "The threat of a broad interpretation of this new statute would compel all who provide access to the Internet to restrict *all* public discussion areas and public information sources from subscribers unless they prove that they are over the age of eighteen," warned Berman. "Under this statute, a service provider could not even provide Internet access to a minor *with the approval* of the child's parent. Since every online service provider would have to similarly restrict access to minors, this proposed statute would create two separate Internets, one for children and one for adults."[7]

AOL's Burrington warned that his company and other service providers would need to adhere to the broadest interpretation of the proposed statute in order to avoid liability. This would force providers into the awkward role of national censor. "Constitutional guarantees of free speech and press should be cautiously guarded," said Burrington. "The online service provider industry should be encouraged to provide *voluntary* editorial control over its service and to continue its research and development of parental empowerment technology tools. This industry should not be cast in the role of national censor, determining which information may be fit for children, but nonetheless subject to criminal liability if it guesses incorrectly in any given instance."[8]

Michael Hart, whose Project Guttenberg places electronic texts of classic literature on the Internet, told the committee that legislative restrictions on indecency might prevent people from enjoying serious works of literature. With great emotion, Hart warned that Grassley's bill would force him to remove some of Shakespeare's plays and books such as *Catcher in the Rye, Lady Chatterley's Lover,* and *Alice in Wonderland,* all of which have been classified as indecent in various parts of the country.

Jerry Berman was critical of both the Grassley and Exon bills, saying the country would be better served if neither one passed. This remark drew a sharp response from Senator Exon, who, although not a member of the Judiciary Committee, had been invited by Grassley to participate in the hearings. Exon defended his Communications Decency Act and accused the CDT of vicious attacks against his bill. He also dismissed parental control technologies as too little, too late.[9]

Filtering, Not Censoring

Unlike the Senate, the House of Representatives was unwilling to dismiss "parental control technologies," the software that enables parents to personally program their computers to filter out any Internet sites they deem objectionable. Just two days after the Senate's 1995 cyberporn hearing, two subcommittees of the House Science Committee held a joint hearing on the parental use of software to "filter" inappropriate sites from the Internet.

The hearing, convened by the subcommittee on Basic Research, chaired by Representative Steven Schiff (R-N. Mex.), and the Subcommittee on Technology, chaired by Representative Connie Morella (R-Md.), included witnesses from the computer industry and from law enforcement agencies. All three law enforcement witnesses agreed that current law is sufficient to prosecute Internet pornography, stalking, and solicitation, and they argued specifically against the Senate-passed Communications Decency Act (CDA). Not a single member of either subcommittee defended Senator Exon's CDA. Representative Zoe Lofgren (D-Calif.) complained that "the Exon bill is a totally wrong approach and a complete misunderstanding of the technology." Chairwoman Morella urged Congress to consider technology that empowers parents before rushing to enact Internet censorship laws.[10]

Internet Society (ISOC) executive director Tony Rutkowski described voluntary Internet rating systems and content tagging and told the subcommittees that centralized content restrictions would be ineffective in the global, distributed network environment of the Internet. As a result, argued Rutkowski, the only effective method of Internet control is to provide parents with the technology to block and filter what they consider inappropriate.

Ann Duvall, president of SurfWatch, described her company's Internet filtering software and stressed that the industry was developing products that are simple to use and inexpensive and that empower parents to make their own choices about what their children see. "There is not a simple, national solution to the problem of children accessing inappropriate material on the Internet," said Duvall.[11]

Steve Heaton, general counsel for CompuServe, described KidNet, CompuServe's proposed interactive service designed for youngsters. "The cyber community, made up of hundreds of thousands of computers distributed across the globe, is truly a world without borders. Directly regulating cyberspace—history's only true functioning anarchy—may prove impossible. This makes it imperative that laws focus on individual responsibility and that education and empowerment among users and concerned parents be emphasized."[12]

Shortly after the House hearings concluded, Representatives Christopher Cox (R-Calif.) and Ron Wyden (D-Oreg.) introduced the Internet Freedom and Family Empowerment Act, which implemented many of the recommendations of the House hearings. In an effort to head off the Senate's censorship bills, the House bill encouraged the online industry to police itself. Rather than censor the Internet, Cox and Wyden said they hoped instead to spur technologies that would help companies, parents, and schools to block out objectionable material. Their legislation would also ensure that online companies could take the initiative to screen out obscene material without becoming liable for every message transmitted over their systems.

Some members of the Senate also seemed to be moving away from Exon's CDA and toward the filtering alternative. "Empowering parents to manage—with technology under their control—what the kids access over the Internet is far preferable to bills . . . that would criminalize users or deputize information-service providers as smut police," said Senator Leahy (D-Vt). "[G]overnment regulation of the content of all computer and telephone communications, even private communications, in violation of the First Amendment is not the answer—it is merely a knee-jerk response."[13]

As congressional support for screening software grew, some conservatives attempted to move the debate from voluntary screening in the home to obligatory screening in public libraries, but First Amendment scholars questioned the constitutionality of such an approach. Jonathan D. Wallace, a prominent attorney and free speech advocate, issued a briefing paper arguing that the installation of blocking software by libraries is an unconstitutional removal of materials from the library. "The blocking of a web site is analogous to the removal of a book from a shelf," wrote Wallace. "Most advocates of the use of blocking software by libraries have forgotten that the public library is a branch of government, and therefore subject to First Amendment rules which prohibit content-based censorship of speech. These rules apply to the acquisition or the removal of Internet content by a library." Wallace argued that even the *voluntary* use of screening software by public libraries would be unconstitutional. His basic legal argument consisted of the following points:

1. Under Supreme Court cases such as *Island Trees Board of Education v. Pico* (1982), the installation of screening software by libraries constitutes an unconstitutional removal of materials from a library.
2. The criteria used by manufacturers of screening software are vague and overbroad, and they do not conform to legal parameters laid out by the Supreme Court.
3. A library may not delegate to a private organization, such as the publisher of screening software, the discretion to determine what library users may see on the Internet.
4. Forcing library patrons to ask that screening software be turned off has an unconstitutional chilling effect under the First Amendment.[14]

A recent district court case in Alexandria, Virginia is expected to influence the law and library policies with respect to screening software. In *Mainstream Loudoun v. Board of Trustees* (1998), Judge Leonie Brinkema, herself a former librarian, ruled that public libraries in Loudoun County, Virginia, may not block sexually explicit material on the Internet. Judge Brinkema pointed out that libraries are not obligated to provide Internet access to their patrons, but when they do, they may not violate the First Amendment rights of adults "just because the material is unfit for minors."[15]

Despite such adverse legal judgments, Congress eventually drafted a number of Internet "filtering" bills, but it first attempted direct censorship of the Internet. The cyberporn hearings had galvanized congressional support for the heavy-handed Communications Decency Act, and a showdown on that bill could not be avoided.

The Communications Decency Act

Senator Exon's Communications Decency Act (CDA) of 1995 criminalized any "comment, request, suggestion, proposal, image or other

communication" on a "telecommunications device" that is found by a court to be "obscene, lascivious, filthy or indecent." The penalties for such expression included fines of up to $100,000 and two years in jail, and they were applied even to privately exchanged messages between adults.

A coalition of public interest groups, including the American Library Association, wrote to Exon expressing concern that his bill posed a significant threat to freedom of speech and the free flow of information in cyberspace. An electronic petition against the bill posted on the Internet generated 56,000 signatures in two weeks. Even House Speaker Newt Gingrich (R-Ga.) condemned the CDA as a clear violation of speech and the right of adults to communicate with each other. Exon characterized Gingrich as out of touch, and House Republicans seemed to agree as they ignored their Speaker and led a landslide 420–4 House passage of the CDA.

Although the House version of the CDA was a considerable improvement over Exon's Senate-passed bill, it included a provision that would make it a crime to use offensive terms about "sexual or excretory activities or organs" in computer communications with someone who is believed to be under eighteen years of age. Like the original Senate bill, the House version provided heavy fines and prison sentences for anyone who "knowingly" transmits obscene or indecent material to minors or to publicly available areas of the Internet where minors might see it.

A discouraged Representative Wyden said, "The idea of a federal Internet-censorship army would make the Keystone Kops look like crackerjack crime fighters. Our view is that the private sector is in the best position to guard the portals of cyberspace and to protect the children."[16]

In December 1995, House conferees voted 17–16 to maintain the bill's indecency standard, rejecting a proposal by Representative Rick White (D-Wash.) that would have replaced the broad term "indecency" with the more lenient "harmful to minors" standard. A joint House-Senate conference committee then met to iron out differences between the House and Senate versions of the CDA but chose to do little more than hand out a list of forty-six items agreed to at the staff level. After addressing a handful of technical issues, the joint committee adjourned.

Representative Pat Schroeder (D-Colo.) complained, "It's like a bag of smoke, and I can't figure out what's going on." Representative Anna Eshoo (D-Calif.) suggested that members had been sandbagged by the leadership and did not have time to understand what they were voting for. The *Washington Post* said the language negotiated by the conferees "combines some of the worst of a broad array of restrictions on speech, none of them likely to protect children. . . . The conferees should dump this disastrous legislation entirely and give the people—and Congress—more time to learn what the medium is about."[17]

In the end, as a result of heavy lobbying from the Christian Coalition, most of the severe provisions of the original Exon bill were retained. On February 1, 1996, Congress passed the Telecommunications Act of 1996, including the Communications Decency Act amendment. President Clinton signed the bill into law, but there was widespread concern, even within Congress, that the law would never withstand constitutional scrutiny by the courts.

Several public service organizations, including the ACLU and the Electronic Frontier Foundation, soon brought suit challenging the constitutionality of the CDA. On February 15, 1996, *American Civil Liberties Union v. Reno* was heard by U.S. District Judge Ronald Buckwalter, who blocked enforcement of the CDA's indecency provision until a three-judge panel could rule on it.

Meanwhile, the Clinton administration continued to defend the CDA, although the Justice Department had earlier written to Senator Leahy admitting that the decency provision would "impose criminal sanctions on the transmission of constitutionally protected speech" and "threaten important First Amendment and privacy rights."[18]

On February 26, 1996, another group of organizations led by the American Library Association brought suit against the CDA. The suit, which was joined by the major online companies as well as the trade and professional associations of newspaper publishers, editors, and reporters, was combined with the ACLU suit. On June 12, 1996, the three-judge panel consisting of Judges Dolores Sloviter, Stewart Dalzell, and Ronald Buckwalter ruled that the CDA violated the First Amendment.

Judge Stewart Dalzell wrote, "[T]he Internet may fairly be regarded as a never-ending world-wide conversation. The Government may not, through the C.D.A., interrupt that conversation. As the most participatory form of mass speech yet developed, the Internet deserves the highest protection from government intrusion. . . . Just as the strength of the Internet is chaos, so the strength of liberty depends upon the chaos and cacophony of the unfettered speech the First Amendment protects. For these reasons, I without hesitation hold that the C.D.A. is unconstitutional on its face."

Chief Judge Sloviter wrote, "Whether Congress's decision was a wise one is not at issue here. It was unquestionably a decision that placed the CDA in serious conflict with our most cherished protection—the right to choose the material to which we would have access."

Judge Dalzell seemed to reject the possibility of rewriting the CDA in the future so that it might pass constitutional muster, saying the Act's broad reach into protected speech "not only renders the Act unconstitutional but would also render unconstitutional any regulation of protected speech in the new medium."[19]

Only Judge Buckwalter left the door open for new legislation regulat-

Senator Patrick Leahy (D-Vt.) (top left) and Representative Pat Schroeder (D-Colo.) (top right) were two members of Congress who worked in vain to prevent the passage of the Communications Decency Act (CDA), which was ultimately ruled unconstitutional. Justice John Paul Stevens (bottom) wrote the Supreme Court's majority opinion that found the Communications Decency Act unconstitutional. He declared, "The CDA, casting a far darker shadow over free speech, threatens to torch a large segment of the Internet community." Photo of Senator Patrick Leahy courtesy of the senator's office. Photos of Pat Schroeder and John Paul Stevens reproduced from the collections of the Library of Congress.

ing the Internet. "I believe it is too early in the development of this new medium to conclude that other attempts to regulate protected speech within the medium will fail a challenge."[20]

The supporters of the CDA, including President Clinton, were not yet ready to turn to new legislation. The government promptly appealed the decision on the CDA to the Supreme Court. President Clinton said he remained convinced that the Constitution allowed laws like the CDA to protect children from exposure to objectionable material. Senators Exon and Coats, cosponsors of the CDA, expressed confidence that the Supreme Court would approve their bill. They were wrong.

On June 26, 1997, the Supreme Court struck down the CDA as an abridgement of " 'the freedom of speech' protected by the First Amendment." The 7–2 opinion actually had the strength of unanimity on the question of constitutionality, because even the minority opinion of Justice Sandra Day O'Connor and Chief Justice William Rehnquist concurred in part and supported much of the majority's approach. The majority opinion, written by Justice John Paul Stevens, forcefully rejected the CDA while endorsing the democratic potential of the Internet.

"[T]he CDA lacks the precision that the First Amendment requires when a statute regulates the content of speech," wrote Stevens. "In order to deny minors access to potentially harmful speech, the CDA effectively suppresses a large amount of speech that adults have a constitutional right to receive and to address to one another. . . . The general undefined terms 'indecent' and 'patently offensive' cover large amounts of non-pornographic material with serious educational or other value." Stevens concluded, "The CDA, casting a far darker shadow over free speech, threatens to torch a large segment of the Internet community. . . . The interest in encouraging freedom of expression in a democratic society outweighs any theoretical but unproven benefit of censorship."[21]

Sons of CDA

Conservatives in Congress were infuriated by the Court's decision. Dan Coats (R-Ind.), a sponsor of the CDA, complained, "A judicial elite is undermining democratic attempts to address pressing social issues. The Supreme Court is purposely disarming the Congress in the most important conflicts of our time."[22]

Several lawmakers quickly declared their intention to pass a new, more carefully drawn law that would pass constitutional muster. On the very day that copies of the scatological Starr Report documenting President Clinton's sexual escapades was being handed out on Capitol Hill, Congress also held hearings on seven bills that would limit access to the Internet by minors. Some of these bills attempted to avoid the constitutional problems of the CDA by imposing Internet content restrictions on public and commercial computer systems, rather than home computers. One bill, S.1482, introduced by Senator Coats on November 8, 1997, was based in large part on the CDA. The Coats bill banned commercial distribution on the World Wide Web of materials that are "harmful to minors," whereas the other bills sought to "filter" cyberporn rather than ban it.

The most prominent of these "filtering" laws was the Internet School Filtering Act, introduced in February 1998 by Senator John McCain (R-Ariz.). McCain's bill stopped short of prohibiting Internet use in schools without blocking software in place, but it would forbid such schools from receiving government-mandated subsidies for Internet access. Failure to comply could cost an average high school several thousand dollars in government funds each year. "Online access places our children in tremendous jeopardy because of an abundance of harmful online material that is as readily available to Internet users as instructional material," said McCain. "Parental supervision can, and does, compensate for this in the home. But parental supervision is impossible when children use the Internet in school."[23]

Although Senator Coats preferred the direct prohibition of cyberporn, he did not oppose the "filtering" bills being offered. "I believe the Court misinterpreted and misunderstood the true nature of the Internet," he said. "Parents don't want to send their kids to school in a red-light district."[24]

Many First Amendment scholars and advocates believed that McCain's bill, if passed, would fare no better in the courts than did the CDA. "We clearly think that use of these filters and blocking applications in libraries and schools violates the First Amendment," said Ann Beeson, national staff counsel for the ACLU. "The question is whether tying this to funding makes it more acceptable. It doesn't. There are a whole series of cases that establish that Congress cannot place unconstitutional restrictions on funding."[25]

Another Internet filtering bill was Representative Ernest Istook's (R-Okla.) Child Protection Act of 1998, which was reported out of a House Appropriations subcommittee in June 1998. Istook's bill, like McCain's, would deny federal funds for computer equipment in schools and libraries that do not install filtering software, but it went farther by requiring the filtering of not only obscene content but "content inappropriate for minors" as well.

The Electronic Frontier Foundation (EFF), the Electronic Privacy Information Center, and the ACLU characterized Istook's bill as a replay of the CDA. Ron Weich, an ACLU legislative consultant, said, "For Congress to adopt the Istook bill would be like ordering every news stand in the country to be wrapped entirely in a brown paper bag to protect any child from seeing any potentially obscene materials."[26]

There were many other Internet filtering bills being proposed. The Safe Schools Internet Act (H.R.368) required schools and libraries to install a system for filtering or blocking "inappropriate" material on the Internet. The Children's Internet Protection Act (H.R.543, S.97) made schools and libraries ineligible to receive or retain universal service assistance unless they install "a technology for computers with Internet access which filters or blocks material deemed harmful to minors." The Neighborhood Children's Internet Protection Act (S.1545) required schools and libraries receiving universal service assistance to install systems for "blocking or filtering Internet access to matter inappropriate for minors."

As Congress was generating a flurry of bills to impose filters on schools and libraries, those institutions themselves were taking a hard look at the advisability of even *voluntary* use of filters. In early 1998 a group of librarians published the findings of The Internet Filter Assessment Project (TIFAP), which neither endorsed nor rejected filters but cast doubt on their effectiveness in a library setting. The TIFAP study, which was conducted from April to September 1997, tested six major commercial filters and concluded that for the filters to be useful in library settings, most of the blocked categories needed to be disabled. Otherwise, reference librarians' ability to answer standard patron inquiries would be compromised by the filters' use. "Over 35% of the time," said TIFAP, "the filters blocked some information they [librarians] needed to answer a question. Keyword blocking obscured everything from nursery rhymes ('pussycat, pussycat'—blocked repeatedly, even, in one case, when the tester used the search terms 'nursery rhymes') to government physics archives (the URL began with XXX) to the word 'button.' "

The filters also blocked Web sites for hate groups, press releases on sex offenders, a list of jockeys, safe sex information, pros and cons on the legalization of drugs, and other information common to many library collections. "Think about it," TIFAP advised fellow librarians. "At some point you probably expended labor to select material in one of these categories—and now you can pay someone to deselect it!"[27]

The Child Online Protection Act (COPA)

As enthusiasm for Internet filtering bills cooled on Capitol Hill, Senator Coats' hard-line bill (S.1482) soon became the frontrunner among the "sons of CDA." Its final version was the Child Online Protection Act (H.R. 3783), introduced in April 1998 by Republican Michael Oxley (R-Ohio). The bill specified, "Whoever knowingly and with knowledge of the character of the material, in interstate or foreign commerce by means of the World Wide Web, makes any communication for commercial purposes that is available to any minor and that includes any material that is harmful to minors shall be fined not more than $50,000, imprisoned not more than 6 months, or both."

H.R. 3783 defines "minor" to mean "any person under 17 years of age." The phrase "material that is harmful to minors" is defined to mean "any communication, picture, image, graphic image file, article, recording, writing, or other matter of any kind that is obscene or that

a. the average person, applying contemporary community standards, would find, taking the material as a whole and with respect to minors, is designed to appeal to, or is designed to pander to, the prurient interest;

b. depicts, describes, or represents, in a manner patently offensive with respect to minors, an actual or simulated sexual act or sexual contact, an actual or simulated normal or perverted sexual act, or a lewd exhibition of the genitals or post-pubescent female breast; and

c. taken as a whole, lacks serious literary, artistic, political or scientific value for minors."

The bill specifies an "affirmative defense against prosecution" if the defendant "in good faith, has restricted access by minors to material that is harmful to minors

a. by requiring use of a credit card, debit account, adult access code, or adult personal identification number;

b. by accepting a digital certificate that verifies age; or

c. by any other reasonable measures that are feasible under available technology."[28]

The COPA had been opposed throughout its committee hearings by the Internet Free Expression Alliance, a coalition of twenty-three groups including the ACLU and the American Library Association. In a letter to the subcommittee considering the bill, the Alliance wrote, "H.R. 3783 should be rejected because it contains many of the unconstitutional provisions of the Communications Decency Act.... Like the CDA, the bill would have the effect of criminalizing protected speech among adults. Whatever governmental interest may exist to protect children from harmful materials, that interest does not justify the broad suppression of adult speech."[29]

The Alliance statement rejected the claim that H.R. 3783 was aimed only at "commercial" Web sites, noting that the term was so broad that it covers anything from an online bookseller like Amazon.com to a non-profit Web site selling T-shirts.

The Child Online Protection Act was the first of the "sons of CDA" to become law. It was passed by the House in August 1998 and by the Senate in September, and President Clinton signed it into law in October.

A *Washington Post* editorial commented, "The new measure is an echo of the original bad idea, blurred just enough to cloud prospects both for enforcement and for court review.... Drafters insist that they mean to target only commercial pornographers and that commercial Web sites can protect themselves by requiring proof of age—a credit card—before making their materials available. Whether that actually will prevent a chill on speech is another question. The argument is far from over on what Justice Sandra Day O'Connor, in the 1997 case, referred to as the possible 'zoning' of cyberspace."[30]

Almost immediately after the passage of the COPA, the argument was joined in a Philadelphia court when a coalition of seventeen plaintiffs, including the ACLU and the online magazine *Salon*, challenged the law. The ACLU argued that serious Internet sites like those maintained by AIDS education organizations could be at risk under the COPA. The editor of *Salon* testified that the ambiguity of the law would make it difficult to know whether groups could publish material like the Starr Report. Allowing the COPA to go into effect, argued the plaintiffs, would do irreparable harm, even if the law were eventually overturned.

Government lawyers argued that the COPA was tailored to meet the guidelines set down by the Supreme Court when it rejected the CDA and that the new bill used the more constitutionally acceptable "harmful to minors" standard, rather than the "decency" standard of the CDA. As for the claim that material like the Starr Report might fail the "harmful to minors" standard, government lawyers insisted that the bill's provision protecting material with "serious literary, artistic, political, or scientific value for minors" would apply to the Starr Report.

Representative Oxley, the House sponsor of the COPA, was not satisfied with the government's defense of the bill, and his office sent a strongly worded letter to the Department of Justice suggesting that "the department assigned a low priority to defending" the law. Oxley's office also complained that civil liberties organizations had "overhyped and overblown" the COPA's constitutional problems.[31]

The first legal judgment on the COPA came in Philadelphia on November 20, 1998, when U.S. District Judge Lowell Reed Jr. granted a temporary restraining order at the request of the ACLU. Implementation of the law was thus suspended until February 1, 1999, when Judge Reed reaffirmed the restraining order by issuing a preliminary injunction against enforcement of the COPA, pending a trial on the merits.

In imposing the preliminary injunction, Judge Reed said, "The plaintiffs have uniformly testified or declared that their fears of prosecution under COPA will result in the self-censorship of their online materials in an effort to avoid prosecution, and this Court has concluded ... that such fears are reasonable given the breadth of the statute. Such a chilling effect could result in the censoring of constitutionally protected speech, which constitutes an irreparable harm to the plaintiffs. . . . For plaintiffs who choose not to self-censor their speech, they face criminal prosecution and penalties for communicating speech that is protected for adults under the First Amendment, which also constitutes irreparable harm."

Reed said the Internet deserved the highest level of protection from the courts, "not because of the risk of driving certain commercial Web sites out of business, but the risk of driving this particular type of protected speech from the marketplace of ideas." He concluded, "Despite the Court's personal regret that this preliminary injunction will delay once again the careful protection of our children, I without hesitation acknowledge the duty imposed on the Court and the greater good such duty serves. Indeed, perhaps we do the minors of this country harm if First Amendment protections, which they will with age inherit fully, are chipped away in the name of their protection."[32]

The COPA's cosponsors in the House, led by Representative Oxley, issued a statement urging the government's lawyers to fight on. "We continue in our steadfast support of the Child Online Protection Act, and we urge the Department of Justice to continue defending this law at trial or on appeal all the way to the U.S. Supreme Court," they said. "Through COPA we seek only to apply the same common-sense standard to the World Wide Web as prevails in the rest of our free democratic society."[33]

On April 2, 1999, the Department of Justice filed a notice of appeal from the district court's preliminary injunction. The COPA now seemed headed down the same path that took the CDA through the federal courts to the Supreme Court.

Hate on the Web

Indecency was not the only congressional concern about cyberspace. Messages of hate, violence, and racism on the Internet were also generating bills and hearings on Capitol Hill. On May 11, 1995, just a few weeks after a right-wing extremist killed 168 people by blowing up a federal building complex in Oklahoma City, Oklahoma, the Senate Judiciary Subcommittee on Terrorism, Technology, and Government Information held a hearing on "The Availability of Bomb-making Information on the Internet." The hearing went far beyond bomb-making, examining the broader implications of Web sites espousing extremist causes.

Subcommittee chairperson Arlen Specter (R-Pa.) opened the hearing by stating, "Among those who communicate on the Internet are purveyors of hate and violence. . . . The media have reported that a variety of hate groups and militias use the Internet to gain adherents, organize, and rally support. Among the issues before us are the extent of such usage of the Internet and whether anything can and should be done about it."

Senator Herbert Kohl (D-Wis.) added, "Mr. Chairman, most Americans don't know what is out there on the Internet. If they did, they would be shocked. While the vast majority of information is useful and valuable, the information superhighway has dark back alleys."

Senator Patrick Leahy (D-Vt.) offered a word of caution. "Before we head down a road that leads to censorship," he said, "we must think long and hard about its consequences. The same First Amendment that protects each of us and our right to think and speak as we choose, protects these others as well. The rule of this free society has long been that it is harmful and dangerous conduct, not speech, that justify adverse legal consequences."[34]

Most of the witnesses before the subcommittee, including current and former members of the Department of Justice, were uneasy with attempts to criminalize Internet speech. Robert Litt, deputy assistant attorney general for the criminal division, acknowledged that materials on building bombs were available on the Internet, but he noted that the same information has been available in bookstores and public libraries for many years. "The basic legal principle is clear," he said. "The First Amendment protects speech, even speech that advocates or teaches illegal action, unless there is imminent danger of, and an incitement to, lawless action, or unless the speech itself constitutes a crime."[35]

Frank Tuerkheimer, a professor at the University of Wisconsin Law School, told the subcommittee that while preparing his testimony he was able to acquire twelve manuals from the University of Wisconsin libraries that contain the same information on bombs that is available on the Internet. Tuerkheimer, who had earlier represented the Justice Department in its failed attempt at prior restraint of a magazine article on "How to Build an H-bomb," appended to his statement eight pages from the *Encyclopedia Britannica* that provided detailed information on bomb-making and noted that the readily available *Blaster's Handbook* tells exactly how to prepare the same mixture that was used in the Oklahoma City bombing.

"I share the concern that there is material on the Internet that I would rather not see," said Tuerkheimer. "[T]here are things in newspapers I would rather not see. There are books I would rather not see printed. However, I believe in a society such as ours, the answer to ideas that we don't want to see ... are ideas that we do want to see."

When subcommittee chairman Specter questioned Tuerkheimer about his experience in prosecuting the Justice Department's case against the publisher of the hydrogen bomb article, Tuerkheimer replied, "Senator, I believe that the lesson of the hydrogen bomb case is that efforts to curtail the dissemination of ideas and thoughts by means of an injunction are doomed to fail. . . . It is just not going to work in an open society."[36]

William Burrington, assistant general counsel for America Online, told the subcommittee, "Our government's role should be to facilitate—not inhibit—the development of national and global information infrastructure. . . . If America's values teach us anything, it is that, particularly at times like these, what we need to foster is more speech, not less."

Jerry Berman, executive director of the Center for Democracy and Technology, testified forcefully in favor of Internet freedom, declaring, "The openness of the Internet and other interactive media should be seen as a great boon to our democracy, not as a threat to order. . . . Speech and advocacy on the Internet, unlike a street demonstration, are pure speech, with no immediate threat of physical violence. . . . As passionate and vehement as speech on the Internet may be, it remains only speech, with no immediate nexus to violence in most situations."[37]

Senator Dianne Feinstein (D-Calif.) disagreed with virtually all the subcommittee witnesses. "I have real problems with what has been said this morning," she declared. "I have a hard time with people using their First Amendment rights to teach others how to go out and kill and to purvey that all over the world." Berman responded by asking Feinstein, "Are you proposing that we outlaw speech of that kind? In other words, for bookstores? . . . We have gone through periods where we have tried to fight speech by criminalizing it, and that has not been exactly the best times of this country. The best way to deal with speech is with more speech."[38]

Perhaps mollified by the cautionary advice of the witnesses, the Judiciary subcommittee and Congress generally assumed a lower profile on the issue of Internet hate and violence—until another national calamity aroused national concern. On April 20, 1999, four years and a day after the Oklahoma City bombing, two teenage students entered Columbine High School in Littleton, Colorado, and sprayed halls and classrooms with automatic weapons fire, killing twelve students and a teacher and wounding twenty-three others.

A subsequent Gallup poll indicated that 82 percent of those surveyed believed the Internet was at least partially to blame for the Columbine attack—compared to 60 percent who thought easy access to guns was to blame.[39] The Columbine disaster once more aroused political fervor and claims that the media were somehow responsible. Some of the dormant Internet "filtering" bills were revived, and new bills were introduced. In June the House debated whether violence in the media or the availability of guns was the primary cause of the Columbine tragedy. A pivotal vote came on a bill offered by Republican Henry Hyde (R-Ill.), the influential chairman of the House Judiciary Committee. Hyde's bill would have made it a crime punishable by up to five years in prison to sell or distribute violent movies, television programs, videos, books, or Internet material to minors. The bill's provisions applied to material that "the average person" would consider "patently offensive with respect to what is suitable to minors." Such material would also have to be devoid of "serious literary, artistic, political or scientific value for minors."

Hyde's bill defined several examples of violence, including "sadistic or masochistic flagellation" and "torture," but it made no mention of terrorist bombing or mass murder with automatic weapons. Despite the frenzied atmosphere on Capitol Hill, the bill was overwhelmingly rejected by a vote of 281 to 146. In explaining his vote, Representative Kenny Hulshof, a conservative Republican from Missouri who voted against the bill, said, "If I believed that passing one additional law would prevent incidences of school violence in America, I would lead the charge."[40]

THE NUREMBERG FILES

Congressional inaction did not calm the emotional public debate on Internet violence, which soon extended beyond the highly publicized terrorist attacks and addressed fundamental religious and social conflicts. During the late 1990s the most controversial Web site of all was The Nuremberg Files, a site maintained by radical abortion opponents whose messages seemed to cross the line from violent speech to violent action. Created in 1997 by Neal Horsley, an antiabortion activist and computer consultant in Georgia, the site published the names, photos, home addresses, and license plate numbers of doctors it identified as "baby butchers." More than 200 doctors were listed on The Nuremberg Files, along with scores of clinic owners and workers, as well as judges and politicians who support the right for a woman to have an abortion. The site provided particular detail on what it called The Dirty Dozen, doctors who perform abortions frequently. Even the spouses and children of these doctors were identified.

Such information may be intrusive, but it is clearly protected speech. The charges of incitement to violence arose over the Web site's advocacy of stalking and its policy of drawing a line through the names and photos of doctors as they are murdered. Doctors who are wounded but not killed are shaded in gray. The site operators claim that they are merely collecting data on doctors who could be prosecuted for crimes against humanity. But in 1999 it was the doctors who chose the legal recourse of suing the Web site under the 1994 Freedom of Access to Clinic Entrances Act and the Racketeer Influenced and Corrupt Organizations Act (RICO). More than a dozen defendants were named in the suit, including Michael Bray, a minister who has spent time in prison for setting fire to abortion clinics and whose book, *A Time to Kill*, suggests that killing doctors who perform abortions is justified.

Defense attorneys argued that nothing in the Nuremberg Files directly advocates violence and that the Web site is a form of expression protected by the First Amendment. "This is a case about the threat to kill or injure, which is simply not there," said defense attorney Chris Ferrara. Michael Godwin, a lawyer for the Electronic Frontier Foundation, agreed. "It's rare that textual material has reached that threshold, because by its nature reading is reflective," he said. "There's no constitutional right in this country not to be scared, and I can see why these doctors are, but there is a right to express hateful, even frightening thoughts."[41]

Attorneys for the doctors and for Planned Parenthood, which joined in the suit, claimed that The Nuremberg Files is an illegal threat because it is produced by people who support killing doctors who perform abortions. They also argued that the style and substance of the Web site implicitly encourage readers to threaten or harm doctors.

"Certainly the strongly implied message here is to go after these doctors by any means necessary," said Sandi Hansen of the National Abortion and Reproductive Rights Action League. "This site should have a responsibility not to yell 'fire' in a crowded movie theater. What they're doing goes beyond free speech. It's a form of terrorism."[42]

On February 2, 1999, the suit was decided by a federal jury in Portland, Oregon, which awarded $107 million in damages to the suing doctors. The jury agreed with the doctors that by listing their names in the form of a "wanted" poster and crossing off the names of those who were murdered the site produced a "hit list" that threatens violence and is therefore unprotected speech. The jury had the authority to award damages but not to shut down the site.

Attorneys for the fourteen defendants vowed to appeal the jury decision and asked that the Web site remain open pending the outcome. Defendant Michael Bray said, "It ought to be appealed not for my sake but for the sake of truth and free speech."

Groups supporting a woman's right to have an abortion praised the decision. "The jury confirmed what we have been saying throughout this case: These anti-choice terrorists have abused this country's precious First Amendment rights," said Lois Backus, head of the Portland chapter of Planned Parenthood.[43]

U.S. District Judge Robert E. Jones had advised jurors that they did not have to determine whether the Web site intended to threaten doctors, only whether a "reasonable person" would interpret it as a serious intent to cause bodily harm. Because jurors used this lesser standard, rather than the Supreme Court's notion of "imminent lawless action," free speech advocates and First Amendment scholars thought the jury verdict might be vulnerable on appeal. "People need to know what they can and what they can't say," said David Fidanque, executive director of Oregon's ACLU.

"And the standard that was applied in this case just isn't clear enough. If political activists don't know what they can and can't say before defending themselves against $200 million dollar law suits, then free speech is in big trouble in this country."[44]

The fact that the convictions were based in part on RICO muddies the First Amendment waters somewhat. RICO says that if a defendant deprives—or conspires to deprive—a person of his or her lawful rights by threats of force, violence, or fear, the defendant is guilty of racketeering. The Portland jury appears to have applied that language in finding the defendants guilty.

Wendy Kaminer, president of the National Coalition Against Censorship (NCAC), concluded, "The verdict in this case suggests, in part, that people have a right not to be terrorized (especially when engaged in constitutionally protected activity), and that the right not to be terrorized may sometimes trump the right to speak."[45]

Suzanna Sherry, professor of civil rights and civil liberties law at the University of Minnesota, took a different view. "Shutting down this frightening Web site won't stop anti-abortion violence," she said. "After all, taking away the murderers' access to speech won't limit their access to guns. But I am afraid that it will do permanent damage to the First Amendment."[46]

After the trial, the doctors' attorneys asked Judge Jones to shut down the site, and he issued a temporary injunction against the site. The injunction ordered the defendants not to republish any of the Web site material or its equivalent, but Judge Jones did not order the closure of the site, saying it was outside his jurisdiction. The site's Georgia-based service provider nonetheless removed The Nuremberg Files from the Net after the site's author announced that he would begin showing live videos of women entering abortion clinics.

The practical effects of the court decision are unclear. The defendants in the case say they have disposed of their assets and therefore can't and won't pay the $107 million judgment. They also vow to continue their Internet agitation. Alex Fowler of the Electronic Frontier Foundation, an Internet advocacy group, says squelching the files will prove impossible. "I think that it's very likely we'll see a proliferation of that same questionable content around the world on multiple sites in response to that one particular site being closed down," he said.[47]

The legal status of the case is also far from resolved. Defendants have appealed, and because of its ramifications for free speech, it is likely to end up in the Supreme Court.

CONCLUSION: FURTHER CHALLENGES TO INTERNET INDEPENDENCE

The Internet's ongoing struggle against censorship, outlined in this chapter, is not the only challenge faced by the fledgling media format. There is strong evidence that the Internet's independence is threatened by its growing reliance on the same corporate monopoly that controls the traditional media outlets.

Perhaps the most sensitive Internet issue of all is privacy. An entire book could be written on the problems of corporate and government snooping in cyberspace. A recent article in *Brill's Content* documents the disturbing extent of personal data collection through the Internet. "Unless you choose to live the life of an unplugged hermit," warns the article, "much of your daily activity is now being recorded in corporate and government databases, whether you know it or not. . . . Once collected and organized, these data can be stacked together to produce a new kind of electronic identity—in other words, an entire profile about you containing the most private details of your life. Many different types of people and organizations can use this path to find you, and find out things about you, for a variety of purposes, not all of which are pleasant—or legal."[48]

The most sinister threat to privacy is cloaked in national security rhetoric. "Suppose, this past weekend, you sent an e-mail to a friend overseas," wrote journalist Jason Vest recently. "There's a reasonable possibility your communication was intercepted by a global surveillance system. . . . That system is called ECHELON and it is controlled by the U.S. National Security Agency (NSA)."[49] ECHELON is an electronic net that catches the millions of phone, fax, and modem signals circling the world, selecting messages that match key words of interest to a five-nation intelligence alliance: the United States, Britain, Canada, Australia, and New Zealand. The list of key words includes personal and organizational names, e-mail addresses, phone and fax numbers, and a wide variety of other identifiers.

The global nature of the Internet makes all users vulnerable to the surveillance proclivities of any nation. For example, Britain's M15 intelligence service is building a new £25 million surveillance center that will have the power to monitor all Internet communications sent and received in Britain. The new computer center, codenamed GTAC, has raised concern among civil liberties groups worldwide, because Internet communications from around the globe will pass through GTAC and Western intelligence services will in all likelihood share that information.[50] With this new facility, the government can track every Web site that a person visits, without a warrant.

NOTES

1. "Free Speech in an Electronic Age," *New York Times* (January 6, 1991), sec. 3, p. 13.

2. "Worldwide Net, Worldwide Trouble," *Washington Post* (January 1, 1986), A20.

3. *U.S. Code*, Title 18, sec. 1461.

4. Philip Elmer-DeWitt, "CYBERPORN," *Time* (July 3, 1995), p. 38.

5. *Congressional Record*, Senate, 104th Cong., 1st sess., June 26, 1995, no. 1055; S9017–S9021.

6. Al Kamen, "In the Loop," *Washington Post* (July 24, 1995), A19.

7. Center for Democracy and Technology, *Policy Post*, no. 22. (July 26, 1995), p. 3, www.cdt.org/publications.

8. Ibid., p. 4.

9. Ibid., p. 6.

10. Ibid.

11. Ibid., p. 7.

12. Ibid., p. 8.

13. Cited in Nat Hentoff, "The Senate's Cybercensors," *Washington Post* (July 1, 1995), A27.

14. "Court Bars Internet Filters in Loudoun County Library," *Censorship News* (winter, 1998–1999), p. 2.

15. Ibid.

16. Cited in "Internet Users Relieved by House Measure's Provisions on Indecent Material," *Chronicle of Higher Education* (August 18, 1995), A20.

17. "Internet Mess: Return to Sender," *Washington Post* (December 15, 1995), A24.

18. "Judge Blocks On-Line Smut Law Enforcement," *Washington Post* (February 16, 1996), B1.

19. *American Civil Liberties Union v. Reno*, 929 F.Supp 824 (E.D. Pa. 1996), at 883.

20. Ibid., at 857–59, 867.

21. *American Civil Liberties Union v. Reno*, in *United States Law Week*, 65 LW 4715, at 4723–27.

22. Cited in "Clinton Readies New Approach on Smut," *New York Times* (June 27, 1997), A21.

23. Cited in Will Rodger, *ZDNN Tech News Now* (February 10, 1998), pp. 1–2, www.zdnet.com.

24. Ibid., p. 3.

25. Ibid., p. 2.

26. Cited in Maria Seminerio, "Controversial 'Filter' Bill Approved," *ZDNN Tech News Now* (June 25, 1998), pp. 1–2, www.znet.com.

27. "Learning from TIFAP" (September 13, 1997), www.bluehighways.com/tifap.

28. U.S. House H.R. 3783 *Child Online Protection Act*, version 2, October 9, 1998, www.lexis–nexis.com/congcomp.

29. Internet Free Expression Alliance, Joint Statement Submitted to the Sub-

committee on Telecommunications, Trade and Consumer Protection, Committee on Commerce, U.S. House of Representatives (September 11, 1998), p. 3, www.aclu.org.

30. "Replay on Internet Porn," *Washington Post* (October 28, 1998), A18.

31. John Schwartz, "Online Decency Fight Brews Anew after Ruling," *Washington Post* (December 14, 1998), F21.

32. *American Civil Liberties v. Reno*, Civil Action No. 98–5591, U.S. District Court for the Eastern District of Pennsylvania, February 1, 1999.

33. "U.S. Judge Blocks Law Curbing Online Smut," *Washington Post* (February 2, 1999), A2.

34. *The Availability of Bomb-Making Information on the Internet*, Hearing before the Subcommittee on Terrorism, Technology, and Government Information of the Committee on the Judiciary, U.S. Senate, 104th Cong., 1st sess., May 11, 1995 (Washington, D.C.: U.S. GPO, 1996), pp. 4–5, 8.

35. Ibid., p. 14.

36. Ibid., pp. 41–42, 46.

37. Ibid., pp. 28, 35–37.

38. Ibid., pp. 50–51.

39. "A Web of Violence?" Online NewsHour, May 1999, www.pbs.org/news hour/forum/may99.

40. Cited in "Politicians Speak Out But Are Wary of Restricting Film Violence," *New York Times* (October 13, 1999), B4.

41. Cited in "Abortion Foes' Internet Site on Trial," *Washington Post* (January 15, 1999), A3.

42. Ibid.

43. Cited in "Doctors Win Suit over Antiabortion Web Site," *Washington Post* February 3, 1999, A1.

44. Cited in "Protected Speech?" Online NewsHour, February 9, 1999, p. 5, www.pbs.org/newshour.

45. Wendy Kaminer, "The Limits of Free Speech," *Censorship News* (spring 1999), p. 4.

46. Suzanna Sherry, "I Hate What They Say But I Won't Stop Them," *Washington Post* (February 14, 1999), B4.

47. Ibid.

48. Charles Jennings and Loni Fena, "Privacy under Seige," *Brill's Content* (May 2000), pp. 110, 113.

49. Jason Vest, "Listening In," *The Village Voice* (August 12–18, 1998) p. 1, www.villagevoice.com/features.

50. Mike Ingram, "New Internet Spy Agency to Be Set Up in Britain," World Socialist Web site (May 18, 2000), www.wsws.org/articles.

CHAPTER

Microradio's Challenge to Spectrum Scarcity

THE ORIGINS OF A BROADCASTING ELITE

In the years before the passage of the Communications Act of 1934, as Congress considered the permanent regulation of radio, many religious groups and civic organizations argued that if commercial interests were allowed to control broadcasting, no amount of regulation would be able to overcome the bias built into the system. The reformers were ignored, and with the passage of the Communications Act and the creation of the Federal Communications Commission (FCC), the reform movement disintegrated.

The text of the Communications Act promised "to make available, so far as possible, to all the people of the United States, without discrimination on the basis of race, color, religion, national origin, or sex, a rapid, efficient, Nation-wide, and worldwide wire and radio communication service with adequate facilities at reasonable charges." But by 1940 the commercial basis of America's broadcast system was irreversibly established, and the system was completely dominated by two enormous national networks, CBS and NBC. The FCC was authorized to review license holders every few years to ensure that they were serving the "public interest, convenience and necessity," but in practice the FCC failed to hold the networks accountable.[1]

The final step in radio monopolization occurred with the Telecommunications Act of 1996, which relaxed ownership restrictions so that one company could own up to eight stations in a single market. In the first twenty months since the 1996 Act came into effect, 4,000 of the nation's 11,000 radio stations changed hands. There were over 1,000 radio company mergers,[2] and as a result, a few massive companies have come to dominate the industry. According to *Advertising Age*, by September 1997 in each of the fifty largest markets, three firms controlled over 50 percent of radio advertising revenue and programming.[3] In twenty-three of the top fifty, three companies controlled more than 80 percent of the ad revenues. CBS alone has 175 stations, mostly in the fifteen largest markets.

In March 2000 radio's biggest merger occurred when Clear Channel Communications, the nation's largest operator of radio stations, acquired SFX Entertainment, the nation's largest concert and sports talent agency. The $4.4 billion deal created a company with unprecedented influence over the radio, concert, sports, and theatrical businesses. The combined Clear Channel–SFX conglomerate would have power to control promotion, marketing, and ticketing for touring shows and concerts and the potential to withhold radio air play from artists promoted by rival companies. Media analysts say the merger raises questions about excessive influence over the public's entertainment choices.[4]

The *Wall Street Journal* concluded that such deals "have given a handful of companies a lock on the airwaves in the nation's big cities."[5] Relative to television and other media, radio is inexpensive for both broadcasters and consumers, and hence it is ideally suited for local control and community service, yet a handful of firms seem to have turned radio broadcasting into nothing more than a conduit for advertising. These giant chains use their market power to provide homogeneous formats with broad national appeal, but the programming has little relevance to the communities in which the stations broadcast.

Today, fewer than ten corporations possess the licenses for over half the radio spectrum. This virtual monopoly of the airwaves has caused the homogenization of the content of licensed radio, what communications attorney Louis Hiken calls the "standardization of ideas." According to Hiken, "As a result of disenfranchising the poor, people of color, women, and other minorities, the FCC has ensured the most undemocratic use of the airwaves. By delegating licenses exclusively to wealthy commercial broadcasters, the FCC has abandoned in full its obligation to carry out the mandates set forth in the Communications Act.... If people are to have any opportunity to communicate their views outside the confines of their own homes, there must be outlets for local participation and dialogue."[6]

Under the modern corporate stranglehold, local participation in radio has all but disappeared, and a growing number of unlicensed radio stations have stepped in to fill the vacuum. In many parts of the United States, these low-power "microradio" stations are the only ones that broadcast news about city council meetings, community gatherings, high school sports events, and the like. In his preface to the fifth edition of *Media Monopoly* (1997) Ben Bagdikian says, "The steady deterioration of local communities' access to their own local broadcast and cable systems has brought illegal rebellions. It is a federal felony to operate a radio station without a government license. But abandonment by the federal government of local needs has led to 'pirate stations,' illegal low-power radio stations reaching individual neighborhoods or whole communities. Typically, these stations are set up secretly in garages, or move nightly by van from hilltop to hilltop, or are tucked into closets and periodically go on the air by sticking their antennas out of apartment windows."[7]

The surreptitious nature of microbroadcasting derives from the fact that since 1979 the Federal Communications Commission has decreed that no radio station can be licensed at a broadcast power of fewer than 100 watts, and the FCC requires all potential licensees to conduct expensive engineering studies, which, with associated legal and hardware costs, amount to over $250,000 for a typical new station.

Hiken says, "It is as if a 'Federal Newspaper Commission,' in the name of efficiency, has said that to conserve paper and ink, only newspapers of at least 1 million general circulation would be legal. All church newsletters, PTA bulletins, and community weeklies would be banned.... The situation in broadcasting is quite analogous."[8]

The rationale for the power restriction put in place in 1979 was the enhancement and strengthening of public radio stations, but today's underfunded public radio is drifting into commercialization and away from community access.

"The American people are essentially voiceless," says Hiken. "We can only express our views when and if the owners of the media permit us to do so.... In reality there is, or should be, little competition between microradio stations and megawatt stations. Whereas megawatt stations broadcast far and wide, microradio stations are limited to a small geographical patch. Therefore, microradio stations should serve local communities and provide a vehicle for two-way communication."[9]

The multiplicity of voices represented by microradio is in dramatic contrast to the 150,000-watt stations that provide entertainment and advertising on behalf of corporate owners. Low-power broadcasters tend to report what is happening in their own communities and why it is important, but they also make use of material from other stations, thereby permitting a far wider distribution of ideas than any small station could have imagined in the past.

The technology involved in microradio can be mastered by any moderately talented high school student with access to $500 and the local electronics shop. Despite heavy federal penalties (including fines of $10,000, seizure of equipment, and imprisonment), the movement has grown to an estimated 1,000 stations across the nation. In 1996 a national convention of microradio broadcasters in San Jose, California, was attended by about 150 persons representing fifteen of these unlicensed stations. Bagdikian says such stations "are a measure of the desire of neighborhood, ethnic, political, and other civic groups for local broadcasting, a desire frustrated by a government-regulated system that has turned over most of the public airwaves to large national and international corporations."[10]

Ron Sakolsky, a leader of the microradio movement, says, "Whether called pirate radio, micropower radio, low watt radio, liberation radio or free radio; collectively we constitute a movement that has the capability of . . . offering a libertarian alternative to both corporate and state controlled radio that has an even broader appeal." Sakolsky asks rhetorically, "Are radio pirates plundering and hijacking the airwaves from their rightful state and corporate owners, or are they better conceived as state-free rebels using culture jamming tactics to challenge the power of the media monopoly and the authority granted by government's normalizing regulations which have created a new interlocking system of enclosure, not merely on land, but in the air itself?"[11]

RADIO PIRATES

On October 5, 1998, a small demonstration outside the FCC in Washington, D.C., caught the attention of the press. About fifty "radio pirates"—low-power radio broadcasters who operate without a license—marched on the headquarters of the FCC and the National Association of Broadcasters (NAB) to protest the failure of corporate radio to serve community needs. To fill this gap, these pirates, like others in the growing microradio movement, were providing alternative programming, usually broadcast from their garages or bedrooms.

In the center of the demonstration were three giant puppets. The largest puppet, symbolizing "Corporate Radio," pulled the strings of the NAB, which in turn pulled the strings of "Kennardio," a Pinocchio-like puppet representing FCC chairman William Kennard, whose nose grew with each lie.

Ironically, Kennard himself showed some sympathy for the aims of the protesting pirates. "When I started in the early 80s," he said, "you could buy a small AM or FM radio station for an amount of money that made it within the grasp of a small business. Unfortunately, with radio consolidation and deregulation by Congress, that's no longer possible. We've got to find other ways for folks like those who were outside the FCC today."[12]

Who are these radio buccaneers, and why does their cause seem just even to their enemies at the FCC?

The term "pirate radio" is often used to describe unlicensed radio stations because the earliest such stations in the United States and Europe broadcast from ships in international waters. The first of these pirate stations was probably RKXR, which operated in 1933 from aboard the SS *City of Panama*, a floating gambling casino off the shores of California. The station, which broadcast popular music, took the Federal Radio Commission (the predecessor to the FCC) by surprise. The agency was not sure that it had authority over a ship registered to Panama and anchored in international waters, so the U.S. government demanded that Panama rescind the ship's registry. Panama complied, and the U.S. Coast Guard seized the vessel and towed it to Los Angeles. RKXR was permanently silenced, and although similar offshore stations later operated in Europe, it would be decades before a genuine microradio movement appeared in the United States.

The American pirates who went on the air in the late 1960s and early 1970s may have been inspired by their shipboard counterparts, but their approach was dramatically different. First, the U.S. buccaneers moved ashore and broadcast from within their communities, most of which had no local radio outlets. Whereas the offshore stations had made themselves attractive to advertisers by reaching as large an audience as possible, the U.S. pirates tried to serve the local folks. They were dedicated to the counterculture of the 1960s, and profit was not their motive. They broadcast a much wider variety of music and programming, including talk shows, call-ins, and political commentary, a format that ultimately became the model for today's micropower stations.

One of the earliest of these stations was WRAD, begun in 1969 by Alan Weiner, a teenager in Yonkers, New York. Weiner felt that Yonkers needed a station of its own, so he began broadcasting on 1620AM from a modified military surplus transmitter located in the basement of his parents' home. Weiner recently recalled, "WRAD was on the air for two weeks before we were ratted on and the FCC came, and my friends and I ran out the back door." Weiner soon started another station, WKOV, that operated in Yonkers from December 1969 to mid-1971. "My friends and I were getting together and getting more political," said Weiner. "We decided to get on the air and discuss what was happening politically. . . . We felt there were no stations on the air that were open to listeners. They were very orchestrated and tightly controlled. It was out of civil disobedience that we went on the air."[13]

Initially WKOV broadcast with 50 watts and later increased to 300 watts, carrying folk and rock music by artists who rarely got air time on the large New York City stations. In early 1970 one of WKOV's listeners, J. P. Ferraro, started WFSR, which shared the 1620 frequency with WKOV. Soon the Yonkers broadcasters began an FM station, WXMN-FM, which was joined by WSEX, both broadcasting on 87.9 MHz FM with 250 watts of power. The stations were operated by about thirty or forty volunteers, mostly teenagers. Community response was largely favorable, especially among the parents of the teens who worked there. The only complaint came from close neighbors who said the station interfered with television Channel 7 during the time that *The Brady Bunch* was on. So the pirates made a practice of shutting down during *The Brady Bunch*.

Eventually the FCC raided the homes of Wiener and Ferraro, arresting them and confiscating their equipment in what Wiener described as "a search and destroy mission."[14]

Although the Yonkers stations were shut down by the FCC, they had sent a message to communities around the country. If a handful of teenagers could keep four radio stations going for over a year and a half, surely community and labor leaders could do the same. In addition, the FCC requirement that potential broadcasters be well financed now appeared to be an artifice designed to ensure that only the rich controlled the airwaves.

Around the time that the Yonkers broadcasters went off the air, Bruce Quinn, a legally blind radio buff in Bloomington, Indiana, began Jolly Roger Radio. Broadcast from his living room on both AM and FM, the station featured rock, folk, and country music interspersed with commentary. Staffed primarily by University of Indiana students, Jolly Roger Radio remained on the air for a decade until it was raided by the FCC in November 1980. Quinn and two of his volunteers were arrested and fined $250.[15]

One of the longest running pirate stations was WTFC in Delaware, which appeared on Christmas Eve 1964 and survived until 1988. During WTFC's twenty-four years of intermittent operation, the FCC searched in vain for its transmitter.[16] Apparently imaginative pirates can indeed elude the radio police.

Another persistent unlicensed station was WCPR, started in 1975 by John Calabro and Perry Calavieri, teenage residents of a Brooklyn, New York, housing project. Like many early radio pirates, Calabro and Calavieri were rebelling against the corporate straight-jacket imposed on radio music programming. They began broadcasting Beatles music using a homemade FM transmitter that covered only a five-block area, but they soon acquired a larger transmitter that enabled them to blanket Brooklyn and outlying areas. WCPR invited listeners to call in and discuss whatever they liked. This was accomplished through the use of "phone-loops," that is, telephone numbers used by the phone company to test lines. Radio pirates discovered that they could call one of these numbers and announce another over the air, and when a listener called, a connection was established. By using these phone loops, radio pirates were able to use untraceable numbers to conduct call-in shows.

Calabro and Calavieri were arrested by the FCC in 1976, but they returned to the air the following year with WFAT, a 50-watt AM station operating on 1620 KHz and located in Cavalieri's apartment bedroom. WFAT used the same transmitter that had beamed WCPR and continued to feature music and call-ins, using phone loops to prevent the FCC from tracing the calls. The station developed a loyal audience from as far away as New England and West Virginia, where the station's AM signal could bounce at night.

Because the large number of apartments near Calavieri's made WFAT difficult to locate and silence, the FCC formed a task force that staked out multiple locations. Finally, at 2 A.M. on April 19, 1979, Calavieri and Calabro spotted FCC agents carrying tracking equipment into the court-yard adjoining the apartment. "This is it," they announced on the air. "WFAT has to leave the air." A caller quickly dialed in and shouted, "Rock n' Roll forever!" after which the station went silent.[17]

Nearly two dozen other unlicensed stations that had emerged in the New York area were also shut down as part of a larger FCC operation, despite the fact that none of them interfered with corporate-owned stations.[18]

"BLACK LIBERATION" RADIO: THE SOUL OF MODERN MICRORADIO

Today's microradio rebels are a natural extension of the earlier pirates. Music is still an important part of their programming, but it is not the *purpose* for broadcasting, as was the case with many of the early rock and roll pirates. The modern microradio station has become a full par-ticipant in the local culture, playing a broad social and political role within the community.

The definitive model of the modern microradio station was begun in 1983 in Springfield, Illinois. When the residents of Springfield's John Hay Homes housing project rioted in response to police brutality, it triggered a microradio revolt that produced unlicensed, low-power stations in the area. That revolt has since spread to other cities, but Springfield remains a vital microradio center.

Springfield's media are owned by a few giant corporations, and no commercial radio station is directed to the city's 15,000 African Ameri-cans, most of whom live in or around the Hay Homes project. In 1983 Dewayne Readus, partially blinded by glaucoma as a child, became a disk jockey at project parties. When one of those parties turned into a brawl, police beat Readus so badly that he was completely blinded. Readus subsequently became involved in social activism and police ac-countability, and in 1985 he helped organize the Tenants Rights Asso-ciation (TRA), which demanded that the Hay Homes housing authority be accountable to project residents.

Readus, who changed his name to Mbanna Kantako, recalled, "We discussed starting a newspaper, but we recognized that a large percentage of our people can't read." So the TRA considered the legality of operating a radio station without a license and decided that the benefits were worth the risks. "We're not even concerned about the FCC regulations," said Kantako. "Clearly they were designed before blacks were allowed to hold their heads up. And, obviously, being designed at that period of time, there was no consideration of what we as people might want to do. It's not even a question of the FCC regulation or anything like that for us. The air belongs to everyone who breathes it."[19]

The TRA purchased a 1-watt Panaxis FM transmitter, assembled it themselves, adjusted it for 107.1 MHz in order to avoid interference with existing stations, and made their first broadcast on November 27, 1986, from the living room of Kantako's apartment. They named the station WTRA for their association. The range of its signal was only about a mile and a half, but it was sufficient to reach most of Springfield's African American residents. Initially WTRA broadcast two nights a week, but in 1988 it expanded to three nights, from 6:00 P.M. to 6:00 A.M., carrying commentary, news reports, and music. As the station's social and political involvement grew, its name changed to Zoom Black Magic Liberation Radio, then Black Liberation Radio, and finally Human Rights Radio, reflecting its broader purpose, which Kantako said was "to build community. We're really trying to raise the consciousness of the people."[20]

The station was largely ignored by the FCC until 1989, when it broadcast a series of local controversies. First, Kantako aired a hospital interview with the victim of a police beating, asking listeners to call the station and relate their own experiences with the police. The responses described everything from police kidnapping to an army of occupation. Next, the station covered a three-day standoff between police and Doug Thomas, a local resident involved in a domestic dispute. On the third day, police stormed the Thomas home and Kantako covered the action live, telling listeners that Thomas had been killed by what he described as a police death squad.

As the result of these broadcasts, Kantako became the target of harassment, first by police, then by the FCC. Responding to a police complaint, FCC agents descended on the station on April 6, 1989, fined Kantako $750, and ordered him to cease broadcasting. Kantako refused. Indeed, he held a press conference demanding that the police arrest him for operating the station. When the police refused, Kantako went to the federal building in Springfield and asked to be arrested by U.S. marshals, who also refused.

At this time the station began broadcasting twenty-four hours a day, seven days a week, a schedule that it continues to maintain. In March 1990, after a federal court ordered Kantako to shut down his transmitter, he contacted Peter Frank, cochair of the Lawyers Guild Committee on Democratic Communications (CDC). "This started the ball rolling on legal research on free radio broadcasting," said Frank.

The CDC prepared "a Brief on the Constitutionality and Human Right to Practice Microradio without Government Interference," which argued that the FCC's ban on microradio stations was unconstitutional. The brief was never filed on Kantako's behalf because in the absence of complaints from commercial broadcasters, the FCC decided not to pursue the case. But the brief was used subsequently to defend Free Radio Berkeley in California.

After initiating its 24-hour-a-day programming, Human Rights Radio introduced some unique features, including *Notes on the Devil's News*, which provides alternative interpretations of news events covered that day by the commercial media. Another program, *Brothers at the Real Table*, is a talk show moderated by Kantako that features guests such as author Zears Miles and reporter Luis Rodriguez.

Human Rights Radio continues to broadcast socially relevant programming to its community, and it has inspired other stations, such as Black Liberation Radio in Decatur, Illinois, to perform the same community role. Decatur's Black Liberation Radio began broadcasting in 1990 from the small home of Napoleon Williams and Mildred Jones, using less than 1 watt of power. Tuned to 107.3 MHz FM, the station was created "to give a voice to those who have no voice of their own through the mass media."[21]

Two weeks after Decatur's Black Liberation Radio took to the air, its criticism of local political officials led police to raid the home of Williams and Jones, close their station, put them behind bars, and take custody of their daughter. As soon as they were released and had regained custody of their daughter, Williams and Jones put Black Liberation Radio back on the air despite a $17,500 FCC fine and an order to stop. Police and family services personnel responded by forcibly entering their home, abducting their daughter, and making her a ward of the court. As the result of their attempts to take their child back, Williams and Jones were jailed once more, temporarily silencing the station.

In May 1996, Black Liberation Radio conducted a one-day fundraiser to enable it to purchase a more powerful transmitter. The money raised was sufficient to purchase not only a new transmitter but a new antenna and a meter to check the transmitter's output as well, and the station was soon broadcasting at increased power. Once again the station's scathing coverage of local politicians provoked official action. On January 9, 1997, the police raided the home of Williams and Jones, charging them with having recorded public officials without their permission. The police seized every piece of broadcasting equipment, effectively silencing Black Liberation Radio.

Once more the station appealed to its loyal listeners. Their donations, along with assistance from other members of the microradio movement, enabled Black Liberation Radio to purchase the necessary equipment to return to the air. Meanwhile the courts prosecuted the station for "eavesdropping," the legal term for recording individuals without their permission. Once again Williams was arrested and released on bond. Jones was arrested for aiding and concealing a fugitive, and she remains in jail. The station is in limbo.[22]

Other stations have been inspired by Mbanna Kantako's example. Black Liberation Radio 2, which broadcast to Richmond, Virginia, was on the air between December 29, 1994, and June 25, 1995. The station featured programs on economics, government, health, and other issues, as well as music and poetry. It challenged the FCC by operating on 91.7 MHz FM twenty-four hours a day, seven days a week, with 30 watts of power. FCC agents eventually located the transmitter and raided the station, seizing the transmitter, the antenna, and all visible equipment.[23]

FREE RADIO BERKELEY AND THE CALIFORNIA RADIO REVOLUTION

Mbanna Kantako's model of radio resistance has spread far beyond the housing projects of Springfield, Illinois. The relevance of Kantako's Human Rights Radio extends not only to black liberation but to political liberation generally, and California has been fertile ground for that message.

In 1991 Tom Reveille started Radio Free Venice, California's first micropower station. "In my view, we have a media government," said Reveille. "If you need information, you can only get it from the media. They control the elections. They have a stranglehold on information." With respect to the struggle between human rights and corporate power, Reveille said, "This is the only war in history where one side gets all its information from the other side."[24]

Reveille decided to break the corporate stranglehold by opening a free radio station on which the listeners could become program producers. He used the porch on his house as his studio, allowing passersby to come in and talk whenever they wished. Reveille made no attempt to conceal the location of the station and provided its phone number to listeners. This openness made him vulnerable.

On May 29, 1991, FCC agents, backed by Los Angeles police, came to Reveille's home, told him he was breaking the law, and handcuffed him. Reveille insisted that the FCC had jurisdiction only over interstate and foreign communications, not over microradio signals that travel barely two miles. Police then uncuffed him and left, and Radio Free Venice remained on the air.

Several months later FCC agents and federal marshals returned to Reveille's home with guns drawn. They not only confiscated his equipment but ransacked the rooms of people who had nothing to do with the station, taking cash, video and audio tapes, files, and anything else they chose.[25]

Radio Free Venice never returned to the air, but another California city, Berkeley, soon became the center of the microradio revolution. Stephen Dunifer, a former broadcast engineer for commercial radio and television, started Free Radio Berkeley in 1993 as a direct challenge to the FCC's ban on low-power broadcasting. Dunifer had created a microradio transmitter costing less than $100 that could broadcast between 5 and 25 watts of power. The simplicity of the transmitter and the accuracy of its signal represented a breakthrough in microradio technology.

In April 1993 Dunifer began broadcasting on Sunday nights from his workshop home, announcing, "This is Free Radio Berkeley, 88.1 on your FM dial." Dunifer frequently denounced the FCC for promoting corporate interests rather than the public interest, charging the FCC with theft of the people's airwaves. Angered by the broadcasts, FCC agents traveled to Berkeley with direction-finding devices. After isolating the location of Free Radio Berkeley, the agents went to Dunifer's door but were denied access to his home.

Dunifer soon turned Free Radio Berkeley into a 24-hour-a-day, 7-day-a-week operation, broadcasting on 104.1 FM with 30 watts of power. It now featured a wide variety of music and political commentary, including material obtained from Radio Free Maine and David Barsamian's Alternative Radio. The station was operated by volunteers including ecologists, anarchists, street activists, musicians, and Latino and African American street youths.

Eventually, programming conflicts developed between the apolitical punk rock crowd and Dunifer, who saw the station as a means to politicize the listeners. A subsequently drafted mission statement said Free Radio Berkeley had an obligation "to be an example to all of microradio broadcasting at its best." The statement concluded, "Consistent with a vision creating an alternative, diverse, hybrid society free of sexism, homophobia, and racism, . . . programming on Free Radio Berkeley will be reflective of those goals and ideals. Equal respect must be given to every member by every other member of Free Radio Berkeley. Any form of disrespect is just not acceptable. Just as we seek further engagement with the community we serve, we must do the same within the membership of Free Radio Berkeley."[26]

One unexpected boost in Free Radio Berkeley's professionalism came when KPFA, the Pacifica Foundation's outlet in Berkeley, began laying off some of its more progressive commentators. KPFA, begun in 1949, was the first noncommercial station to be licensed in the United States, other than stations at educational institutions. Although characterized as a "community" station, KPFA was not owned by the community, and this produced a series of disputes culminating in a 1993 decision by Pacifica's executive director to pursue funding from national sources. Inevitably this process made KPFA's veteran firebrands expendable, and many of them ended up on microradio stations like Free Radio Berkeley.

Former KPFA correspondents such as Bill Mandel and Sue Supriano brought a level of professionalism to Free Radio Berkeley that it previously lacked. Programmers were now required to arrive at the station on time or lose their time slot. They could also be dismissed for two or more violations of station policy, which prohibits smoking or drinking alcoholic beverages in the studio, theft of studio equipment, violence, and actions contrary to the mission statement. If an applicant for work had little or no radio experience, he or she was usually sent to Flea Radio Berkeley, a low-power portable station that broadcasts on weekdays from the Ashby Flea Market and serves as a training ground and advertisement for Free Radio Berkeley.

When one of Free Radio Berkeley's comedy shows, *Heaven & Hell*, consistently featured sexist material, a rift developed that eventually forced Free Radio Berkeley out of its Oakland home. Dunifer then relocated to an office near upscale North Berkeley but subsequently moved to a larger space in a low-income neighborhood.

Meanwhile, Dunifer was building more transmitters for eager microradio activists around the country. Radio Libre in San Francisco's Mission District used a Dunifer-built transmitter to begin broadcasting on 103.3 MHz during the summer of 1994. Radio Libre featured music, political commentary, and Latino community news. The station served as a unifying voice for the white and Latino residents of the Mission District, but the FCC saw Radio Libre as an illegal voice.[27]

In October 1994, FCC agents demanded to inspect Radio Libre's transmitter but were turned away because they didn't have a search warrant. Anticipating another raid, Radio Libre moved to another location, from which it now broadcasts sporadically.

Free Radio Berkeley Goes to Court

Almost from the beginning, Dunifer had intended to provoke the FCC into citing him in order to challenge the microradio ban in court. Indeed, his first broadcasts were deliberately made from a fixed location. However, once the FCC had located and visited Dunifer's home, the station went mobile and operated that way for a year and a half until the end of 1994. Dunifer would put the transmitter and other portable equipment in backpacks and take them up into the hills of Berkeley, where the battery-powered signal was broadcast as usual on Sunday nights.

As long as the station was not broadcasting from Dunifer's home, the

Louis Hiken, an attorney for the Lawyers Guild Committee on Democratic Communications, has represented microradio activists such as Stephen Dunifer. His proposal for a low-power radio regime also formed the basis for the FCC's subsequent low-power FM rules. Photo courtesy of Louis Hiken.

FCC could not get a search warrant to enter his residence and seize his broadcasting equipment. Nonetheless irate FCC agents served Dunifer with a Notice of Apparent Liability, claiming that Free Radio Berkeley had previously been monitored broadcasting from his home. Dunifer was given a $20,000 fine, far in excess of the $1,000 called for in FCC regulations.

At this point Dunifer turned to the Lawyers Guild Committee on Democratic Communications (CDC), which had earlier prepared a brief on behalf of Mbanna Kantako. Louis Hiken, an attorney for the CDC, drafted Dunifer's response to the Notice of Apparent Liability, stating that the FCC's fine was "grossly disproportionate to the alleged violations . . . and exceeds the maximum amount set by statute." He noted that FCC policies were developed "before the advent of FM broadcasting" and "failed to keep pace with . . . technological advances," such as highly stable micropower stations, which provide democratic access to the broadcast spectrum. Hiken argued that the FCC's ban on low-power broadcasting was illegal, because the "FCC is constitutionally required to develop a regulatory procedure appropriate to the medium rather than simply creating and enforcing a complete and absolute prohibition on microradio."[28]

On November 8, 1993, the FCC rejected all of Hiken's arguments, claiming that the FCC had the sole power to determine the public interest in broadcasting. It also justified Dunifer's $20,000 fine on the grounds that the $1,000 amount in the regulations was for routine violations, whereas Dunifer was a "recalcitrant individual" who had willfully challenged the FCC.[29] Hiken promptly filed an appeal.

Meanwhile, Dunifer took his case to the public through his regular broadcasts, on which he not only defended his right to operate a station but encouraged others to do the same. He also sent press releases to local and national media and made himself available for interviews. Nationally syndicated columnists Alexander Cockburn and Norman Solomon took up Dunifer's cause, and stories about Free Radio Berkeley began appearing in newspapers such as the *San Francisco Chronicle*, the *New York Times*, the *Washington Post*, and the *Los Angeles Times*, as well as on CNN. Even the FBI's attempt to link Dunifer to Theodore Kaczynski, the "Unabomber"[30] whose mail bombs killed three people and injured 23, served only to increase media coverage of the microradio cause.

The FCC was most concerned about Dunifer's campaign to teach others how to start micropower stations and his sale of low-power FM transmitters to potential broadcasters. Inspired by Free Radio Berkeley, another Bay area micropower station, San Francisco Liberation Radio (SFLR), appeared in May 1993 on 93.7 MHz FM. Run by Jo Swanson and Richard Edmonson, the station initially operated in a mobile manner, broadcasting two nights a week from different locations. FCC agents tried to track down SFLR, but the station eluded the agents for four months. When the FCC finally located SFLR's mobile signal, it requested the help of San Francisco police in stopping Edmonson's "getaway" car.

"There were so many cops out there, I thought I was right in the middle of a riot zone," said Edmonson. "To think they were all there because of me is a little mind-boggling." Edmonson said the police "were mad that they were being called out for something so insignificant" as a micropower broadcast.[31] After identifying Edmonson, the FCC issued him a Notice of Apparent Liability and imposed a $10,000 fine. Edmonson, like Dunifer, continued to broadcast.

Meanwhile, the FCC chose to ignore Dunifer's appeal of the fines imposed under the Notice of Apparent Liability, instead filing an injunction in U.S. District Court ordering Dunifer to stop broadcasting. Hiken believes that the FCC adopted this strategy so that whenever Dunifer broadcast, it could cite him for violating the injunction rather than for violating FCC regulations, thus avoiding a constitutional challenge to its rules. In addition to its request for a permanent injunction, the FCC asked that an immediate temporary injunction be imposed, claiming that

Free Radio Berkeley's broadcasting represented "immediate and irreparable harm." The FCC also claimed that the court need only address the question of whether Free Radio Berkeley was operating without a license, leaving all constitutional issues to the FCC.

Hiken pointed out that the FCC had repeatedly monitored Free Radio Berkeley for eighteen months, during which time it had discovered only two instances in which the station's signal interfered with those of other stations, and in one of those cases the interference was actually caused by the FCC. As for the broader constitutional issues, Hiken said that the "myriad of constitutional violations . . . which arise as the result of the FCC's decision to preclude the poor from having any access to the airwaves must not be sanctioned by this court. There are numerous less restrictive alternatives to the current licensing scheme enforced by the FCC that would provide the American people with use of the airwaves."[32]

On January 20, 1995, District Court Judge Claudia Wilken denied the FCC's request for a temporary injunction. The FCC's desire to avoid any discussion of constitutional issues was also dashed when Judge Wilken ruled that "the FCC is arguably violating its statutory mandate as well as the First Amendment" by enforcing its ban on microradio. Wilken concluded that "the record does not support the . . . assertion [that] because Defendant's equipment is not FCC-approved, it must be considered likely to emit spurious signals without a warning."[33]

Nine months after Judge Wilken's denial of the temporary injunction against Free Radio Berkeley, the FCC issued its opinion on Dunifer's appeal of the Notice of Apparent Liability. In rejecting the appeal, the FCC said Dunifer's constitutional arguments directly challenged the FCC's authority to license broadcast transmissions. After issuing its ruling, the FCC filed in federal district court for a summary judgment and *permanent* injunction, not just against Dunifer but against the entire Free Radio Berkeley collective as well as Free Radio Santa Cruz and other stations that the FCC believed were operated by Dunifer. As for the constitutional issues, the FCC claimed that the jurisdiction of the courts extended only to the constitutionality of laws, not rules and regulations.[34]

On June 16, 1998, the FCC gained an important legal victory over microradio when Judge Wilken issued a permanent injunction against Dunifer and Free Radio Berkeley. Wilken enjoined "Dunifer, and all persons in active concert or participation with him . . . from making radio transmissions in the United States until they first obtain a license from the FCC."[35] Two days later, Free Radio Berkeley was off the air.

Dunifer appealed the injunction, and oral arguments for the case were heard before the 9th Circuit on April 13, 2000. Dunifer says his attorney Louis Hiken "did a splendid job," and "at least two of the judges seemed well disposed to what he had to say and had very good questions." Despite Dunifer's optimism, on July 20, 2000, the U.S. Appeals Court for the 9th Circuit affirmed the district court's permanent injunction against Free Radio Berkeley, though on different grounds. The decision by Judge A. Wallace Tashima said the Communications Act requires that anyone seeking to broadcast must "first go through the FCC, or be subjected to injunctive relief, even if the underlying regulatory (as distinct from statutory) scheme is claimed to be unconstitutional." In short, Dunifer could not challenge the constitutionality of the FCC's prohibition on low power radio without first going through the bureaucratic process of requesting a license. According to the appeals court, "[I]t is important to note that this is not a case in which Dunifer had no means to obtain judicial review of the regulations. . . . Dunifer could have applied for a license and sought a waiver of the applicable FCC rules, or he could have filed a petition for a rulemaking for new low power regulations, a denial of which would be reviewable by a court of appeals."[36] Thus the court once more avoided constitutional scrutiny of the FCC's regulations.

MICRORADIO COMES OF AGE AND THE FCC TAKES IT SERIOUSLY

The court judgment against Free Radio Berkeley may have been a pyrrhic victory for the FCC. During the drawn-out process of legal deliberations, hundreds of new free radio stations took to the air. This period also saw the creation of the Association of Micropower Broadcasters (AMPB), which sponsors conferences, serves as a clearinghouse for technical and legal advice, and provides assistance to fledgling stations.

The growth of interest in microradio during this period was so dramatic that potential broadcasters actually began contacting the FCC for information about setting up micropower stations. The FCC acknowledged that it received 10,000 inquiries, and it felt obliged to establish a Web page called "Low Power Broadcast Stations." The Web page summarized the FCC's position with the warning, "DON'T DO IT!" The warning was accompanied by a statement that unlicensed broadcasters would be fined "a total maximum amount of $75,000" and their equipment "confiscated."[37]

As microradio stations proliferated around the country, the FCC apparently felt the need to take more aggressive action to silence them, and it enlisted the National Association of Broadcasters (NAB) in this process. Beverly Baker, the chief of the FCC's Compliance and Information Bureau, appeared at the NAB's 1997 conference in Las Vegas, addressing a forum on "pirate radio." Baker described the "tools" available to the FCC for silencing the pirates, beginning with warnings and forfeitures. "We can go in and seize the equipment that the unlicensed operator is using," said Baker. "That is my personal favorite. We can also go for injunctions . . . and in some cases there are criminal penalties."

Baker derided the idea that there were First Amendment issues involved in the FCC's suppression of microradio, and she advised the commercial broadcasters on how to help silence free radio operators. "You can help us by first of all letting us know about the pirates in your area," said Baker. "The more you can tell us about them, the easier it will be for us to deal with them."[38]

A number of broadcasting corporations responded to Baker's offer. For example, the Milwaukee Area Radio Stations (MARS) trade organization promptly filed a complaint with the FCC, asking it to take action against unlicensed stations in the Milwaukee area. In addition, the NAB asked the FCC to ensure that " 'pirate' radio broadcast operations are terminated promptly" and operators "are prosecuted to the fullest extent of the law."[39]

Indeed, the FCC initiated a nationwide crackdown on microradio. Stations were raided and closed in New Jersey, California, Florida, Missouri, Massachusetts, Tennessee, Kansas, and Pennsylvania. Many of the broadcasters were handcuffed and taken to jail. Responding to charges that the FCC was using disproportionate tactics against these low-power operators, an FCC official explained, "Ninety illegal broadcasters have been shut down in the past year with no more action than sending letters or visiting them and delivering warnings. Still, we do want to get across to the public that this is a serious matter, and what consequences there are to public safety and to the broadcasters themselves."[40]

The FCC's overzealous action against micropower broadcasters apparently strengthened the resolve of many. Free Radio Memphis, Radio Mutiny (Philadelphia), and KAW-FM (Lawrence, Kansas), stations that had been temporarily closed, vowed to fight on. Radio Mutiny said it would put ten micropower stations on the air for every one that the FCC shut down. "We are going to fight this in the courts and streets," said one Radio Mutiny supporter.[41]

Radio Mutiny organized a tour of the eastern states to promote microradio and demonstrate the ease of operating a free radio station. In Boston, supporters of Radio Free Allston filed petitions opposing the license renewal of WROR, the station that had urged the FCC to silence the unlicensed station. Indeed, the free radio movement began holding its own conferences, one in New York in February 1998, another in Philadelphia in April 1998, and another in Las Vegas, scheduled to coincide with the NAB's annual convention there in mid-April.

The New York conference included a dance and fund-raiser to help pay for the upcoming Philadelphia conference. Workshops were held in various parts of New York, and as a result, four new microradio stations were begun in New York City. The Philadelphia and Las Vegas conferences included technical and legal sessions and workshops for local community organizers, who were shown how to start a microradio station.

Nevertheless during the first three months of 1998 the FCC shut down sixty-seven microradio stations and sought cease and desist orders from the courts against operators who continued to broadcast after being warned by the FCC. In an interview with the *New York Times*, William Kennard, now FCC chair, took a strong position against unlicensed stations but added, "I am personally very concerned that we have more outlets for expression over the airwaves. I have made it a point of my tenure here as chairman to try to spotlight the fact that the broadcast industry unduly is consolidating at a very rapid pace. And as a result of this, there are fewer opportunities of entry to minority groups, community groups, small businesses in general."[42]

PARTNERSHIP WITH THE FCC

William Kennard's acknowledgment of corporate radio's failure to provide democratic access to the airwaves suggested that there is common ground between the positions of the FCC and the radio pirates. In response to Kennard's claim of concern about inadequate access to the airwaves, the Association of Micropower Broadcasters (AMPB) issued an open letter to Kennard proposing that the FCC create a micropower FM band between 88 and 92 megahertz, that the band have a minimal filing fee and that limits be placed on the number of stations that could be owned by a single company in a community.[43]

Initially the FCC would have none of the AMPB proposal, but apparently the pressure of publicity led the Commission to reconsider an old petition to establish a minimal microradio broadcasting system. The petition had requested that the FCC assign "one AM broadcast and one FM broadcast channel to [a] microstation radio broadcasting service." The channels would be shared by the licensed microstations, which would be limited to just one watt of power. Educational institutions, rather than community groups, would be given licensing priority, but the microstations would be commercial, providing access for "entrepreneurs" who are "motivated by the prospect of genuine wealth."[44]

Clearly this proposal did not address the major inequities of the commercial broadcast system, yet even this effort was strongly opposed by the NAB and the commercial broadcasters generally. This seemed to confirm the widely held belief that they were not opposed to microradio because it was unlicensed, but because it represented competition. Lawrence Soley, author of *Free Radio* (1999), says, "Free stations attract listeners who are disenchanted with commercial radio programming, demonstrate that commercial stations fail to serve the public interest, and represent an alternative to corporate station ownership. Thus, microradio stations, regardless of whether they are legal or illegal, threaten the very raison d'être of the U.S. system of corporate broadcasting."[45]

The NAB had a historic opportunity at its meeting on April 6, 1998, to demonstrate a willingness to share some of the electronic spectrum with grass roots stations. The microradio community, led by Louis Hiken, came forward at that meeting to present a simple, practical, and democratic proposal for a low-power radio regime. That proposal[46] is summarized here:

a. A micropower station may be established on any unused frequency within the FM broadcast band and extending down to 87.6.12 where there is no TV on Channel 6. A micro station broadcaster shall send one copy of a simple registration form with an appropriate registration fee to the FCC and a second copy to the voluntary body set up by the micropower broadcast community to oversee the stations.

b. Maximum power shall be 50 watts urban and 100 watts rural. In the event of interference due to power level, a station shall have the option to reduce power to remedy the situation or else be shut down.

c. Equipment shall meet basic technical criteria with respect to stability, filtering, modulation control, and so on.

d. Only one station may be owned by any organization. The organization must be nonprofit and based in the local community. Local origination of programming is encouraged as much as possible.

e. No commercial sponsorship shall be allowed.

f. There shall be no content requirements. Stations shall deal with "community standards" issues on an individual basis and in accordance with their own particular mission statements.

g. When television broadcast stations go digital, leaving Channel 6 free, it shall be allocated as an extension to the bottom of the FM band strictly for low-power community FM service. This would add thirty new channels, because TV Channel 6 is 6 MHz wide and an FM broadcast is only 200 KHz wide.

h. Registration shall be valid for four years.

i. Problems, whether technical or otherwise, shall be resolved, if at all possible, at the community level, first by technical assistance or voluntary mediation. The FCC shall be the court of last resort.

j. Micro broadcasting of special events does not need to be registered but is encouraged to meet all technical specifications.[47]

The NAB ignored the proposal, but the FCC showed surprising interest. In February 1999 it initiated a process to consider "rule-making" for some form of low-power radio. The big broadcasters and the NAB immediately lobbied against the initiative. Representative Michael Oxley (R-Ohio), who had received large political donations from media giant Viacom and from the NAB itself, introduced legislation in November 1999 that would outlaw low-power radio. Despite such pressure, the FCC proceeded with a vote on a micropower proposal.

On January 20, 2000, after decades of opposition to microradio, the

FCC began the new millennium by voting to approve a low-power FM radio service (LPFM) that would authorize: (1) stations with 50 to 100 watts of power with a service radius of about 3.5 miles (LP100), and (2) stations with 1 to 10 watts of power serving a radius of 1 to 2 miles (LP10). In a press release acknowledging "broad national interest" in microradio, the FCC said the new service would "enhance community-oriented radio broadcasting."[48]

Applicants for LP100 or LP10 stations would be required to meet minimum separation distances to protect the service contours of existing stations and anticipated LP100 stations. Eligible licensees could be noncommercial government or private educational organizations or nonprofit entities that serve an educational purpose or provide local public safety or transportation services. The FCC said the noncommercial requirement was "the best way to bring additional diversity to radio broadcasting and serve local community needs."[49] To further the FCC's goal of encouraging diversity and local opportunity, the new regulations would prohibit any existing broadcaster or media entity from having an ownership interest in or operating agreement with any LPFM station. In addition, LPFM stations would be prohibited from operating as translators (i.e., transmitters that repeat broadcasts originating elsewhere).

LPFM stations must broadcast for a minimum of 36 hours per week, as is currently required of full-power noncommercial educational licensees, and they must adhere to existing statutory rules such as sponsorship identification, political programming, and prohibition of obscene or indecent programming. LPFM stations will be licensed for eight-year renewable terms. During the first two years of their license eligibility, licensees must be located within ten miles of the station they operate, and no entity may own more than one station in any community. After the first two years of the LPFM program, licenses may be granted to nonlocal entities who may own up to five stations nationwide, and after three years, up to ten nationwide.

Entities that continue illegal broadcasting will be ineligible for a broadcast license. FCC chair Kennard explained, "If someone had a pirate station and, once it was brought to our attention, we contacted them and they shut down, they're more likely to get a license." However, Kennard warned that if a pirate station continued to broadcast in defiance of the FCC, "we wouldn't have the confidence they would operate as a responsible [licensed] broadcaster."[50]

The FCC's vote in favor of the LPFM system was 3 to 2, although in fact only one commissioner voted against the full proposal. In his statement supporting the proposal, FCC chair Kennard said, "Every day, it seems, we read about a bigger merger and more consolidation, all of which leads to the perception that the interests of small groups and individuals are being lost, and that important voices and viewpoints are being shut out. The possibility of opening up available spectrum in the

FM band has sparked creativity. Among those who propose new uses for the FM spectrum, the excitement is palpable. And the fact is, there is more room at the table; there is spectrum available for these and other uses." As for the fear that low-power stations would interfere with existing signals, Kennard said, "I have pledged all along that I would not support any proposal that threatens the integrity of existing radio services. I am pleased to say that my support of today's proposal is consistent with that pledge."[51]

Commissioner Gloria Tristani echoed Kennard's support for LPFM, noting that since the passage of the 1996 Telecommunications Act, the number of radio station owners has decreased by 12 percent even as the number of stations has increased. "As radio has been concentrated in fewer and fewer hands," said Tristani, "I've grown increasingly concerned about the effect of consolidation on localism and the diversity of voices on the public airwaves. The new low power radio service we are adopting is a partial antidote to the negative effects of consolidation. It promotes localism and diversity, not by limiting the rights of existing voices, but by adding new voices to the mix. Under the First Amendment, this is the best kind of response—the answer is more speech, not less."[52]

The only commissioner to vote against the entire LPFM proposal was Harold W. Furchtgott-Roth, who wrote, "Perhaps there *is* a demand for lower power noncommercial stations. Theoretically, however, any such demand could be met by the dispensation of licenses within our existing rules—i.e., by giving out 101 watt licenses consistent with the 100 watt minimum requirement.... [T]here is no evidence in the behavior of license applicants that suggests any pent-up demand for the stations in question." In addition to questioning the existence of genuine demand for LPFM, Furchtgott-Roth doubted the assurances that such broadcasts would not interfere with existing stations. He concluded, "In short, the Commission has, at the expense of existing service quality, created: a handful of new stations in primarily non-urban areas; stations that may not meet their licensing requirements if they air religious programming; stations that may well be unlistenable by fixed listeners due to interference received from higher power stations; a threat to the development of digital radio services; a heavy regulatory scheme, including cross-ownership, political programming rules, and EEO [Equal Employment Opportunity] outreach duties, to govern these very small operators; and more enforcement and administration burdens for the Commission. This is not a wise balance of interests."[53]

PREPARING FOR LICENSED MICRORADIO

Shortly after the FCC's approval of a low-power FM service, this author spoke with Louis Hiken, attorney and activist in the micropower movement. "We're all in a state of shock, because what they have adopted is almost verbatim what we had recommended," said Hiken. "They have approved low-power radio and single ownership. No corporation or group can own more than one station for the first two years. They have required that it be nonprofit or noncommercial. If you look at what the FCC just passed, it's amazingly close to our own proposed rules for microradio."

Asked if he had any concerns about the FCC's regulations for LPFM, Hiken said, "There are a few tricky things. For example, they have said there will be no amnesty for those who have recently violated licensing requirements. In other words, everybody can sit on the bus except Rosa Parks.[54] They still say they're going to look at character when assigning licenses. We said fine, why don't you look at General Electric and its sordid history. Why don't you shut down these corporate monsters."

Ironically, Hiken believes that the manipulation of the FCC by the powerful National Association of Broadcasters (NAB) may have led to the LPFM breakthrough. "The NAB has had such a lock on the FCC for all these years that it became a public embarrassment," said Hiken. "Because the NAB was so intransigent and inflexible, they gave the FCC no space to save face. We in the microradio movement assumed the clear moral high ground. Our position was that the FCC does nothing but whore for the NAB, and the NAB does nothing but silence the American people in order to make money. The NAB actually threatened to close down the FCC if it didn't support the Telecommunications Act of 1996. The FCC acquired such a negative public image from bowing to the NAB's demands that they realized they had to democratize communications."

What happens now? "The FCC has seventy days within which to issue the new expedited regulations," said Hiken. "They've gotten rid of that massive application form that nobody could fill out, along with the engineering studies and other expensive requirements that discouraged people from applying. After the new regulations appear, the many groups that have been lobbying for microradio will have a five-day window to submit applications for licenses. There will likely be no problems in most of the country, especially the rural areas. The difficulty is going to be in the big cities like New York, Chicago, and San Francisco."

Does this suggest another "spectrum scarcity" crisis in which LPFM stations compete for inadequate space within the radio spectrum? "We're arguing that the spectrum scarcity problem results from their [the FCC's] allocation of the airwaves and not from a lack of space," said Hiken. "There's some debate right now as to what's available and what isn't. Stephen Dunifer and I have made several serious offers to them about the use of the audio portions of TV's Channel 6. There are a lot of ways that they can make space available to local voices in the cities."

Asked whether the 10-watt or 100-watt categories of LPFM service would be more significant to the microradio movement, Hiken said, "It depends. In a rural area you're obviously going to need more wattage. You can't cover an Indian reservation with one watt. But there are many cities that will not need 100 watts. You know, 25 or 30 watts would cover a lot of small cities."

After many years of underground "pirate" operation, will the proposed LPFM regulations energize and expand the microradio movement? "That's certainly our hope," said Hiken. "The main reason we feel so positive about it is that the FCC's statement of their purpose for LPFM is precisely the language we used in our lawsuits and our analyses of how the repression of microradio violated the Constitution. Having acknowledged this, they can't renege on their stated obligation under blatant pressure from the NAB. They're a public agency. They can't do that."

Despite such optimism, Hiken feared that the power wielded by the NAB would ultimately influence Congress to quash LPFM. "With recent media mergers, the NAB now has assets in the trillions of dollars," he said. "It is probably the most powerful lobbying agency in the world, and no politician will take it on."[55]

CONGRESSIONAL ATTEMPTS TO KILL LPFM

The Radio Broadcasting Preservation Act, introduced in November 1999 by Representative Michael Oxley (R-Ohio), was an impressive display of the lobbying power of the NAB. The bill would prevent the implementation of the FCC's LPFM regulations by prohibiting the Commission from prescribing "rules authorizing the operation of new, low power FM radio stations, or establishing a low power radio service." Anticipating that the legislation might not be passed in time to prevent the issuance of the LPFM rules, the bill's authors wrote part (b) to state: "Any rules prescribed by the Federal Communications Commission before the date of enactment of this Act that would be in violation of the prohibition in subsection (a) if prescribed after such date shall cease to be effective on such date. Any low power radio licenses issued pursuant to such rules before such date shall be null and void."[56]

Representative Oxley is one of the NAB's many "friends" in Congress, who have responded to a massive NAB lobbying campaign.[57] Committee hearings on Oxley's bill began, predictably, with NAB president Fritts, who declared, "NAB believes the FCC has abandoned its mandate and primary function of spectrum manager and has crossed over to social engineering at the expense of the integrity of the spectrum for existing FM broadcast stations and their listeners."[58]

The reference to "social engineering" was Fritts's way of characterizing the FCC's attempt to diversify the airwaves in the wake of massive media mergers. Fritts declared, "[T]he FCC's assumptions that consolidation permitted by the Telecommunications Act of 1996 has eliminated independent voices in the radio industry and reduced format diversity are unfounded." Having rejected the social benefits of LPFM, Fritts claimed that low-power radio would cause interference with existing stations and cause them economic hardship. He concluded, "The FCC has rushed to judgment by substituting social engineering for rational, prudent policy-making by adopting a service that lacks any benefit that outweighs the substantial costs that will be produced."[59]

Not all the committee witnesses followed the NAB's line. Don Schellhardt, national coordinator of the Amherst Alliance, a microradio organization, testified, "In the eyes of Representative Oxley's bill, there is no place in America where the spectrum is open enough, and no wattage where the signal is low enough, and no technology—past or future—where the signal is controlled enough. Now and forever, from sea to shining sea, FM stations of 100 watts or less pose an inherent risk of unacceptable interference to all of those helpless, endangered 30,000 watt and 50,000 watt stations." Schellhardt noted that currently there were thousands of unregulated microradio stations on the air, many of them broadcasting in crowded urban areas, yet the evidence of reported interference has been minimal. "Whatever the actual level of interference from unlicensed broadcasters might be, why would it increase—rather than decrease—after some or most of these broadcasters obtain licenses and become regulated?" he asked. Schellhardt said the benefits of microradio would include "more choices for radio listeners, more opportunities for innovation, the return of decent community coverage and—most important of all—a much-needed increase in the free flow of ideas, without which our country cannot remain a representative democracy for long."[60]

On March 29, 2000, the Oxley bill was sent to the floor of the House of Representatives amid strong public controversy. The *Washington Post* urged Congress not to scuttle the FCC's LPFM program, stating that "this potentially useful area should be allowed some space to grow." The *Post* acknowledged that "an immense lobbying effort has begun to stop the commission in its tracks," but it characterized Oxley's bill as "a bad idea."[61]

Oxley's bill passed the House on April 13, 2000, by a vote of 274 to 110. The vote followed a deal between Oxley and Democrat John D. Dingell of Michigan under which the bill would allow a small number of LPFM stations to be licensed after a lengthy "testing period." In return for this "compromise," the bill required the FCC to maintain three "separations" between one FM station and another. For example, if a station is currently broadcasting on, say, 91.1, no other broadcaster could use

91.3, 91.5, or 91.7. This means that the only FM frequencies available to new low-power stations would be in virtually uninhabited regions of the country, a total of only about seventy low-power stations nationwide, most of them in the desert.

Companion legislation introduced in the Senate by Senator Judd Gregg (R-N.H.) would eliminate low-power radio entirely. Alexander Cockburn, writing in *The Nation*, declared, "If the Senate concurs, Congress will have issued a stark NO to free speech and democratic communications, just as ruthlessly as any dictator sending troops into a broadcasting station." Cockburn pointed out public broadcasting's disturbing complicity in the lobbying blitz against LPFM and noted a sinister factor in its opposition. Both Kevin Klose, president of National Public Radio (NPR), and Robert Coonrod, head of the Corporation for Public Broadcasting, had earlier careers in what some people would consider government propaganda. Klose ran Radio Liberty and Radio Free Europe, and Coonrod oversaw the Voice of America and Radio/TV Marti, all of which had originated as CIA-funded media operations. Peter Frank of the National Lawyers Guild says Klose and Coonrod come out of "the national security state" and "see federally funded public radio as an actual or potential propaganda arm of government, and they're terrified of independent voices."[62]

THE FUTURE OF MICROBROADCASTING

Despite the seemingly inexorable power of the NAB over Congress, a prestigious coalition led by the American Library Association (ALA), the Public Media Center, and the Media Access Project has been formed in an effort to save microradio. The battle lines are eerily similar to those drawn during the congressional fight over the Communications Decency Act (CDA). Oxley was the originator of that now-discredited legislation, and the ALA was at the head of the opposition. As it turned out, Oxley won the congressional battle (Congress passed the CDA) but lost the war (the Supreme Court ruled the CDA to be an unconstitutional infringement on free expression).

On May 2, 2000, as the Senate approached its crucial vote on Oxley's Radio Broadcasting Preservation Act, the coalition opposing the bill ran a full-page ad in the *Washington Post* under the heading:

> **Low-Power Radio vs. High-Powered Lobbyists:**
> **Act Now to Save America's Last Chance for Local Radio**

The ad described how the NAB spends over $5 million a year in lobbying and hands out more than $1,000 a day to federal candidates. The ad declared, "The broadcast lobbyists want to keep broadcasting in the hands of a few corporations. Which means that all radio, once the most diverse and local of mediums, sounds the same everywhere. They also want to weaken the FCC and win final say on how America's airwaves, a priceless *public* resource, are allocated in the future. This gives big broadcasters even more power and profits than they had before. *But democracy doesn't mean that the richest, loudest voice wins. Not every time. Not this time.*"[63]

The coalition ad concluded by asking all Americans to contact their senators and urge them to save low-power radio. Meanwhile, the Senate added several amendments to Representative Oxley's Radio Broadcasting Preservation Act. The final version of the act, sponsored by outgoing Sen. Rod Grams (R-Minn.), would allow a few low-power stations to be licensed in rural areas, but none in the cities, where microradio was intended to serve minorities, churches, community groups, and schools. The Grams bill would also rescind the FCC's future licensing authority and make that power contingent on a subsequent act of Congress. The controlling influence of the broadcasting lobby on Capitol Hill would effectively give them a veto over any effort to create a real low-power program.

Senate support for the bill was lukewarm, and in any case, it appeared unlikely that it could be brought to a vote before Congress adjourned. Just when it looked like low-power radio might survive the 106th Congress, Senate Republicans employed a stealthy stratagem. They buried the Radio Broadcasting Preservation Act as a rider inside an appropriations bill. Many congressional critics decried this maneuver, prominent among them FCC chairman William Kennard, who emerged as a forceful public advocate for microradio. In an op-ed article for the *Washington Post*, Kennard wrote, "It's Halloween time on Capitol Hill, and who's that skulking around the halls of Congress in the dead of night? Not ghouls or goblins, but special interest lobbyists up to their old tricks and looking for more treats. And this time, they're out to devour small community radio."[64]

The FCC had already received more than 1,200 applications for low-power FM licenses, and Kennard was outraged that any representative of the people could think of "colluding with big radio to stifle the voices of our schools, churches and local organizations." He warned that the NAB had dispatched high-powered lobbyists to use the congressional appropriations process to bury the micropower program. "These attempts to kill low-power FM behind closed doors smack of everything that Americans have come to distrust about our democratic process," said Kennard. "I very much hope Congress will do the right thing and snuff out the broadcasters' protectionist plot to make an end run around our democratic process."[65]

Kennard's hopes were soon dashed. Protected from debate and scrutiny, the Radio Broadcasting Preservation Act was passed as part of a spending bill that President Clinton was obliged to sign. Senate Commerce Committee chairman John McCain promised that he would make it a high priority to overturn the rider when Congress reconvened, but there has been little movement in that direction in the 107th Congress.

The *Washington Post* concluded, "[L]ow power radio isn't dead, but it's hardly poised to serve as the democratization of the airwaves and counterweight to media consolidation that FCC Chairman William Kennard had envisioned. The passage of the bill is a sad triumph of powerful campaign donors over reasonable policy."[66]

Stephen Dunifer, one of the pioneers of microradio, is opposed to the Radio Broadcasting Preservation Act, but he is defiant in the face of current congressional hostility. In May 2000 this author asked Dunifer for his thoughts on the Oxley bill. "It's really not that much of a concern to me, quite frankly," he said. "I don't feel these legislators have any authority, any legitimacy, and they certainly don't represent me in any way, shape, or form. I do not assign the responsibility for my representation to people like this. They can continue to do whatever the ruling class wants them to do, and we in the free radio movement are going to continue to do what we're doing."

Asked whether the microradio movement would continue to grow in spite of Congress and the NAB, Dunifer replied, "We'll do everything we can to ensure that it does. The NAB has basically been in a state of declared war against us for three or four years, and we decided to return the favor, particularly now with the Oxley bill. There is a really wonderful opportunity to point out to the people the extent to which the corporations are trying to control and dominate our lives. So we've called for a micropower council of war, a national strategy meeting in Berkeley on May 27.

"The Oxley bill has been a great organizing tool. It removes any doubt about the ability of raw, corporate muscle power, influence, and money to get anything they want. In this regard, they have really done us a great favor."

Although he is contemptuous of the political power structure, Dunifer is encouraged by grass roots developments in society and technology. "We're working to bring together the Internet, microradio, and other forms of local community media activism and content promulgation," he said. "What happened recently during Seattle's World Trade Organization protests is a major positive hope.[67] It was a watershed event in many ways, not just in the streets, but in doing an end run around the corporate media filters. An independent media center was set up in the heart of downtown Seattle, right at ground zero, within what became known as the 'Constitution Free Zone.' It was a collaborative effort among hundreds of media activists, community radio people, journalists, and similarly inclined folk.

"It took a lot of heavy lifting to get it up and going, but it was a phenomenal operation. There was an audio section where people who had been out in the field could come back with their tape recorders and essentially dump everything onto the computer, quickly edit 5- or 10-minute pieces, pull them up and make them immediately available on the Web site in streaming content. I was involved with a facility called Studio X, located off the periphery of downtown Seattle, but still within the Constitution Free Zone at night. We had a Webcasting studio set up there, an Internet radio station whose feed was being picked up and sent around the world. Micropower stations and other free stations were picking up our feed and rebroadcasting it."

Asked whether Internet radio was becoming a dominant format, Dunifer responded, "In our work, we see it largely in the distribution media. For example, while we were operating our feed from Studio X we got a call from a guy at Radio 100, a free station in Amsterdam. They were picking up our feed and rebroadcasting it to Amsterdam. On the local level, we had a micropower station that was picking up the feed from Studio X and broadcasting it throughout Seattle. We had another micropower station that was located up in a tree platform where it was beaming a signal into Seattle with a high-gain beam. They ran night after night, using roaming reporters on the street with VHF radios calling back reports to the tree. They would go up on a high parking garage and point their antennas toward the station and file reports from the top of the garage. There were also independent media centers and a microradio station running in D.C. during their WTO protests."

Given such growing use of Internet distribution of microradio, might Internet radio soon replace broadcasting? "No, absolutely not," Dunifer said emphatically. "For us as media activists the Internet is an incredible distribution medium. Through the combination of microradio and the Internet, communities can maintain their own local flavor in broadcasting through microradio, but they can become part of a global community of newsgathering and media activism through the Internet. This combination makes a wealth of material content available for microradio rebroadcast, either on a live action basis as happened in Seattle or by downloading whatever information is posted. We in the microradio movement were actually well ahead of the curve on this issue. As the Internet evolved, we began discussing how we could share program content. The process came together after some gnashing of technical teeth over which format to use, and we decided on MP3. We were one of the first entities to widely use the Internet for distribution in the MP3 format. That was 1997. But the transmitter will remain the heart of microradio, because everyone in a community can afford a $5 radio. Not everyone can afford a computer, and some people just don't want to be bothered with it."[68]

NOTES

1. *U.S. Code*, vol. 47, sec. 151, as amended in August 1996.

2. David Johnston, "U.S. Acts to Bar Chancellor Media's L.I. Radio Deal," *New York Times* (November 7, 1997), C10.

3. Ira Teinowitz, "Westinghouse Deal Fuels Consolidation in Radio," *Advertising Age* (September 29, 1997), p. 61.

4. "Clear Channel to Merge with SFX," *Rini, Caran & Lancellotte-Industry News*, March 9, 2000, www.rdpc.com/ind_news.

5. Eben Shapiro, "Wave of Buyouts Has Radio Industry Beaming," *Wall Street Journal* (September 18, 1997), A1.

6. Louis N. Hiken, "Microradio: The Struggle for America's Airwaves," in *Censored 1999*, ed. Peter Phillips (New York: Seven Stories Press, 1999), pp. 185–86.

7. Ben H. Bagdikian, *The Media Monopoly*, 5th ed. (Boston: Beacon Press, 1997), pp. xxix–xxx.

8. Louis Hiken, Alan Kom, Allen Hopper, and Peter Franck, "Broadcasting, the Constitution and Democracy," in *War, Lies and Videotape: How Media Monopoly Stifles Truth* (New York: International Action Center, 2000), pp. 239–40.

9. Hiken, "Microradio: The Struggle for America's Airwaves," p. 186.

10. Bagdikian, *Media Monopoly*, pp. xxix–xxx.

11. Ron Sakolsky, "Introduction: Rhizomatic Radio and the Great Stampede," in *Seizing the Airwaves: Free Radio Handbook*, eds. Ron Sakosky and Stephen Dunifer (San Francisco: AK Press, 1998), p. 11.

12. "Yo Ho Ho and a Battle of Broadcasters," *Washington Post* (October 6, 1998), D2.

13. Cited in Lawrence C. Soley, *Free Radio: Electronic Civil Disobedience* (Boulder, Colo.: Westview Press, 1999), p. 55.

14. Ibid. p. 56.

15. Soley, *Free Radio: Electronic Civil Disobedience*, pp. 56–57.

16. Ibid.

17. Frances Cline, "New York: A Sound of Silence on WFAT, Pirate Radio," *New York Times* (April 2, 1979), p. 27.

18. Cited in Soley, *Free Radio: Electronic Civil Disobedience*, p. 60.

19. Ibid, p. 73.

20. Cited in Eric Harrison, "Out of the Night," *Los Angeles Times* (November 19, 1990), E1.

21. Leaflet for "Black Liberation Radio, Decatur, 107.3 FM," undated.

22. Cited in Soley, *Free Radio: Electronic Civil Disobedience*, p. 81.

23. Ibid, p. 83.

24. Ibid, p. 82.

25. Ibid.

26. Stephen Dunifer, "Open Letter to All FRB Folks," (March 1997), www. freeradio.org/frb/openlet.html.

27. Soley, *Free Radio: Electronic Civil Disobedience*, p. 92.

28. Response to the Notice of Apparent Liability by Louis N. Hiken, addressed to Philip M. Kane, Acting Engineer in Charge, FCC, Hayward, California, June 28, 1993.

29. Soley, *Free Radio: Electronic Civil Disobedience*, p. 89.

30. Ibid, p. 90.

31. Cited in John Batteiger, "Radio Rebels," *San Francisco Bay Guardian* (October 6, 1993), p. 11.

32. "Defendant's Motion in Opposition to Plaintiff's Motion for Preliminary Injunction," *United States v. Stephen Paul Dunifer*, United States District Court No. C94–03542CW (December 2, 1994).

33. "Memorandum and Order Denying Plaintiff's Motion for Preliminary Injunction and Staying Action," *United States v. Stephen Paul Dunifer*, United States District Court, No. C94–03542 CW (January 30, 1995).

34. Soley, *Free Radio: Electronic Civil Disobedience*, p. 99.

35. Charles Burress, "FCC Wins License Battle with Free Radio Berkeley," *San Francisco Chronicle* (June 18, 1998), A27.

36. *USA v. Dunifer*, No. 99–15035, U.S. 9th Circuit Court of Appeals, June 20, 2000, http://caselaw.lp.findlaw.

37. "Low Power Broadcast Radio Stations" (April 1996), http://www.fcc.gov/asd/lowpwr.html.

38. Beverly Baker, "Radio: Technical-Regulatory Issues" (panel discussion at Broadcast Engineering Conference, National Association of Broadcasters 1997 Annual Conference, Las Vegas, April 5–10, 1997).

39. Statement of NAB President and CEO Edward O. Fritts, Release S23/97, September 5, 1997, http://www.nab.org/statement/s2397.html.

40. Mary Curtius, "Defiant Pirates Ply the Airwaves," *Los Angeles Times* (March 5, 1998), A20.

41. Yvonne Latly, "Mutiny on the Airwaves," *Philadelphia Daily News* (December 2, 1997), p. 12.

42. Cited in Julie Lew, "Radio's Renegade," *New York Times* (December 8, 1997), D12.

43. Soley, *Free Radio: Electronic Civil Disobedience*, p. 132.

44. "Before the Federal Communications Commission: Petition for a Microstation Radio Broadcasting Service." Petition submitted by Nickolaus Legget, Judith Legget, and Donald Schellhardt, June 26, 1997.

45. Soley, *Free Radio: Electronic Civil Disobedience*, pp. 133–35.

46. Louis N. Hiken, "Broadcasting, the Constitution and Democracy," in *War, Lies and Videotape: How Media Monopoly Stifles the Truth*, ed. Lenora Foerstel (New York: International Action Center, 2000), pp. 242–43.

47. For example, in the San Francisco Bay Area, 87.9 serves this purpose.

48. "FCC Approves New Non-Commercial Low Power FM Radio Service," FCC news release, January 20, 2000, MM Docket No. 99–25, p. 1.

49. Ibid.

50. Cited in Frank Ahrens, "Power to the Pirates?" *Washington Post* (February 9, 1999), C2.

51. "Separate Statement of Chairman William E. Kennard, Re: Creation of a Low Power Radio Service" (January 20, 2000), www.fcc.gov/speeches/Kennard/.

52. "Separate Statement of Commissioner Gloria Tristani, Re: Creation of a Low Power Radio Service" (January 20, 2000), www.fcc.gov/speeches/Tristani/.

53. "In the Matter of Creation of Low Power Radio Service, Dissenting Statement of Commissioner Harold W. Furchtgott-Roth" (January 20, 2000), www.fcc.gov/speeches/Furchtgott-Roth/.

54. Rosa Parks was the black woman who challenged segregation in Montgomery, Alabama on December 1, 1955, by refusing to give up her seat on the bus to a white man. Her arrest and trial led to a 381-day bus boycott and a November 1956, Supreme Court ruling that segregation on transportation is unconstitutional.

55. Louis N. Hiken, interview by author, San Francisco, California, January 30, 2000.

56. H.R. 3439, 106th Cong., 1st sess., U.S. House of Representatives. Introduced November 17, 1999. Congressional Universe, web.lexis-nexis.com/congcomp.

57. Frank Ahrens, "Political Static May Block Low Power FM," *Washington Post* (May 15, 2000), A10.

58. "Prepared Testimony of Edward O. Fritts, President and CEO, National Association of Broadcasters, before the House Telecommunications & Finance Subcommittee" (February 17, 2000), web.lexis-nexis.com/congcomp/.

59. Ibid.

60. "Prepared Testimony of Donald Schellhardt, National Coordinator of the Amherst Alliance, before the House Telecommunications & Finance Subcommittee" (February 17, 2000), web.lexis-nexis.com/congcomp/.

61. "Let Low Power Flower," *Washington Post* (March 30, 2000), A20.

62. Cited in Alexander Cockburn, "Low-Power Radio: Mayday! Mayday!" *The Nation* (May 8, 2000), p. 8.

63. "Low-Power Radio vs. High-Powered Lobbyists," *Washington Post* (May 2, 2000), A20, advertisement.

64. William E. Kennard, "The Voice of the People," *Washington Post* (October 23, 2000), A23.

65. Ibid.

66. "Low Power Mugging," *Washington Post* (December 25, 2000), A44.

67. The World Trade Organization met in Seattle, Washington, November 29–December 2, 1999, causing 50,000 people to protest WTO policies.

68. Stephen Dunifer, interview by author, Berkeley, California, May 21, 2000.

Selected Bibliography

Barnouw, Erik. *The Golden Web: A History of Broadcasting in the United States.* New York: Oxford University Press, 1968.

Bennett, James R. *Control of the Media in the United States: An Annotated Bibliography.* New York: Garland Publishing, 1992.

Bogart, Leo. *Press and Public: Who Reads What, When, Where and Why in American Newspapers.* 2d ed. Hillsdale, N.J.: Lawrence Erlbaum, 1989.

Bollinger, Lee. *Images of a Free Press.* Chicago: University of Chicago Press, 1991.

Bradlee, Benjamin. *A Good Life.* New York: Knopf, 1995.

Broder, David. *Behind the Front Page: A Candid Look at How the News Is Made.* New York: Simon & Schuster, 1987.

Capella, Joseph N., and Kathleen Hall Jamieson. *Spiral of Cynicism: Press and Public Good.* New York: Oxford University Press, 1997.

Cirino, Robert. *Don't Blame the People: How the News Media Use Bias, Distortion and Censorship to Manipulate Public Opinion.* Los Angeles, Calif.: Diversity Press, 1971.

Cohen, Jeff, and Norman Solomon. *Through the Media Looking Glass: Decoding Bias and Blather in the News.* Monroe, Maine: Common Courage Press, 1995.

Cutlip, Scott H. *The Unseen Power: Public Relations. A History.* Hillsdale, N.J.: Lawrence Erlbaum, 1994.

Fallows, James. *Breaking the News: How the Media Undermine American Democracy.* New York: Pantheon, 1996.

Fuller, Jack. *News Values.* Chicago: University of Chicago Press, 1996.

Goldstein, Tom, ed. *Killing the Messenger: 100 Years of Press Criticism.* New York: Columbia University Press, 1989.

Hazen, Don, and Julie Winokur, eds. *We the Media: A Citizens' Guide to Fighting for Media Democracy.* New York: The New Press, 1997.

Herman, Edward S., and Robert W. McChesney. *The Global Media: The New Missionaries of Corporate Capitalism*. London: Cassell, 1997.

Kurtz, Howard. *Spin Cycle: How the White House and the Media Manipulate the News*. New York: The Free Press/Simon & Schuster, 1998.

Lichtenberg, Judith, ed. *Democracy and Mass Media*, Cambridge: Cambridge University Press, 1990.

Mazzocco, Dennis W. *Networks of Power: Corporate TV's Threat to Democracy*. Boston: South End Press, 1994.

McChesney, Robert W. *Corporate Media and the Threat to Democracy*. New York: Seven Stories Press, 1997.

Neuman, W. Russell. *The Future of the Mass Audience*. Cambridge: Cambridge University Press, 1991.

Parenti, Michael. *Inventing Reality: The Politics of Mass Media*. New York: St. Martin's Press, 1986.

Povich, Elaine S. *Partners & Adversaries: The Contentious Connection between Congress & the Media*. Roslyn, VA.: Freedom Forum, 1996.

Sabato, Larry J. *Feeding Frenzy: How Attack Journalism Has Transformed American Politics*. New York: The Free Press/Simon & Schuster, 1991.

Saunders, Francis Stoner. *The Cultural Cold War: The CIA and the World of Arts and Letters*. New York: The New Press, 1999.

Schiller, Herbert I. *Culture, Inc.: The Corporate Takeover of Public Expression*. New York: Oxford University Press, 1989.

Schudson, Michael. *The Power of News*. Cambridge, Mass.: Harvard University Press, 1995.

Squires, James D. *Read All about It! The Corporate Takeover of America's Newspapers*. New York: Time Books, 1993.

Stauber, John, and Sheldon Rampton. *Toxic Sludge Is Good for You: Lies, Damn Lies and the Public Relations Industry*. Monroe, Maine: Common Courage Press, 1995.

Trimble, Vance H. *The Astonishing Mr. Scripps: The Turbulent Life of America's Penny Press Lord*. Ames: Iowa State University Press, 1992.

Index

About the Author

HERBERT N. FOERSTEL is the former Head of Branch Libraries at the University of Maryland, College Park. He currently serves on the Board of Directors for the National Security Archives. He is the author of seven previous books for Greenwood Publishing, including *Banned in the Media* (1998).